The Joan Palevsky Imprint in Classical Literature

In honor of beloved Virgil—

"O degli altri poeti onore e lume . . ."

—Dante, *Inferno*

The publisher gratefully acknowledges the generous support of the Classical Literature Endowment Fund of the University of California Press Foundation, which was established by a major gift from Joan Palevsky.

Summoned to
the Roman Courts

Summoned to the Roman Courts

Famous Trials from Antiquity

Detlef Liebs

Translated by
Rebecca L. R. Garber and Carole Gustely Cürten

UNIVERSITY OF CALIFORNIA PRESS

Berkeley   Los Angeles   London

University of California Press, one of the most
distinguished university presses in the United
States, enriches lives around the world by
advancing scholarship in the humanities, social
sciences, and natural sciences. Its activities are
supported by the UC Press Foundation and by
philanthropic contributions from individuals
and institutions. For more information, visit
www.ucpress.edu.

University of California Press
Berkeley and Los Angeles, California

University of California Press, Ltd.
London, England

Library of Congress Cataloging-in-Publication Data

Liebs, Detlef.
    [Vor den Richtern Roms. English]
    Summoned to the Roman courts : famous trials from
antiquity / Detlef Liebs ; translated by Rebecca L. R.
Garber
        p.   cm.
    Includes bibliographical references and index.
    ISBN 978-0-520-25962-1 (cloth, alk. paper)
        1. Trials—Rome—History.   2. Justice, Administration
of (Roman law).   3. Rome—History.   I. Title.
    KJA127.L5413   2012
    347.37'6307—dc23   2011041260

21   20   19   18   17   16   15   14   13   12   11
10   9   8   7   6   5   4   3   2   1

CONTENTS

PREFACE

This book grew out of my experience teaching. In particular, it evolved from a course that focused on the history and comparison of law, within the curriculum at the Law School at Albert-Ludwigs-Universität in Freiburg im Breisgau. To deepen our understanding of Roman law, I gave a lecture entitled "Seminal Trials in the Roman Empire," in which I acknowledged the contributions of Roman judicial practices to the evolution of Roman law. The trials discussed in this book were thus selected on the basis of their importance to legal history, that is, their ability to illuminate specific legal precedents that were essential to the development of law in Roman antiquity and quite possibly beyond. I am grateful to Stefan von der Lahr of the Beck Verlag, whose encouragement and unfailing support ensured that these lectures were first published. This book would not have been possible without the help of my youngest son, David, who patiently showed me the ways of word processors and remained ever ready to spring to my assistance. To David, therefore, I express my deepest thanks here as well.

I dedicate this book to the University of Freiburg, my alma mater, on the occasion of its 550th anniversary. I was a professor of law at Freiburg for forty years (with sabbaticals in Paris, Princeton, and Oxford), and I am deeply grateful for the academic opportunities there from which I have benefited. My career as a teacher and scholar would not have been as rewarding without the well-trained staff and excellent facilities at the University of Freiburg, particularly in the Departments of Law, History and Classics, and Theology. Not least, I would like to thank my students, whose commitment and curiosity were a constant inspiration.

Rebecca L. R. Garber took on the demanding task of translating this book into American English at a considerable distance from the author (her task was made even more difficult by his weakness for complex sentences). Nevertheless, she succeeded in completing a very fine, even intuitive translation of this book. I have revised her excellent translation, fine-tuning the legal concepts and vocabulary, together with Carole Cürten and Albert Furtwangler, who made innumerable suggestions to improve the flow of the text. During this revision, I seized the opportunity to make minor corrections in the content as well, to incorporate new knowledge and to eliminate information of interest only to German readers. In conclusion, I wish to express my deep gratitude to the University of California Press, especially classics editor Eric Schmidt, for allowing me to reach the English-speaking public with these fascinating tales, and last but not at all least to Marian Rogers, for her diligent and very helpful editing.

Freiburg im Breisgau
July 2011

Introduction

The acts of Roman politicians have often been described: how their deeds blazed a path of legislation that is still followed today. The decisions of Roman jurists have also been extensively studied: how they interpreted laws and attempted to fill in legal lacunae. The development of Roman law by civil authorities has also been well researched: how they helped establish lines of precedence in case law.

Far less attention has been paid to the most direct contributors to case law, the Roman judges themselves. The men who ultimately made the decisions in legal cases were, during antiquity and well into the Middle Ages, simply honorable men from the upper classes. They were, as a rule, not trained as jurists; legal experts were relatively rare in the Roman world. The contributions of advocates who prepared cases for judges and those of the parties have also been relatively ignored. Such men influenced legal decisions through their public speeches in crucial cases in favor of one party or the other, which were often well received. Advocates were not trained as jurists as a rule either.

In addition, from the early days of the imperial period, the emperor's opinion carried weight. As he was of course never selected for his legal expertise, we can generally assume that he had none. Judges, advocates, interested parties, and authorities were advised by jurists as a matter of course, although they were often guided in their legal decisions by public opinion, their own experiences, and their personal attitudes about justice.

We shall follow the course of sixteen trials that ended in trailblazing decisions, examining to what extent these participants in the public discourse on law were also able to effect change that contributed to the development of Roman law, which in turn forms the basis for European and world law. Although Roman law was later referred to as world law, its beginnings were fairly ordinary. Initially, it contained many wayward standards cobbled together from older conventions, including the sophistry of experts (by which means critics, who were not among the illuminati, could be effectively muzzled), as well as bold innovations and no-frills solutions, which attempted to create an equilibrium between old and new. Over the course of several centuries, civil law developed relatively undisturbed by other systems, from a specifically Roman system into a new mutation that gradually became *the* classical law. This law sought to treat all citizens, not all people, with reasonable fairness and thus was adopted throughout Europe and from there in the rest of the western world, Africa, and even the Far East. On its path through the centuries, this legal system, or at least a large portion of it, was almost universally applicable, with the general exception of penal law. But that is no reason to ignore the less-felicitous verdicts in this branch of law, which have so troubled posterity.

CHAPTER ONE

Killing a Sister
for Mourning a Fallen Enemy

The Horatius Trial

Allegedly circa 670 B.C.E. (fifth century?)

THE STORY

According to Livy, Rome and another Latin city, Alba Longa, came into conflict in what would amount to a battle for hegemony over the Latin-speaking part of Italy. So as not to exhaust either army, which would have left the cities vulnerable to attack by power-hungry third parties, they agreed that a duel should determine which city would dominate Latium. Now it happened that each army had triplets, the Horatius brothers from Rome and the Curiatius brothers from Alba Longa. These six young men were instructed to fight until one side was obviously victorious. Initially, things went badly for the Roman triplets: two of them fell early in the duel, although the third was uninjured. All the Alba Longa triplets sustained injuries of greater and lesser severity. At this point, the surviving Roman, Horatius, fooled the trio from Alba Longa by pretending cowardice and fleeing, and immediately the three Curiatius warriors set off in pursuit. Because of their various wounds, the warriors from Alba Longa ran at different speeds, so that when the surviving Roman turned suddenly to face them, he could fight each individually, slaying them one after the other. Rome was victorious, and Alba Longa had to submit to Roman hegemony.

The triumphant Publius Horatius strode home at the head of the returning Roman army, carrying the weapons and equipment he had captured from the Curiatius brothers. He was met by his sister, Horatia, who had been engaged to marry one of the triplets from Alba Longa. When she saw the war cloak that she had made for her fiancé hanging from her brother's shoulders, she tore her hair and tearfully called the fallen enemy by name. Her impassioned brother was deeply offended by his sister's lament: he had, after all, only just survived by the skin of his teeth, and his victory was the reason for the Romans' great jubilation. He drew his sword and approached his sister saying: "Get lost! Join your betrothed, with your misplaced love, since you have forgotten your brothers, both the dead and the living, and forgotten your country! So shall perish every Roman woman who mourns a foe!" And with that, he drove his sword through her.

The senate and the people of Rome were appalled by his action. His killing of his sister, however, was counterbalanced by his accomplishments on behalf of the city immediately before the killing. He was brought before the king to be tried. Yet the king wanted nothing to do with pronouncing the sentence, which had to be harsh, and which the crowd that had gathered would not understand. Therefore, he summoned the people's assembly and declared: "By the power of the law, I appoint two men (*duumviri*), who shall sit in judgment over Publius Horatius in this case of treason." The law at that time read: "Two men shall pass judgment in cases of treason. If he (the accused) is convicted, and appeals the conviction in the people's assembly (right of *provoca-tio*), then he may contest for his rights in the appeal proceedings. If the *duumviri* win the case, then the head of the accused shall be veiled and he shall be hanged, before which he shall be flagellated, either inside or outside the city walls."

Two men were thus appointed in accordance with the law. They concluded that there was no point under which they could acquit Horatius: his deed was inexcusable. They proclaimed the sentence, "Publius Horatius, the court adjudicates against you in the case of treason," telling the executioner to bind his hands. The executioner approached and was about to bind him when Horatius made an appeal on the advice of the king. Thus the trial proceeded publicly before the people's court. The citizens, who were now responsible for passing judgment, were impressed most of all by this statement from Horatius's father: In his opinion, his daughter had been justifiably killed; had that not been the case, he would have initiated legal proceedings against his own son as befits the *paterfamilias*. He then begged the citizens not to take his last remaining child from him, a father who until recently had had four children. At this point, the father hugged his son, pointed at the captured weapons still known as the "Horatian Spears," and declared: "Citizens, can you stand by and watch while this man, who only recently returned as the triumphant victor bearing the spoils of war, is bound to the stake, flagellated, and ultimately hanged? Even the people of Alba Longa could not endure such an appalling spectacle. Go, executioner; bind the hands of the man who just now, with sword and shield, prevented the Roman people from losing their freedom! Go, veil the face of the liberator of this city! Hang him from the gallows tree! Whip him! But if you flagellate him inside the city walls, then you must do so next to these spears and the other captured weapons; if outside the walls, then you must beat him while standing among the graves of the Curiatii! For where could you take him where the brilliance of his deeds would not denounce such a gruesome punishment?"

The people could not withstand the father's tears, and they were likewise impressed by his son's demeanor, as neither had he shown fear in the face of danger, nor had he begged for mercy. He was thus acquitted, more due to admiration for his courage than according to law and justice. In order that the public homicide be atoned for in some fashion, the father was ordered to make the necessary offerings: he brought many expiatory sacrifices and vowed that they would continue eternally, a promise the entire Horatius clan assumed. He laid a beam across the street, veiled the head of the young man, putting him in a manner of speaking under the yoke. This beam is known as the "Sister's Beam," and it still exists, being restored at state expense when necessary. An ashlar block monument was erected to Horatia at the site where she finally collapsed.[1]

HISTORICAL BACKGROUND

That is how Livy (59 B.C.E.–17 C.E.) recorded this incident. As with everything written by this historian, when he refers to events so long ago, the factuality of this narrative remains highly dubious. According to him, all of this occurred early in the reign of King Tullus Hostilius, the third king after the fabled founding of the city in 753 B.C.E. Tullus Hostilius was said to have reigned from 672 to 640 B.C.E.; however, there were no urban centers in Latium over which a king might rule at that time, only rural settlements, even if the latter were indeed organized along military lines. Also, and this is the primary cause for doubt, Rome did not conquer Alba Longa until the fifth century B.C.E., when it was no longer a significant rival for power. The duel, which plays out in a manner worthy of a Hollywood epic, could have been a Roman myth used to justify Rome's own supremacy within Latium.[2] On the other hand, transmission of the tale, in which the hero murders his sister and is then sensationally acquitted (we are interested only in this part of the story),[3] appears, by the second century B.C.E., remarkably uniform in numerous sources.[4] Therefore, it is entirely possible that the deed and trial did take place, but in connection with a different military endeavor, namely one from the fifth and not from the seventh century B.C.E.

THE TRIAL

According to Livy, the king was responsible for rendering judgment in cases like this. But he could also hand the case over, provided he had the agreement of the people's assembly, although this does not appear to be strictly necessary from Livy's report. Yet the law just cited strictly dictates that it was not the king who would sit in judgment, but rather a judicial collegium consisting of two men (*duumviri*) who would adjudicate. If convicted, the accused could then appeal to the people's assembly. The two men in question, however, were not appointed by the assembly, but by the king. These peculiarities, in addition to the king's further behavior, which is highly inconsistent with royal prerogative, make sense if one assumes that there was, in fact, no longer a king serving as head of state at the actual time of this trial. According to the records, kingship ended by 510 B.C.E. While it is probable that Livy, or his original source, did not create the trial out of thin air, he may have set it in an earlier period, which would tend to involve some kind of fabrication.

In order to form an opinion about the character of the accused, the people's assembly listened intently to his father, assessing the defendant's behavior during the trial. In so doing the assembly endeavored to determine more completely than before all facts that might be significant for a comprehensive evaluation. The father, however, did not limit himself to the presentation of actual events; instead, he appended his own legal opinion, which the court took very seriously. The people's assembly was obviously not limited in its legal judgment, as the assembly diverged widely in this matter from the pertinent law, the *ius causae*, as Livy expressed it.

Nevertheless, as in the trial of Socrates, the only options available to the assembly were to condemn, which meant a death sentence, or to acquit the accused. In this case, the people's assembly chose acquittal. It is true that the father was obliged to atone for his son's deed in another manner; however, the records do not state that the assembly imposed this upon him. It is more probable that the order came from the priests, who stood next to the magistrate governing the assembly in order to ensure that religious procedures were followed, so as not to offend the gods.

SUBSTANTIVE LAW

According to modern understanding, Publius Horatius committed homicide; moreover, he killed a close relative, his sister. The killing of any close relative, not just the father or grandfather, was called *parricidium*. According to Roman law, this was an especially heinous crime, deserving an exceptionally severe punishment. The perpetrator was "sacked," that is, sewn into a leather sack with unclean animals—monkeys and snakes are most commonly cited—and thrown into a river or the sea. In this case, however, Horatius was accused of *perduellio*,[5] which included treason. It was Horatia who could have been accused of treason, had her mourning been specifically meant as a desire for her fiancé's survival. Had her wish been fulfilled, her third brother would have had to perish; he was, after all, involved in a battle to the death. Rome would have fallen under the rule of Alba Longa.

The question remains whether her brother committed treason. He first accused his sister of betraying her dead brothers, himself, and her country, and then usurped judicial powers, disregarding the rule of law. He high-handedly issued a death sentence and immediately carried it out. In addition, his behavior could be considered a presumption of paternal rights over his sister and their autocratic execution. As the authority of the *paterfamilias* may well have held the same legal status as the constitution at that time, this could be considered treasonous.

The father presented three points to exonerate his son, whom he understandably did not want to lose in addition to his other children. First he argued that the son had justifiably killed his daughter; otherwise he, the father, would have taken action against him as *paterfamilias*. Modern scholars tend to consider this argument to be rather weak, as it assumes that the speaker would always behave in a law-abiding manner and never allow himself to be influenced by personal feelings. The lack of logic of this claim is, in fact, demonstrated by the father's next argument: he had just lost three of his four children in quick succession; therefore the people should not also take his last child from him. This extremely personal point implies that he would never have initiated a lawsuit against his son in which this son would have to forfeit his life to the father. In the end, the father's actions also undercut his first argument: if the son had indeed acted justifiably, then he would have been spared the acts of atonement that his father imposed on him. Of course, another possible explanation for this atonement is that even justifiable killing, for example in self-defense, had to be expiated at that time.

The final, third point upon which the father dwelled at great length, and which must have made quite an impression on all of the assembled Romans, was the deed that the accused had performed for the city. He had very recently placed himself in mortal danger, thus saving all Romans from subjugation by a neighboring city. Legally, this argument is not without its own dangers, because even serious crimes could theoretically be counterbalanced by service to the city: whoever provided Rome with extremely meritorious service would, if we carry this thought further, be permitted to commit *one* serious felony. And yet it was this argument that tipped the balance for Horatius's contemporaries, who had just been in fear of subjugation, even if Livy does phrase it in a more positive light: everyone admired the courage of the accused. Livy's positive formulation hides the fact that, in a strict sense, all who heard this argument, including the magistrates, were biased. They were impressed by the accused's calm in the face of this additional mortal peril, tantamount to the bravery he had demonstrated in the face of great danger on the battlefield. He did not beg for mercy. His behavior at the trial confirmed that his "flight" during the duel must have been a ruse.

EFFECT

Whether this trial actually took place or not, it remained firmly imbedded in the collective memory of Rome's citizens. Its pre-

cedence was repeatedly extended by people's laws to any citizen
sentenced to death or flogging by a magistrate in the court of the
first instance, and allowed that citizen to demand that the people's assembly reassess the sentence. This "right to legal challenge" (*provocatio*) was upheld by many laws, allegedly already in
509 B.C.E.,[6] at the beginning of the Republic; then in 449 B.C.E.;[7]
with greater historical probability in 300;[8] and, after a futile
attempt in 133, again in 123 B.C.E.[9]

In 63 B.C.E., when Cicero was consul, the story acquired a
rather lurid postscript involving Gaius Rabirius, then a senator.
Thirty-seven years previously, after the senate had proclaimed
emergency rule, Rabirius had participated in the violent down-
fall of the plebeian tribune, Appuleius Saturninus. Saturninus,
who had surrendered upon formal assurance that his life would
be spared, was subsequently murdered in prison by young supporters of the conservative senatorial party. In 63 B.C.E., Rabirius
was suspected of having taken part in the murder. The *plebicola*
party, representing the common people, believed the time had
come to mount a counterstrike against the senatorial ranks and,
with the judiciary's help, challenge the entire law of exception,
which by its nature favored the upper classes. The initiative was
taken by Titus Labienus, a relative of another man who had been
murdered at that time. Labienus served as plebeian tribune in 63
B.C.E. However, before this case could come before the courts, a
people's decree was enacted (with Gaius Julius Caesar's assistance), according to which a collegium of two magistrates was
appointed to decide upon cases of treason, as in the Horatius
story. Gaius Caesar and his uncle were appointed to the collegium. They put Rabirius on trial and condemned him to death
because the murder of a sacrosanct tribune, particularly an invi-
olate plebeian tribune, represented a case of treason. But they

allowed Rabirius, according to the people's law, to appeal to the people's assembly, which he of course did.

During this public procedure, when it appeared that an outcome unfavorable for Rabirius would prevail, Cicero, who then supported the senatorial party, had a loyal augur (an interpreter of divine omens) lower the flag on top of the Janiculum, which was a hill on the right bank of the Tiber. By lowering the flag there, he gave a sign of imminent danger, although, in this case, there was no danger. At this sign, all legal proceedings should have been terminated, including the vote in the case of Rabirius. As soon as possible, Labienus renewed his accusation before the people's assembly. Yet this time, the accused was defended by two famous legal advocates, Hortensius and Cicero. The latter's speech in support of the defendant is still largely extant: Hortensius proved that someone else had received the bounty paid for Saturninus's death, while Cicero impressively explained that the emergency law was absolutely necessary. In the end, Rabirius was acquitted largely because Caesar's political bias became gradually obvious.[10]

The right of any Roman citizen to appeal for judgment before the people against far-reaching encroachments by those in authority, even when those authorities were judges, remained a *palladium,* a refuge forever ensuring the freedom of each Roman citizen, a kind of fundamental human right. Cicero referred to it as the "patron" of the citizenry and the guarantor of freedom (*patrona civitatis ac vindex libertatis*).[11] During the imperial period, of course, the people's assembly no longer passed judgment over such cases: the emperor assumed this responsibility. When the provincial governor Festus had the apostle Paul imprisoned and threatened to have him tried in a Jewish court, Paul claimed his right as a Roman citizen, delaying the *provocatio,* the right to legal challenge. For this reason alone, he had to be transferred to Rome.[12]

The trial of Horatius long remained a vivid example that continued to influence customs in the Roman private sphere. It simply became unacceptable for Roman women to greet their men with emotional outbursts whenever the latter had to make war.

CHAPTER TWO

Temporary End to Trials Involving Black Magic

Furius Cresimus Defends Himself

Circa 191 B.C.E.

THE STORY

Gaius Furius Cresimus was a freed slave who owned a small plot of land near Rome. His land was surrounded by larger properties belonging to longtime Roman citizens who scraped by using old-fashioned agricultural methods and whose harvests, as a result, had stagnated. Cresimus, on the other hand, put all of his effort into his small plot and grew proportionately far more produce than his neighbors with their larger properties. When Cresimus's neighbors compared earnings, his productivity initially aroused jealousy, then the suspicion that there was no possible way this could happen if Cresimus were playing fair. They accused him of using magic to lure the crops from his neighbors' fields onto his own. One of the two curule aediles (authorities exercising the highest policing power in Rome), the *patricius* Spurius Albinus, summoned Cresimus to appear before the people's assembly, making the farmer fear for his life. It was common knowledge that to win in this court the accused (or the accuser) had to stir the emotions of the masses, but Cresimus could not afford a professional advocate with such skill. Therefore, on the day set for the trial, he planned his court appearance carefully, bringing along his workers, farming tools, and draft animals to the assembly, which met near the Forum in Rome. His workers looked strong, well fed, and sufficiently and appropriately clothed; his iron tools, including heavy rakes and powerful plowshares, were innovative and well made; and his oxen were muscular and healthy. Pointing at them, he said: "These, citizens, are my magical implements. However, I cannot demonstrate to you my labor after the sun has set, nor my nocturnal vigils, nor the sweat I have shed." He was unanimously acquitted.[1]

TEXTUAL TRANSMISSION

We know about this case from Pliny the Elder, a natural scientist from the second half of the first century C.E. He left behind an encyclopedia containing all the knowledge worth knowing in thirty-eight scrolls or books, each holding the equivalent of thirty to forty modern pages. Botany is covered in books 12 to 19, and agriculture appears in the book 18, which is where we find this report. Medicines and magic are dealt with in books 20 to 32, the latter in book 30. In citing this case, Pliny merely wanted to demonstrate that a farmer's earnings had less to do with his financial investment in the farm and everything to do with his own hard work and ingenuity. Pliny knew about the trial, he noted, only from the literature, namely the *Annales* of Lucius Calpurnius Piso Frugi. Frugi had published this work in seven books two hundred years before Pliny as an edifying representation of Roman history from its beginning, and covering the more than six hundred years up to Frugi's own time, that is, around 115 B.C.E. Frugi moralizes, uses anecdotes, and embellishes the historical record, but his very concrete and detailed report on this trial may well draw from an actual incident.[2]

THE PARTICIPANTS

The accused was a freedman—that is, he had been a slave and was then freed.[3] Provided his freedom had been formally granted (at the time there were hardly any other alternatives), he must have attained Roman citizenship. In fact, he bore the traditional three Roman names. The surname and usually the first name, in this case Gaius Furius, would have been adopted from the master who freed him, while his former slave name became a cognomen: Cresimus, from the Greek Χρήσιμος, meaning "the competent one," was a typical slave name. Our Cresimus thus had a Hellenistic background; he may have arrived in Rome as a prisoner of war. In any case he ended up belonging to a man named Gaius Furius of unknown cognomen, who had freed Cresimus while he was still in the prime of life. Cresimus acquired a modest piece of property—the text calls it a small acre—which he cultivated quite successfully.

Regarding his accuser, we know only his first name, Spurius, and his cognomen, Albinus; his surname is not mentioned in the text. However, every Roman would have known that this combination was restricted to the Postumius family, longtime members of the patrician class: the two names never appear together elsewhere. The Spurius Postumius Albinus who is most likely our accuser here served as consul in 186 B.C.E. and was best known for opposing the secret cult of the Bacchanalia and its debauched festivals. According to contemporary rules for the course of hon-

ors (*cursus honorum*, the ranks and offices through which noble-
men passed on their political path), he would have held the office
of aedile, a one-year post, approximately five years before his
consulship, perhaps even a little earlier.[4]

THE "CRIME"

The newcomer enjoyed substantially greater economic success
than the long-term, large-scale property owners. The freedman
became increasingly wealthy, while the others grew correspond-
ingly poorer. In fact, the freedman seemed to be actually threatening their traditional ways of cultivating the land on his small
plot. The freedman was obviously significantly more involved
in his farm, possessing great initiative and introducing creative
innovations.

This type of dynamic in the lives of freedmen can usually be
traced back to their release, which often gave those affected a
huge socioeconomic boost. During the late Republic and imperial period, freedmen contributed greatly to commerce, especially to retail, skilled crafts, and small businesses in Rome and
Italy; the volume of income they produced was far out of pro-
portion to their actual numbers.[5] When involved in agriculture,
freedmen tended to reverse the fortunes of run-down farms, and
a significant number of innovations can be attributed directly to
them.[6] More recently, the emancipation of the European Jews
in the nineteenth and twentieth centuries led to similar success.

SUBSTANTIVE LEGAL SITUATION

Practitioners of *maleficium*, black magic, were threatened with
severe punishments up into the modern period. Beliefs that some

men used supernatural arts to harm others have varied greatly over time and in different jurisdictions and social classes. The "Twelve Tables," the old Roman code, enacted circa 450 B.C.E., contained three penal provisions regarding this issue, all presumably on the eighth tablet. All three provisions included capital punishment, even if it was explicitly documented only in the first and third provisions. The death penalty was applied to anyone who intoned evil verses against someone aloud (*qui malum carmen incantassit* or *occentassit*),[7] sang the crops out of fields (*qui fruges excantassit*),[8] or lured another's grain onto his own property (*qui alienam segetem pellexerit*).[9] According to the extant text, the object of the crime (crops, *fruges*) could be brought under the second provision, and the alleged act (luring, *pellicere*) under the third; but it must also have been possible to punish deeds that combined elements of the two provisions.

THE TRIAL

The trial was initiated by a curule aedile, that is, a magistrate elected by the populace, who was responsible for public safety and order in Rome. In addition, he held supreme authority over all questions relating to the running of the slave and animal markets. When he summoned the accused before the people's assembly, he may have done so as the accuser, in antiquity normally a male commoner, or he may have embraced the role of the magistrate, who convoked and presided over the assembly. If he acted as the accuser, then he was not a common, private accuser but instead was serving as a magistrate in the public interest, which is why he may have believed it necessary to uphold public order pursuing this offense.

The people's assembly (the *tribus* according to the text, originally and probably also at this time representing the thirty-five residential districts) served as the court of law in this case. However, this statement raises questions. The larger centurial assembly (*comitia centuriata* or *maximum comitiatum*) was not convened according to *tribus*, but instead, at least originally, it was structured in 193 centuries (one hundred-strong units), organized according to the various levels of wealth represented by the group of participating citizens. The centurial assembly was convened and presided over by one of the two consuls or a praetor (a high-placed official involved in the administration of justice). The smaller tribal assembly (*comitia tributa*), which was convened according to *tribus*, was likewise presided over by a consul, or a praetor in exceptional cases, and was responsible for minor offenses in which only a monetary penalty could be imposed. The latter penalty applied to the plebeian assembly as well (*concilia plebis*, the assembly of nonpatricians), which was convened and presided over by a plebeian tribune.

This specific case concerned a capital offense; however, the tribal and plebeian assemblies could not impose the death penalty, a right that only the centurial assembly could exercise.[10] Meanwhile, several decades before this case, even the centurial assembly was organized according to the *tribus:* the centuries continued to exist, but within the residential districts.[11] Therefore, the larger centurial assembly may also be considered as the trial site for this case, and it was probably this assembly that Pliny refers to in his account of this case. Be that as it may, Albinus could not have presided over this assembly, as he was just an aedile at that time; therefore, he must have been the accuser.[12]

The freed slave appeared before his patrician accuser in person and without an advocate in an attempt to convince the court through visual inspection of his ingenious and well-tended agricultural implements, his well-fed draft animals, and his strong, well-fed and sensibly dressed slaves. It would have taken a major effort to get all this evidence from the countryside to Rome. But the freedman's trouble paid off.

He was unanimously acquitted. It is conceivable that this meant that every citizen voted for acquittal in the final vote, which was still public at that time. Yet it could also mean that a majority in each of the voting bodies that were polled (here it is immaterial if the groups were centuries of residential districts, *tribus*) voted to acquit. During sessions of the larger centurial assembly, voting was discontinued once a majority was reached within the 193 centuries polled. Because voting was organized according to rank, this often meant that only the richer classes voted.

EFFECT

Some eighty years later, Frugi's *Annales* appeared, stressing the importance of this case by presenting it in unusual detail. Frugi may have realized that it had had lasting effects. In fact, there are no records of prosecutions for black magic over the next two hundred years, although the late Republic is the era whose history is particularly well documented. It appears that the ruling class no longer believed in black magic. Among the common people, however, such superstitions continued to circulate, as can be inferred from certain references in Virgil and Tibullus, both of whom lived during the first century B.C.E.[13] By the mid-first and mid-second centuries C.E., Seneca and Apuleius wrote as if no one believed in such things any longer.[14]

However, in the early imperial period, there was renewed interest in passing laws concerning *maleficium*. A senatorial decree was enacted in the first century C.E., as early as under Tiberius, which supplemented the homicide law enacted under the reforms by Lucius Cornelius Sulla in 81 B.C.E. This decree read: "Whoever hosted or arranged for sacrilegious or nocturnal ritual actions in order to enchant, cripple, or shackle someone, and whoever sacrificed a human being to petition favorable omens with their blood, defiling a shrine or a temple, is to be capitally punished for manslaughter."[15]

In 53 C.E., Titus Statilius Taurus, who served as consul in 44, and in 52–53 as proconsul of the important province of Africa (then the middle of the North African coast area), was accused before the senate by one of his closest associates from Africa (who happened to be a confidant of Empress Agrippina) of engaging in magical ritual acts (*magicae superstitiones*). Taurus took his own life before the senate rendered its judgment. Tacitus implies that he would very likely have been acquitted, and a suicide generally halted legal proceedings. Nevertheless, the accused man's properties were confiscated, among them the Horti Tauriani, the Taurian Gardens (located in the northeastern part of the city), on which the empress had cast her eyes.[16] Taurus must have been accused of committing the first crime listed in the senatorial decree, even if it also appears that most of the senators and magistrates were skeptical regarding this matter. Taurus's suicide was apparently construed as an admission of guilt, to the benefit of the empress.

Soon afterward, Agrippina arranged an accusation of *maleficium,* claiming that her own life had been threatened by black magic. She did this to eliminate her contemporary Domitia Lepida, a distant relative and former sister-in-law who was about her age. Agrippina was vying with Lepida for Nero's affection, as Lepida had raised him, while Agrippina, his mother, was banished. Agrippina's accusation led to Lepida's condemnation and execution.[17]

In 158/9 C.E., Apuleius, the itinerant rhetorician, philosopher, and poet known for his picaresque novel *Metamorphoses,* also called *The Golden Ass,* was accused in Sabratha near Tripoli of practicing magical arts to the detriment of his fellow men. Although a foreigner living more than six hundred miles east of his native city, he had won a rich widow as his wife, allegedly by using magic. After the wedding, the widow's eldest son died suddenly, and a slave boy whom Apuleius may have used as a medium for his prophecies collapsed. The judge in this case was the provincial proconsul, Claudius Maximus, the renowned Stoic philosopher and one of the tutors of the young Marcus Aurelius, later emperor. Claudius Maximus acquitted Apuleius.[18]

It seems that under the rule of the Five Good Emperors (96– 180 C.E.) accusations of black magic were no longer taken seriously by the ruling class, regardless of the legal situation.[19] However, the first setback came just a few decades later, in 205 C.E., following the fall of Plautianus, Emperor Septimius Severus's former close associate and eventual father-in-law of his son Caracalla. The emperor was worried that a continuing belief in the efficacy of magic to discern the future, in particular the future of his reign, could undermine his authority as well as his ability to bequeath power to his then very young sons.

This affected Popilius Pedo Apronianus most directly, the proconsul of the important province Asia, which is western Anatolia today. His former nurse had dreamed that he would become emperor. He may then have used magic to learn more details about her dream. At least that is what the other household slaves reported when questioned under torture (slaves had to be questioned under torture). The senate condemned Apronianus to death, along with other high officials who had supposedly consulted Chaldean seers to learn about the emperor's future.[20] A Spanish eunuch from the house of Plautianus was exiled to an island as a magician and preparer of poisons, although Severus's son and successor, Caracalla, rehabilitated him.[21]

These practices hid very real dangers. The last trial mentioned above offers only a foretaste of what the fourth century would bring. Ammianus Marcellinus, the historian of late antiquity, reported at length about the use of accusations of *maleficium* under the reigns of emperors Constantius II (337–361 C.E.), Valentinian I (364–375), and above all his less capable brother Valens (364–378). These trials, which originated out of a fear of competition, ran rampant and led to the extermination of several entire prominent families throughout the Roman Empire.[22] In spite of the enlightened emperors of the second century C.E., belief in the efficacy of magic persisted. Few emperors and judges were able to acknowledge that it was merely an illusion, and thus free themselves from a widespread belief.

CHAPTER THREE

A Dowry Hunter Loses Out

Fast-Living Fannia

100 B.C.E.

THE STORY

Minturno, a harbor city appoximately sixty miles south of Rome, was so strategically significant that its inhabitants had qualified for Roman citizenship several centuries before this case. It was in Minturno that Gaius Titinius married the prosperous Fannia, even though he knew of her bad reputation. After all, she did bring a sizable dowry into the marriage. They lived together for some time and had a son, Quintus Titinius.[1] Yet in 100 B.C.E. she divorced Gaius Titinius, or he rejected her: our two sources differ on this point. Regardless, both sources agree that Titinius accused Fannia of adultery. We know for a fact that she had an illegitimate son, Gnaeus Fannius;[2] what we do not know is whether Gnaeus was born before or after Fannia's marriage to Titinius; and even if this boy was born after the divorce, we have no idea how long afterward.

What we do know is that when Fannia asked for her sizable dowry back, Titinius refused, citing her adultery: at that time, if a marriage ended in divorce due to the wife's infidelity, the husband could retain the entire dowry. This dowry exceeded the amount about which the municipal court in Minturno was authorized to judge, so Fannia sued her ex-husband before the urban praetor in Rome for restitution. As neither party was willing to concede, the praetor assigned the matter to be examined and judged by a *judex,* a judge appointed by the praetor to hear a dispute.

Fannia and Titinius agreed that the case should be heard by the more famous of the two acting consuls, Gaius Marius. Marius was then serving his sixth term as consul. He was a successful general and as a politician popular with the common people. He sought once again to bring things to an amicable conclusion, and with this goal in mind he took Titinius aside in an attempt to convince him to yield. Titinius, however, convinced that he was in the right, remained impervious to argument and insisted on a formal judgment. As a result, Marius acceded to Fannia's suit in its entirety. According to him, Titinius knew exactly whom he was marrying, and that he had had his eyes on Fannia's fortune from the beginning. But Marius also passed sentence on Fannia for adultery. Although her penalty was only the symbolic amount of one sesterce, her reputation was forever tarnished.

TEXTUAL TRANSMISSION

It is thanks to a Roman and a Greek that we have knowledge of this case. Valerius Maximus, of plebeian heritage, traveled throughout Greece and the Near East as a member of a Roman senator's entourage and published his "Memorable Deeds and Sayings" in nine books (*Factorum et dictorum memorabilium libri IX*) around 32 C.E. He dedicated his text to the ruling emperor,

Tiberius. Maximus provided instructive examples (*exempla*) from Roman and foreign history about religiosity, state institutions, virtues, and vices. Organized systematically, his examples were meant to provide a professional rhetorician with illustrative material for arguments, and they are accompanied by evaluations ranging from the incisive to the obtrusive. This case appears under the rubric "About Important Civil Trials."[3]

Plutarch, born in Greece a good half century later, was also interested in our story as it played out within the context of his biography of Marius,[4] whom he compared positively to King Pyrrhus of Epirus. Although Pyrrhus won important battles against the Romans in the third century B.C.E., his losses were so great that he was forced to retreat—hence the term "Pyrrhic victory." Compared to Maximus, Plutarch reports in a refreshingly sober manner. He also has a specific point of view; his ultimate aim was instruction in morals.

HISTORICAL BACKGROUND

Consul Gaius Marius was a social climber. He was immensely popular because of his military genius, which had enabled him to lead Roman troops out of dire situations, snatching victory from the jaws of defeat. He was elected consul six times in succession, a feat that appears a bit dodgy when viewed from modern perspectives about fair elections. He became the leader of the *populares,* the party of those politicians supported primarily by the common people, and whose opponents were the systematically conservative *optimates,* the senatorial party. Although standing at the head of the government for a sixth term, he condescended to accept the relatively minor duty to serve as *judex* in a lawsuit between private persons. He had neither a high level of education nor any legal training. However, accepting such tasks would have enhanced his popularity.

Twelve years after this judgment, his luck had turned, and he was on the run, so Marius appealed to the city of Minturno. The city council detained him, while acknowledging his position by giving him a private jailer. He was delivered to Fannia, who obviously had more than enough property and guards to keep watch over the prisoner. It was also assumed that she would be motivated to keep the fugitive under strict supervision. Treating Marius like an outlaw would allow her revenge for the insult to her reputation that Marius had inflicted on her years earlier. However, the opposite occurred: grateful for the return of her fortune, she looked after him solicitously, and then proceeded to assist him in his escape across the sea.[5]

THE LEGAL SITUATION

All Roman men expected to receive a substantial dowry upon marrying: this "gift" was provided by the father-in-law (if still alive and able to do so), the bride herself, her distant relatives, or other benefactors (the granting of a dowry was considered a meritorious charitable activity among wealthier Romans). Legally, a dowry was not required, but as there was no registry office where a couple could document their legal status, a marriage without a dowry might be considered an improper alliance, that is, a case of concubinage.

In our case, Fannia obviously brought the dowry to her marriage to Gaius Titinius herself, which was possible only if she were not under paternal authority. This could mean that her father, paternal grandfather, great-grandfather, and so on were already dead, that she had been emancipated, or that she was herself illegimate and thus had never had a paternal guardian. In any case, she had a substantial fortune. She may have pursued a lucrative trade before her marriage, or she may have inherited her wealth. We cannot even be certain that she was independent of paternal authority (*patria potestas*) at her marriage. All that we can be sure of is that she had a reputation as a loose woman before her wedding and that she independently, that is without paternal support, sued for restitution of her dowry. Perhaps her father was unable or unwilling to provide her with a moral education and had given her a dowry nonetheless, but died before the divorce.

This case involved a sizable fortune, which does not necessarily mean that it included everything Fannia owned or that her father had set aside for her. If a woman or a family was wealthy, it was common to put only a part of the fortune into a dowry (the portion was determined according to the specific living circumstances) and to place the remainder at the disposal of the woman herself. The father or, if he were no longer in the picture, the woman's legal guardian would enforce this. Any woman no longer under paternal authority had a legal guardian whose agreement was required in all important legal transactions, especially the establishment of a will, land transactions, the sale of slaves and heavy livestock, and dowry provisions.[6]

Upon marriage, the bride's dowry became the husband's property. However, at the end of the marriage, in particular in the case of divorce, he was obliged to return everything as a matter of principle and to pay restitution if the dowry had lost value because of his actions. The obligation to return the dowry was nevertheless restricted. While regulated in a more sophisticated fashion during the imperial period, in earlier times it roughly came down to this: in a divorce (freely available to both parties in pre-Christian times) caused by the wife's infidelity, she had to forfeit her entire dowry.[7] Under these circumstances, it did not matter who initiated the divorce. Titinius believed in this legal proposition, while Fannia defended herself against it. She considered the application of this custom to be unjust in her case.

THE DECISION

This case was not all that cut and dried for the *judex* either, at least not for a man like Gaius Marius, as Titinius had believed. Marius hesitated to arrive at a judgment that would have contradicted the law as it had been applied to that point. Therefore, he initially attempted to bring the suit to an amicable close, insofar as we can trust Valerius Maximus. It is also possible that Maximus allowed his fantasy free rein in this case and augmented and exaggerated the story on his own to make it more interesting.

Whatever path the court proceedings may have followed, Marius ultimately delivered a verdict that apparently no one had expected, and that Fannia had only hoped for. Marius agreed to Fannia's suit in its entirety. Simultaneously, however, he denounced her and her behavior in a way that did not have serious financial consequences for her but seriously damaged her reputation: she still had to pay punitive damages, to her former spouse.[8] Either Titinius had demanded this in a countersuit (above all, he had filed for a complete dismissal of her claim), or the damages were imposed on her as a sum deducted from the judgment amount (Roman judges always awarded the monetary value of an alleged claim). Marius obviously adjudicated only a symbolic amount: one single sesterce, one silver coin, or according to Plutarch four copper asses, equivalent to one sesterce. This judgment implied that Titinius should not emerge from his lawsuit a wealthy man; his calculating behavior should not be rewarded. Another effect of this judgment was the public and irreparable harm to Fannia's reputation. From that point on, no man who valued his status in society would marry her.

Today, the fate of the couple's children would have become the focus of postmarital conflicts. What happened to Quintus Titinius, their son? Our narrators confine their interest to the trial: there is no mention of her two sons, let alone any daughters who may have lived and died without leaving a trace of documentary evidence. Other sources, however, reveal that the younger Titinius became a senator and that he had a lively association with Cicero, who was only a few years his elder, and Cicero's friend Atticus. Quintus Titinius also engaged in business dealings with Cicero and ultimately collaborated with the victorious Caesar. According to the law, legitimate children remained with their father, who retained paternal authority in case of a divorce: they belonged to him alone. In fact, however, many divorced men allowed small children to remain with their mother and paid for their upkeep, even without being legally obligated to do so. Gnaeus Fannius, Fannia's illegimate son, attained equestrian rank, and it was common knowledge in Rome that he and Quintus Titinius were half brothers. In any case, both of Fannia's sons did well, considering the possibilities, which may also reflect positively on their mother's efforts in raising them.

LEGAL REASONING

Our primary interest in the present case is the dismissal of Titinius and his argument that, because of Fannia's infidelity, he was entitled to keep her dowry. Marius's refusal to subject the wife's adultery to punitive sanctions was a highly novel step and contrasted with prior case history. However, it becomes evident from Marius's justification that he was making an exception only in this specific case: he denied financial satisfaction to the cuckolded husband because said husband had known *before* the marriage that his bride had a questionable reputation, a fact that he was willing to overlook because of the size of the dowry. It should therefore be a given that money was more important to Titinius than his wife's reputation. Furthermore, Marius considered that such an attitude on the husband's part should not be rewarded when events took their very predictable path. That is, a man should not secure a financial windfall when his marriage founders because of the loose reputation of the woman. Marius's response was designed to put an end to such temptations.

Today, we would probably object to this mind-set, claiming that Titinius may have hoped that Fannia would change her ways and be a faithful wife. This ultimately Christian argument, that every sinner can repent and return to a godly life, was unknown in antiquity. Women in particular were tarred their entire lives for one immoral act, as it was widely believed that a loose lifestyle left an indelible imprint on a woman, who could not help but return to old habits. In the imperial period, it was simply assumed that prostitutes and procuresses, as well as actresses, and women who owned or worked in taverns or public houses, were simply incapable of marital fidelity. If such women entered into a marriage and then committed adultery, the routine charges of infidelity were dropped.[9] Marius may have even found it repugnant that Titinius had honored a woman like Fannia by marrying her, and may have wanted to publicly rebuke him for thus legitimizing her as if she were a respectable Roman woman. Since Marius could only interpret Titinius's actions as having been caused by avarice, he labeled Titinius a dowry hunter.

EFFECT

It remains true that in the centuries following this case, we have no documentary evidence of judicial decisions, legal advice, or imperial decisions that correspond exactly to it; however, there is a comparable legal opinion that relates to a similar, if more extreme set of participants. A married man opened a brothel and made his wife work there as a prostitute. If the marriage ended in divorce, the man could retain nothing of her dowry. A general legal doctrine that developed over time held that a husband was entitled to just a sixth of a dowry because of adultery. But the late classical jurist Cervidius Scaevola objected in the case of the brothel keeper. Why, he asked, would such a man condemn morals that he himself had initially corrupted, or at least adopted?[10] In any case, it remains true that one should not blame another for behavior that was acceptable when the contract was closed.

CHAPTER FOUR

A Naive Buyer

*Publius Calpurnius Lanarius
Seeks Recourse*

Circa 98–95 B.C.E.

THE STORY

Titus Claudius Centumalus was the owner of a tall tenement
building on the Caelian Hill, one of the seven hills of Rome. At
the beginning of the first century B.C.E., he was ordered by the
priesthood of the augurs (one of whose roles was to observe and
interpret the flight of birds from the Capitol Hill) to reduce the
height of the tenement so that it no longer interfered with their
observations. Instead of complying, Centumalus advertised the
property for sale and found a buyer, Publius Calpurnius Lanarius, to whom he revealed nothing about the augurs' decree. Following the sale, the augurs forced Lanarius to comply with their
order. When Lanarius learned that they had issued their decree
against the previous owner, and that this had occurred before
the property was put up for sale, he sued Centumalus. Lanarius's complaint regarding the purchase included the clause "in
the monetary value of the obligation, you, *judex* [judge], must

sentence Claudius Centumalus to pay to Calpurnius Lanarius whatever he [Centumalus] was obliged 'in good faith' to pay to him [Lanarius]." The *judex* in this case was Marcus Porcius Cato, a member of the famous Porcius Cato clan. Since the seller had not revealed a known, substantial defect in the object being sold, the judge ruled against Centumalus.

At about the same time, Marcus Marius Gratidianus sold a residential property to Gaius Sergius Orata, from whom he had recently purchased the very same property. This piece of land had long been encumbered with an easement, for example, some right of way for the benefit of third parties, or a right to draw water. This easement was well known to Orata, the buyer and previous seller. In spite of this, he sued Gratidianus, claiming that the latter had not mentioned a defect in the land at the time the contract was drawn up. This lawsuit was dismissed with the rationale that someone who already knows something need not be (re)informed.

TEXTUAL TRANSMISSION

Cicero is our primary source for both of these trials, which we find in his *De officiis*, written around the end of 44 B.C.E. and in which he discusses in depth the widespread opinion that usefulness (*utilitas*) and integrity (*honestas*) are often in conflict in business. He cites many individual cases as well as the discourse of Greek philosophers on this topic, concluding with trials from Roman history, including these two cases.[1] He had already summarized the second case in his *De oratore*, published in 55 B.C.E., where his description takes the point of view of Crassus, the advocate for the losing side.[2] Valerius Maximus, the author of the aforementioned "Memorable Deeds and Sayings," also referred in that text to the first of these two trials, apparently according to Cicero's record. Like the case presented in chapter 3, this trial also appears under the rubric "About Important Civil Trials."[3]

HISTORICAL BACKGROUND

The first trial took place during the early 90s of the first century B.C.E. It can be closely dated because we know that Marcus Porcius Cato, the judge, died between 95 and 91 B.C.E.[4] He was the grandson of the famous censor, Marcus Porcius Cato, and father of Cato Uticensis, the staunch republican and opponent of Julius Caesar. Our Cato may have been a jurist; we know for certain only that his uncle, his father's half brother, was a famous legal thinker.[5] The buyer, Lanarius, belonged to a large plebeian family that had attracted little or no attention before this case. He may be the same Lanarius who later emerged as a partisan for Sulla in 81 B.C.E. This Lanarius is recorded as having murdered the commander of remaining Marian forces in the Pyrenees after the Marians' defeat in Italy (see chapter 3).[6]

We know nothing about the seller, Claudius Centumalus, beyond what we can glean from his name, which tells us that he may have belonged to the Claudian family. Therefore, he may have been a patrician, a freedman released from slavery by a member of the Claudian clan, or a descendant of such a person. We do know that the Caelian Hill was at that time a densely populated, less-than-fashionable quarter with many tenement buildings.[7]

Our second trial can be dated more precisely. In Cicero's dialogue *De oratore,* which he predated to 91 B.C.E., he names Crassus, the advocate in this trial, as having recently (*nuper*) argued in this case. This is how we can be sure that it occurred a few years before 91 B.C.E.[8] The plaintiff, Orata, was known as a resourceful entrepreneur and man-about-town, first, because he operated a successful fish farm in pools heated from below, and because of another trial in which he sued the municipal leaseholder of fisheries on Lucrine Lake (*Lucrinus lacus*), a case that he may also have lost.[9] Our trial involving Orata may also have had something to do with this fish farm,[10] although this is far from certain, as he operated another fish farm on the coast near Baia as well.[11] In any case he had many other businesses. Gratidianus was a businessman who eventually turned to politics and was later adopted by one of Marius's brothers. He became a partisan supporting the people's party.[12]

LEGAL ISSUES CONCERNING THE FIRST CASE

To what extent is the seller of a property liable if the buyer discovers after the sale closure that the property had defects that were not revealed during the sale transaction and permanently detract from the value of that property? In this case, the parties had agreed upon a piece of land on which stood a very specific tenement building of a very specific height according to the number of floors. Now, however, the buyer is being impelled to demolish one or more floors, which will incur additional costs and reduce the rental income. Thus the property has lost substantial value. Can the buyer therefore hold the seller liable?

According to Roman law, a transfer of land became completely valid only through the participation of those involved in an intricate mancipation ceremony. In this ceremony, the buyer, holding in his hand a small piece of copper ore, solemnly stated in the presence of six mature male Roman citizens (one of whom was equipped with a copper scale) that he had bought this land for this piece of copper. He then touched the scale with the copper piece and gave it to the seller, who could respond with a statement describing the property, its size, and other characteristics important to the parties involved. Only if the seller said something untrue was he liable to the buyer, indeed for twice the relative difference in value between the declared and actual state of property, as determined by the actual sales price; the actual price was contracted and paid outside the ceremony. Let us say, for example, that an undeveloped piece of land that actually measured forty *jugera* (a *jugerum* measured 120 x 240 feet, about two-thirds of an acre) was sold for 1 million sesterces. If the seller had stated fifty *jugera* during the mancipation ceremony, the buyer would have received a fifth too little land, or have paid too much, and could thus demand double the difference back, that is, two-fifths of the sale price, or 400,000 sesterces. If, on the contrary, the seller said nothing during the mancipation ceremony, he could not be held liable according to the laws as they were understood in earlier times. Previously, a seller was not liable to any agreements or statements not mentioned during the mancipation ceremony. Likewise, if a buyer had casually said he might be willing to pay interest on the purchase price if he could not immediately pay it in full, he could not be sued for that interest. Centumalus was evidently relying on the traditional understanding that he was not responsible for something he had not said during the mancipation ceremony.

By the time of the trial, however, the rules had changed. The praetor, the Roman magistrate who determined which civil cases could be heard, and who drafted the formulas for their prosecution, had revolutionized the possibilities for bringing a lawsuit related to the purchase of an object. Many buyers, even those purchasing valuable items like slaves or large animals for which a mancipation ceremony to transfer ownership was likewise required, spared themselves the effort and simply took delivery of the object purchased. When everything proceeded above board, this could also be a means of acquiring property, also land, even though it meant that full ownership was delayed. When this occurred the purchaser received clear title of ownership only through usucaption, that is, by keeping an item for a period of uninterrupted possession: one year for slaves and large animals, two years for land. With smaller movable goods, the buyer got full ownership as soon as the goods were received.

In addition, Roman law had also arrived at the radically simplified conclusion that every informal purchase and every informal sale were considered legally binding. The praetor introduced formal legal writs that made everything specific and enforceable, not just the transfer and payment obligations, but all particulars of the sale agreed upon within the context of the purchase as well, even informal agreements. Let us say, by way of example, that someone purchased grapevines, including their delivery. The buyer could, if he had the cash on hand and no vines were delivered, demand both from the seller: vines and delivery; more exactly, if the seller did not deliver the vines, the buyer could demand their monetary value plus that of their transport to him, less the agreed price. This was because the party liable was always sentenced to pay cash for everything so that the buyer could purchase such goods on the market—a trait of capitalism.

The new legal writ stated in reference to our case, in the author's translation: "Marcus Porcius Cato shall be the *judex*. Concerning the fact that Publius Calpurnius Lanarius purchased from Titus Claudius Centumalus the residential property xyz on the Caelian Hill, the matter we address herein, whatever Centumalus is obliged to pay and deliver to Lanarius in good faith, you, Cato, must sentence Centumalus to pay this [the money sum] to Lanarius. If this [this purchase] cannot be proven, then you must acquit him." The broad terms "whatever" (*quidquid*) and "in good faith" (*ex fide bona*) were understood to refer primarily to informal promises, as long as they were meant to be binding—for example, the assurance that this tenement would provide a certain amount of rental income per year. The distinction between this and nonbinding advertising claims, which admittedly should not lead to liability (e.g., "By buying this knife you can fend off every attack!"), could be very difficult in cases like this. This difficulty, however, was accepted as part of the process: the jurists of the period were confident they would be able to draw the line in individual cases.

Over the course of time, purchase agreements tended to include more and more items. Following Cato's decision, even tacit assurances were thus often understood as binding, provided that was the desire of both parties. In the present case, the tacit understanding was that the tenement would continue to stand as it did at the time of purchase and could be used as it had been in the past. After all, income from the tenement was more important to Lanarius than the value of the land it stood on. Thus Centumalus had been obliged to reveal the augurs' demolition decree to Lanarius.

Perhaps the model for these more extensive disclosure requirements was the edict issued by the Roman market authorities, the curule aediles. As stated in their decree, the sellers on the slave and cattle markets had to inform any interested party about certain defects in their wares, according to a list drawn up by the aediles. Otherwise, sellers concealing such defects would have to pay predetermined fines to the buyer. Later, the diminished value of the defective goods was determined individually, and the buyer could also take the option of revoking the entire purchase.

A seller's liability was determined by whatever loss the buyer of an article suffered because of undisclosed defects. In this case, it was the value lost from the floors that had to be demolished in relation to the original whole building, plus the costs for their removal. If a purchased item was worthless, or nearly so, due to defects, then the buyer may have been allowed to demand reimbursement of the entire sales price. Indirect damages did not play much of a role in such cases—for example, slaves injured during the demolition process. Such damages were probably not originally incorporated in the fines, but over the course of time, the buyer could demand cash for them as well, if the seller was aware of the defects at the time of purchase, and the losses were predictable. Julian cites two examples from the second century C.E. In the first, a seller knowingly sold an animal whose disease was not obvious, but which then infected the buyer's entire herd. In the second case, a vendor knowingly sold wood that was rotten, a condition not immediately detectable by visual inspection; the house built from that wood collapsed. In such cases the buyer could demand compensation for all consequential damages, regardless of their amount.[13]

LEGAL ISSUES CONCERNING
THE SECOND CASE

Our second trial concerns a defect of title, namely that the value of the land the buyer had purchased was reduced because of particular rights a third party had to the property, in this case an annoying easement. The plaintiff,[14] who was depicted as shrewd, even greedy, openly sought to enforce what the current legal system seemed able to provide. The decision in this case brought about an exception to the law as practiced at that time. In this case we are still dealing with a buyer's claim based on "in good faith" and incorporating "whatever." Moreover, our seller was liable for knowingly concealing defects in the goods he had sold. Now, however, we learn that the *judex* did not consider this principle to be unconditionally valid, in particular not when the seller and the buyer shared this knowledge. It would be a silly formality (Romans called this "Greek loquacity," *loquacitas Graeca*) if the law insisted that a defect must be revealed to someone with probably more concrete knowledge about the case than the seller had.

FURTHER DEVELOPMENTS

The jurist Alfenus Varus (active ca. 55–35 B.C.E.) reported a similar case. His teacher, Servius Sulpicius (active ca. 75–43 B.C.E.), had told him about the buyer of a piece of land in the countryside the dimensions of which were given as one hundred *jugera*. However, during an inspection, the buyer was shown boundaries that extended substantially beyond the one hundred *jugera* that the seller actually owned. When a third party contested this additional land, the seller was obliged to compensate the buyer for the value of this lost additional property.[15] This case concerned a defect of title: the additional land did not belong to the seller and thus when sold could not become the buyer's property. The seller had gone a step farther and shown the buyer the boundaries of "his" property himself, pointing out incorrect boundaries. This closely resembles our first case, in which the seller showed a buyer a building at its given height. The buyer naturally concluded that was the actual building he was purchasing, just as our later buyer concluded that the property boundaries he was shown were correct and legally enclosed the property he was buying. Ofilius, another of Servius's pupils, stated that if a seller knowingly sells a sterile stallion or slave to a buyer who remains ignorant of this fact, then the seller is liable, even if sterility is not a defect in and of itself. Ulpian explicitly takes this opinion as precedent in the third century C.E.[16]

We learn from a consultant of Modestinus, a pupil of Ulpian's in the mid-third century, that late republican jurists held that the seller of a property was liable to the buyer if the seller had failed to disclose easements associated with the property that were known to him, and that this was true even if the sales contract ruled out any liability. Modestinus himself agreed with this, although his statements on the subject are rather general.[17] Sabinus, a legal scholar, formulated a policy addressing defects of title already in the first century C.E., that is, the seller of a piece of land who knew of easements on the property yet concealed them was liable if the buyer was unaware of them. Ulpian expanded this precedent by insisting that the seller was liable for *every* violation of good faith (*bona fides*). According to him, no matter how expertly phrased clauses of nonliability might be, they were invalid if something important had been deliberately concealed.[18] This opinion eventually was adopted in most European civil law codes.

CHAPTER FIVE

The Party's Intention vs. the Pedantry of Jurists?

The Trial of Curius

93 B.C.E.

THE STORY

An inheritance trial in Rome attracted major attention in the first century B.C.E. Manius Curius took possession of an inheritance later contested by Marcus Coponius, a relative of the deceased also named Coponius. The deceased Coponius had been married but was childless, and had executed a will that read: "If, within ten months, one or more sons [*filii,* also referring to children in general] are born to me, they shall be my heirs. . . . And if my son dies before his maturity, then the inheritance shall pass to Curius." Obviously, the deceased had assumed that his wife was pregnant while executing his will, but when he died shortly thereafter, his wife had neither borne him a child, nor had she been pregnant.

Marcus Coponius was related to the deceased through the male line; he might have been a brother, a nephew of a previously deceased brother, a cousin, or an uncle through the father's line. He engaged the most prestigious jurist of his time, Quintus Mucius Scaevola the Pontifex, as his advocate; the *pontifices* were one of the most important colleges of priesthood, whose responsibilities included the exclusive administration of civil law for many centuries. Mucius Scaevola was born around 140 B.C.E. into a prominent family of jurists whose numerous members had held government offices for generations. Following the death of his father, our Scaevola, then twenty-five years old, was accepted into the same priestly collegium that he would later head as the *pontifex maximus.* In 95 B.C.E. he was consul, and in 94 he served as governor of the wealthy province of Asia (western Asia Minor), where he developed a reputation for protecting the local inhabitants from exploitation by Roman capitalists. Marcus Coponius, together with his advocate Scaevola, filed suit against Curius for surrender of the inheritance before the *centumviri,* the court for inheritance law (the centumviral court, or the court of 100 men). Curius, as the defendant, was represented by the most famous rhetorician of the time, Lucius Licinius Crassus.

Crassus was about the same age as Scaevola, came from an even more prominent family, and had served with Scaevola as consul in 95 B.C.E., during which time they had worked very well together. The following year, however, the senate proposed granting Crassus a triumphal parade to honor his military success while governing Cisalpine Gaul (northern Italy). Crassus's triumphal parade never took place, as Scaevola thwarted it by objecting that Crassus's achievement was minor. Unlike Scaevola, Crassus was merely an advocate, not a qualified jurist. At that time, advocates did not normally study law;[1] instead, they studied rhetoric intensively—the art of using refined speech to persuade the assemblies, committees, and lay *judices* (judges) who decided legal cases.

The plaintiff's representative, Scaevola, spoke first, explaining with impressive earnestness that the events, as they actually occurred, were simply not accounted for in the will; Curius had not been appointed heir in this situation, but rather only in the case specifically described in the will. Consequently, the intestate successor and Scaevola's client, Marcus Coponius, was entitled to the inheritance. Crassus responded for the defendant. He adopted a jovial tone from the outset and sought to make Scaevola's argument appear ridiculous before the audience and the court, an attempt at which he succeeded. The court decided in favor of Curius.

TEXTUAL TRANSMISSION

We know about this trial primarily thanks to Cicero, who repeatedly invoked it as an example of the superiority of rhetoric over a narrow interpretation of the law that focuses on the exact wording of legal documents.[2] This rivalry between the two disciplines, rhetoric and jurisprudence, which Cicero highlights, still dominates modern discussion of this case;[3] however, this is a simplification.

Cicero himself admits that Crassus's position found support outside the class of professional rhetoricians: indeed, Cicero lists a prominent jurist among those supporting Crassus, namely the eponymous uncle of our Scaevola, Quintus Mucius Scaevola the Augur (the augurs were another priesthood of great importance for Roman public law). Cicero also tells us that several well-qualified individuals, no doubt including other jurists, shared the opinion of Scaevola the Augur and Crassus.[4] On the other hand, it is worth noting that Publius Mucius Scaevola, our

Scaevola's father and a *pontifex* himself, principally had taken the same position as his son. This reveals how controversial this question was among legal experts at the time.[5]

THE LEGAL QUESTION IN DETAIL

This case revolves around the correct interpretation of the last will and testament of someone who can no longer be consulted. A properly written will establishing the distribution of a person's estate always took precedence; the succession of inheritance *ab intestato* applied only when the deceased had not left a will. But what exactly had the deceased stated in his will? How should we interpret his words? Obviously, he had sincerely believed that his wife was pregnant and would soon bear him a child. It is insignificant whether the child would have been a boy (perhaps his preference) or a girl or even multiple children. *Filius* (son) was also used in a gender-neutral sense, meaning "child"[6]—this was beyond dispute. There would have been no legal difficulty had a child been born to the deceased after his death. According to an old legal provision that still applies, one not yet born but already in utero can be appointed an heir.[7]

We currently use an author's manner of speech and that of his circle to guide our interpretation whenever a word, expression, or sentence used by someone living, and especially by someone dead, can have several interpretations; section 133 of the German Civil Law Code expressly prescribes this.[8] Crassus reproached Scaevola, saying that a consequence of his rigid adherence to the testament's exact wording would mean that only the language used by jurists, in fact, only the speech of Scaevola the Pontifex, would be legally binding.

Because the testator had obviously believed that his wife

was carrying his child, and she would deliver a live infant, he had made a provision in his will only for the birth of his child. Nevertheless, he was aware of the likelihood at that time that this child might die before reaching the age of maturity. In that case, the child would indeed have received the inheritance, and a guardian would have been appointed for him until he reached the age of maturity. Yet if the child died beforehand, Curius would inherit. "Maturity" (*pubertas*) was defined individually at that time by an *inspectio corporis.* Obviously an "immature" (*impubes*) child would lack progeny of his own, nor would he be qualified as competent to make a legal will and name his own heirs. Had there been a child that died before its maturity, it would have been the primary heir, and Curius would have been what jurists call the subsequent heir. Technically, Curius would have been the heir to the deceased child, although named by the child's father.

But in this case there was no child and never had been. The question was thus whether Curius was the immediate heir to the childless deceased. Modern jurists would call him the substitute heir, substituting for the primary heir named in the will—here the child that the deceased man hoped and believed would exist. This distinction between a subsequent heir and a substitute heir is crucial to this case, and it figures in many others, as we will see. To be precise, this case did not involve the interpretation of ambiguous wording, but rather the question as to what should apply when circumstances arise that the testator had not considered and for which no provision had been made.[10] Should we try to determine what the deceased would have decided in this case? That is, should we attempt to ascertain his hypothetical will, for which only conjectures of greater or lesser validity are possible, and declare which assumption outweighs all others?

Crassus argued that the deceased had in fact willed his estate to Curius, if in an oblique way.[11] He argued in this manner in order to avoid the complications and almost certain defeat of claiming a "hypothetical" will. Lawyers and jurists still discuss "supplemental interpretation" in such cases, and explore possible intentions when there is nothing written in the will that applies to an unforeseen situation. The ruling authority has to fill in the gaps, sometimes by guesswork or sheer, tedious speculation. In the modern period, judges or the judiciary fulfill this function; in classical Roman law, the jurists would have had that authority. The question in this case became whether one should judge by interpreting what the will stated (and perhaps favor Curius) or follow the rules of intestate succession, as if there were no will at all (and certainly favor the other claimant). Crassus argued for the first of these options and yet pretended to avoid guesswork and stick to the wording of the will.

A will always takes precedence over intestate succession. In this case it was clear that there was a will and that Curius was named as some kind of heir, even though the deceased had not accounted for what actually occurred. It was by pursuing this line of argument that Crassus won the case for Curius. Even today, scholars considering the case believe that if Coponius had thought he might die without leaving a child of his own to inherit, he still would have wanted Curius to be his heir. But if Coponius entertained doubts about his wife's pregnancy and a healthy child, why didn't he save himself the trouble of executing a will until he knew more? He was probably so looking forward to having a child that he immediately executed a will. Yet it is also true that a legitimate child would have inherited before other relatives, even without a will. Coponius's will, viewed objectively, was unnecessary for the sake of the child. For Curius, however, the existence of a will was absolutely necessary. One can only wonder whether Curius alone would have been a sufficient impetus for Coponius to draw up a will. Was the execution of a will not only induced by the joyful expectation of a legitimate child? And was Coponius not simply taking this opportunity to name Curius as well?

WAS SCAEVOLA THE PONTIFEX TOO INFLEXIBLE CONCERNING THIS WILL?

Scaevola, the other claimant's representative, seems to have been stiff and inflexible when arguing for his client, so much so that Crassus made an effective rhetorical counterargument simply by appearing jovial, reasonable, and satirical. However, this contrast may have been exaggerated in the accounts we have of the case. Scaevola also wrote a systematic treatise on civil law, and centuries later Justinian's *Digest* (533 C.E.) included fragments from a commentary on the treatise written by Pomponius (active ca. 130–170 C.E.).

According to Pomponius, Scaevola reported that he had known a senator who loved to wear female clothing in public.[12] Because high-ranking Roman men usually wore a toga with a tunic underneath instead of trousers, their traditional costume was thus not all that different from women's. Modern readers should also be aware that, according to Roman law, the eldest male family member owned all of the goods used by his offspring, including his daughters' clothing. Scaevola hypothesized a case in which this senator had bequeathed the "female clothing" to a certain female relative. Scaevola questioned whether the female clothes the senator wore were to be included in the bequest. He answered no, those garments were not included. This case is an example of someone using his possessions in a way that differed from the norm; thus his words should be understood according to how he used his possessions. That is, when this senator wore them the clothes became "male" rather than "female." The generally used, objective meaning of the words that the senator used was not legally binding according to Scaevola (see the similar point in §133 of the German Civil Law Code, cited above).

Does Scaevola's aforementioned opinion contradict his opinion in the trial against Curius? In the case of the clothing, it was clear what the senator meant when he bequeathed the "female clothing." We accept a certain amount of personal eccentricity in the use of individual objects and words, contrary to the way they are generally used, as long as that eccentricity is readily apparent. Such eccentric usage does not make a contract or bequest about such objects invalid, nor does it distort the intent. On the contrary, such an eccentricity is accepted, even when very peculiar. Suppose, for example, that someone owned few books but had a full wine cellar, which he always referred to as his library. If he bequeathed his "library" to a friend, the friend should thus inherit not the few books, but all those bottles of wine.

This was indeed the collective view among Roman jurists. In the Middle Ages, this legal principle was enshrined in the sentence *Falsa demonstratio non nocet* (A false—or mistaken—designation does not harm).[13] It is usually easy to determine what an author meant when making a commonly known false designation. However, in the Curius case we cannot be completely certain as to what the testator Coponius would have wanted, because the unforeseen had occurred.

FURTHER DISCUSSION
DURING THE IMPERIAL PERIOD

Julian was an influential imperial jurist active circa 130–170 C.E. and served under the emperors Hadrian (117–138), Antoninus Pius (138–161), and Marcus Aurelius (161–180). Julian had preferred in his younger years to accept testamentary designation of heirs only in those instances in which the testator had made an explicit designation, and only in the manner in which it had been made.[14]

However, Justinian, emperor from 527 to 565, ultimately interpolated Julian's result in a more liberal direction,[15] a position Emperor Marcus Aurelius had already taken in the 160s. According to Modestinus (active ca. 215–250),[16] Marcus Aurelius had reopened the case of Curius and issued the following ruling. If a father appoints an immature son as heir and substitutes a third party for his son, one of two cases could result: the first, that the son is alive when his father dies, but then dies himself before attaining maturity; and the second, that the son dies before the father or is unable to accept it for any other reason. In either case, the testament should be regarded as if the father had substituted the third party in both instances as his substitute heir and subsequent heir.

Obviously, modern claims—that the case of Curius was completely forgotten by the jurists of the Roman imperial period—are unfounded.[17] Moreover, Scaevola the Augur's prevailing opinion, which Crassus represented, did ultimately triumph as a legal precedent about 250 years later, indeed by imperial decree. About 370 years after Marcus Aurelius, in an effort to end this argument once and for all, Emperor Justinian attributed this opinion to Julian as well, who still enjoyed great authority.

MODERN REGULATION

The German legislature addressed this issue in section 2201, paragraph 1 of the German Civil Law Code.[18] Here, however, the principle is formulated only as a rule of interpretation, a more conservative rule than Marcus Aurelius's judgment, at least according to Modestinus. The principle is applied only in cases of doubt, that is, when it cannot be proven that the testator truly wanted to appoint the third party only as a subsequent heir and not as a substitute heir as well.

In addition, the current German ruling applies only in one direction. In other words, if one is currently appointed only as the substitute heir (the substitute heir is appointed only when the primarily appointed heir is unable to inherit at the time of the inheritance accrual), then one does not also become the primary heir's subsequent heir, as Marcus Aurelius had decided. His decree functioned because according to Roman law the subsequent succession could be prescribed only if the primarily appointed, first heir was immature at the inheritance accrual, and only if the primary heir had died before reaching maturity. In contrast, subsequent succession can nowadays be prescribed under much broader circumstances. It is unlikely that Justinian's rule, were it to be applied now in reverse, would still accommodate the corresponding hypothetical will of the testator, as it would lead to too many unwanted subsequent inheritances.

CHAPTER SIX

Cicero Thwarts the Intrigue of a Powerful Man

The Rescue of Sextus Roscius the Younger

80 B.C.E.

THE EVENT AND
ITS HISTORICAL BACKGROUND

In the year 80 B.C.E., Sextus Roscius the Younger was accused in Rome of having murdered his affluent father. Although both father and son were from Ameria (present-day Amelia), a small town about sixty miles from Rome, the murder had taken place in Rome on the southern edge of the Campus Martius the previous August or September. The elder Sextus Roscius had been walking back to his lodgings in Rome after an evening spent with friends when he was struck down. His son was accused by Gaius Erucius, a man reputed to be a professional accuser, who surely had his eyes on the considerable bounty he would earn if the accused were condemned. A once-impoverished (but now newly endowed) relative of the Roscius family seconded the accusation.

A note on the role of the accuser in the Roman criminal justice system: the office of the public prosecutor or district attorney did not yet exist in antiquity. Criminal offenses could be brought to court and tried by any Roman citizen who served as the accuser. Minor misdemeanors resulted in fines determined during a civil trial and payable to the injured party, the plaintiff. In the case of serious felonies, if the accuser was successful in getting a conviction, then he was rewarded with a fraction of the value of the property confiscated from the defendant. If the accuser were to lose his case against the defendant, he could expect to find himself the defender in a countersuit for frivolous litigation in which the former defendant was now the accuser.

Marcus Fannius, one of the eight praetors in Rome, presided over the murder court, which dealt with both homicides and plots leading up to them. This court had been recently restructured by a law enacted by Lucius Cornelius Sulla in 81 B.C.E., and this was to be the first case held there according to the new law. The trial was to be heard by a jury of senators selected by the chairman, in this case Fannius.[1] The entire procedure was held outside in a plaza near the Forum.

In 83 B.C.E., three years before our case, Sulla had initiated a bloody military uprising and overthrown the government. Once he gained power, he imposed martial law and had himself named dictator by the senate. His authority was confirmed by a people's law, "for as long as he wished until he had restabilized the city, Italy, and the entire Empire, which had been rocked by revolutions and wars." According to conventional Roman constitutional law, a dictator could hold this office for no more than six months, yet Sulla did not relinquish his position for two and a half years. While in power, he instituted several changes to Roman government: he reformed the constitution, the courts, and the criminal law system. The powers of the people's tribunes were strictly limited; the senate was expanded from 300 to 600 members; judges had to be members of the senate; and new laws were established for the prosecution and punishment of the most serious crimes.

But before enacting these reforms Sulla took subtle, legal revenge on his defeated opponents' supporters by applying a very different set of laws. Those affected found their names published on an official list of the "proscribed" (outlaws). Proscribed persons could be killed by anyone, no one was allowed to help them, and their possessions were confiscated *ipso jure* (automatically) and auctioned off, with the proceeds going to the state. Sulla's friends and allies grew rich from such auctions, as they could purchase properties and assets for a fraction of their real value. In all, about 4,700 Roman citizens were proscribed, among them 90 of the then 300 senators and 2,600 holders of equestrian status. Sulla also freed approximately 10,000 slaves, who adopted, as was the custom, the first and family names of their benefactor, Lucius Cornelius, to which they appended their slave names as surnames. They also became reliable party supporters of the new order, like the 120,000 veterans whom Sulla settled as landholders in military colonies.

Sextus Roscius the Elder, our murder victim, had owned thirteen properties in the best locations in Ameria, of which the three most valuable were in the possession of another relative, Titus Roscius Capito, at the time of the trial. The victim's estate, valued at 6 million sesterces, had been auctioned before the trial because his name was on the list of the proscribed. His assets had been purchased for just 2,000 sesterces by one Lucius Cornelius Chrysogonus. The surname Chrysogonus means "sprouted from gold," a typical slave name, as catchy names were given to obtain a higher price on the slave market. This Chrysogonus

was a freedman and one of Sulla's influential associates. Chrysogonus had bought the estate and then given the best properties
to Roscius Capito. He also engaged Roscius Magnus, the man
who later seconded the accusation against the son, to adminis-
ter the remaining ten properties, and he had also granted Magnus the right to take possession of the movables associated with
the estates. The accused son and his mother, the victim's widow
(the murder victim's only brother had predeceased him),[2] were
immediately thrown onto the street.[3] The young man ultimately
found refuge in Rome at the home of one of his father's influential female patrons. He appeared before the court accompanied
by bodyguards, a telling indication of the powers arrayed against
him.

Because the powerful Chrysogonus backed the accusation,[4]
the opposing side had believed the younger Roscius would not
find an advocate of sufficient status to defend him. Indeed, no
advocate of stature stepped forward at first. Cicero was then
twenty-six years old and had only been involved in inconspicu-
ous civil cases until that time. His friends included a younger
relative of the accused's patron, and they convinced him to take
on this case. It would be a unique opportunity, they claimed, to
make his name as an advocate. Cicero finally agreed and threw
himself into the case.

Among the first things he must have considered was that the
murdered man had been on the list of proscribed persons, meaning that anyone could have killed him with impunity, even his
own son. This fact would normally make the accusation null
and void. However, Cicero did not want to apply this argument,
because that would have meant that he and the younger Roscius
had accepted the validity of the proscription, and along with
it the legal auction of the family properties. Cicero discovered

that the victim had been murdered several months after he could have been listed among the proscribed. That is, a law had been passed stating that from 1 June 81 no additional names could be added to the list of the proscribed, and the name of the murder victim was not on the final list published at that time. His name only appeared on a list produced after his murder. Cicero made little reference to the point that the murder victim had in fact been a supporter of the victorious senatorial party; he knew that the proscription list was being manipulated for profit and personal revenge, sometimes against friends as well as foes, and that those in power were turning a blind eye to these events.

Cicero also turned up other odd circumstances. Magnus and Capito had been enemies of the victim, and Magnus had fought with the elder Roscius over a lot of money.[5] The accused son, on the other hand, was in Ameria on the night of the murder, managing the family properties. Moreover, one Mallius Glaucia told Cicero that Magnus had sent Glaucia with the murder weapon, a dagger, via speedy carriage to Ameria, more than fifty miles away, immediately after the crime. Glaucia arrived in Ameria at dawn, where he did not tell the victim's immediate family of the tragedy but delivered the dagger to Magnus's cousin Roscius Capito and told him about the murder.

As the crowning point in this web of intrigue, Cicero also learned and could prove that Capito and Magnus had met with Chrysogonus four days after the crime. On that date, Chrysogonus had been outside Volterra, where Sulla was besieging the last citadel held by the *populares*. Moreover, both Roscius Capito and Roscius Magnus had known Chrysogonus for a long time. From this chain of evidence, Cicero concluded that they had gone to Chrysogonus to ask for his assistance in acquiring the victim's assets. Chrysogonus was in a position to manipulate the list of the proscribed after the fact, and Cicero concluded that he had used his power to do just that.

However, shortly after dividing the booty, its new possessors came under fire. In Ameria, where the victim had been held in high esteem, the locals refused to accept the results of these machinations, especially the fate of his son, who had been left penniless. A delegation of the ten most eminent Amerian city councillors was sent directly to Sulla at Volterra, where they planned to explain to him the numerous irregularities in the proceedings and to advocate for the young man, who they believed should have his inheritance returned to him.

According to a long-standing Roman tradition, this delegation was chosen by wealth and thus included Capito, thanks to his having acquired the victim's properties. With Capito on the committee, Chrysogonus was forewarned and prevented it from meeting with Sulla. He delayed the party and finally fobbed them off with the promise that the father's properties would be returned to the son. Capito had been instrumental in reaching this agreement and even promised to return his gains to the victim's son. Once the delegation had departed, the conspirators caused delay after delay to avoid fulfilling their promises.

It was now clear to the conspirators that they would never be able to enjoy their new wealth as long as the younger Sextus Roscius was alive. Their next step was a direct attempt on his life. But the young Roscius was smart enough to flee to Rome and the protection of his father's influential female patron. The conspirators then began the process of destroying him through a criminal trial. They trusted that Chrysogonus's power would be enough to intimidate the relevant court. Believing that the trial would be easy to win, the accuser gathered compliant witnesses.

Cicero foiled their plans with his well-prepared and bold per-

formance during the public proceedings. The accuser, who presented his claims first, had prudently avoided mentioning that
the victim had been on the list of the proscribed and that his
estate had been auctioned off. The conspirators had assumed
that Cicero, too, would overlook these points out of fear of pro-
voking Chrysogonus.[6] Instead, Cicero brought these matters
up and proceeded to reveal all of the other irregularities. As a
result, Sextus Roscius junior was acquitted, and Cicero became
a renowned defender. But Cicero, fearing revenge for his denun-
ciation of Chrysogonus, immediately withdrew to Athens,
Rhodes, and Asia Minor, where he stayed for years far from
Rome. He was quoted as having wanted to complete his rhetorical education.

TRANSMISSION

We know about this trial and its details from Cicero's speech
for the defense, which is almost completely extant.[7] In addition,
there are brief reports about his speech's repercussions, which
extended well beyond the dramatic acquittal. Cicero's plea was,
naturally, biased; it was carefully targeted to achieve his client's
acquittal. Nothing else was expected from an advocate in court
at that time.

Modern historians are therefore left with the problem of
determining what exactly happened based on Cicero's notori-
ously one-sided representation and a few supplemental notes.
Earlier scholars often fell into the trap of reading uncritically,
believing Cicero's account to be factual in all its detail and
scope. In contrast, two more recent historians dealing with this
case, an Australian and an American,[8] not only cast doubt on
Cicero's claims, about which there is reason to tread carefully;

but they also question the very basis of all of Cicero's evidence. Instead of building on historical sources such as Plutarch and Jerome, in addition to Cicero, these two scholars neutralize the historical record by forming their own, rather personal theories. A path between these two extremes is required.

EVIDENCE

Cicero assumes that there were two conspiracies. According to him, the murder was planned by Magnus and Capito and carried out by Magnus, either alone or with an accomplice, perhaps his associate Glaucia. Cicero deduced this first conspiracy after learning that Magnus and Glaucia were present on the scene immediately after the murder, and that Magnus had ordered Glaucia to bring the news and the murder weapon as quickly as possible to Capito, who was at bitter odds with the victim. Meanwhile, the person most affected by the crime, the younger Sextus Roscius, was deliberately left uninformed. The trip was made by carriage, as it seemed that the slightly built Glaucia would not have managed the trip on horseback.[9] Glaucia traveled without resting and covered the approximately sixty miles by dawn the next day—a tour de force for a Roman carriage on ancient roads at night. Why were Magnus and Glaucia on the scene? Why did Magnus want to inform Capito as quickly as possible? And why inform Capito at all?

The second conspiracy Cicero suspected was hatched after the successful commission of the murder. In order to acquire the victim's wealth, the murderers would have needed an extremely powerful ally, one who was greedy, unscrupulous, and yet worthy of their trust. Chrysogonus was just such a man. The three met just four days later; Chrysogonus was won over to the plan, and they succeeded in having the victim listed among the proscribed.

The next step was to auction off the victim's properties. Thanks to the Roman penchant for keeping records, it must have been quite easy to prove exactly when this happened, as well as that Chrysogonus bought everything for 2,000 sesterces, and that he then transferred the three most valuable properties to Capito, permitting Magnus to obtain the remaining transportable possessions. Chrysogonus was not normally this generous, which is why Cicero deduced the second conspiracy. Manfred Fuhrmann maintains that Cicero "spared" the powerful Chrysogonus by not accusing him of participating in the murder conspiracy.[10] Fuhrmann is right in that it is intrinsically probable that Chrysogonus participated in the first conspiracy as well. However, the defense was probably incapable of producing sufficient evidence to support his supposed involvement; thus they intentionally refrained from even mentioning it as a possibility. In any case, Cicero did not spare Chrysogonus in his speech, for he did accuse him of involvement in the later attempts to murder the accused, Cicero's client and the victim's son.[11]

Cicero did not debate statements made by the witnesses for the prosecution in his speech because they had not been heard at this point in the trial.[12] Nevertheless, he did cast doubts on their veracity in advance; he described them as having been bought.[13] According to Cicero, the primary accuser, Gaius Erucius, was completely unreliable; Cicero even dwelled on Erucius's uncertain parentage as widely accepted grounds for doubting his word.[14] Cicero further informed the court that Erucius was known for making accusations solely in pursuit of profit and that nothing mattered to him except money.[15] In this case, had the accused been found guilty, his property would have yielded very little profit, since the estates were already confiscated and the son left utterly destitute. Therefore, Erucius must have expected payment from Magnus, something the public was presumed to know.[16] The documents Capito would present,[17] who was summoned as a witness for the prosecution, would have been doctored, as Cicero proclaimed in advance.[18]

THE LAW OF PROSCRIPTION

High treason was punished by prohibiting the condemned from sharing fire and water, in other words, by ostracism. Following Sulla's victory in the civil war, the victors proclaimed thousands to be guilty of treason, and it goes without saying that not all of them could be granted a trial. The losing party's guilt was simply proclaimed to be obvious, and particular traitors were named in an official list of the proscribed.

At the beginning of his tenure as dictator, Sulla enacted a law according to which the possessions of the proscribed were forfeited *ipso jure* to the state. The state then sold any such property at auction, usually the entire holdings as one lot. Many of the proscribed had never adhered to the losing party, but Sulla could not count on his followers to restrict themselves to the freedoms allowed by his laws, even though they had already profited so richly from the overthrow of the previous government. Many of them used the general chaos to enrich themselves whenever the opportunity presented itself. Because so many estates were being auctioned off, the bids became increasingly lower. Moreover, they were often kept artificially low, as many of those interested in a certain set of holdings refrained from bidding if they became aware that one of the powerful had his eye on those properties. Such intimidation enabled Chrysogonus to purchase the murder victim's estate for one three-thousandth of its value.

However, if someone appeared on the list of the ostracized (proscribed) only after the closing date (1 June 81), the law of proscription did not apply to him. His property could not be auctioned, and all other transactions concerning his assets being thus legally void, his estates remained in his possession. Those who had acquired such property in good faith were not exempted from this ruling; at best, they could have acquired property through a prescription after the necessary period, which was set at two years for immovable properties, such as land. And even if the property's owner had died in the meantime, the land still belonged to his heirs.

In the case of the elder Sextus Roscius, only the younger Sextus Roscius could be considered his heir—unless he were now outlawed for some reason. Otherwise, he could reclaim the individual assets, no matter where they were or to whom they had been sold, by using the action for the return of property (*rei vindicatio*); in case of damage to these assets, or some act obstructing his use of them, he could bring suit for damages. Cicero repeatedly emphasized that according to the law the estate still belonged to his client.[19]

THE PUNISHMENT THAT THREATENED THE ACCUSED

For those who killed close relatives, especially their fathers, the punishment from time immemorial was the "patricide sack," whereby the murderer, together with "unclean" animals (usually a snake and a monkey), was sewn into a large leather sack that was then thrown into a river. This was the sentence that threatened the young Sextus Roscius.[20] However, at the beginning of his defense, Cicero just mentions that his client will be *eiectus,* cast out, if found guilty (§6 of Cicero's speech). This generally meant self-imposed exile as a consequence. However, we should not take Cicero's lenient sentence too literally. He only introduced his plea in section 6 and at that point mentions what a guilty verdict would impose only in very general terms.[21] The patricide sack was imposed only if the deed had been proven without a doubt, that is, if the accused confessed to the crime, if it had been witnessed, or was otherwise overt.[22] In Sextus Roscius's case, there was little likelihood of the crime being proved without a doubt.

EFFECT

The victory was really Cicero's. This is unanimously and unambiguously attested throughout late antiquity.[23] Sulla, who was still dictator, did not get involved, and even Chrysogonus appears to have remained silent on the matter. However, we do not know of any legal consequence of this victory. To prove the trial and Cicero's defense to have been a clear, legal success, all thirteen properties would have to have been returned to Sextus Roscius junior, and at the very least Erucius should have been prosecuted, and possibly Chrysogonus, Roscius Magnus, and Roscius Capito as well. At the end of his speech (§§128–29), Cicero indicates that his client might be satisfied with an acquittal without demanding damages—we do not know whether this was true. We have no further information concerning the younger Roscius's fate, nor that of the other primary figures in this affair.[24]

The acquitted son and heir had such distinguished contacts among the aristocracy that he probably demanded and received some or most of his inheritance back. But it is unlikely that his enemies were prosecuted—Erucius for frivolous litigation, or Chrysogonus for falsifying the list of the proscribed. To take Erucius and Chrysogonus to court, one would have needed an accuser. But it is very unlikely that anyone came forward, as we know that even the courageous Cicero preferred to distance himself from Rome and Italy for several years.[25]

And yet some significant consequences of the trial become apparent. The atmosphere of intimidation, fear, and repression that had characterized Sulla's early reign now began to subside. The tendency also to ignore the illegal proscriptions and auctions was indeed broken, even if it did not subside everywhere immediately. It again became possible to speak candidly in public, and freedom of speech could not be suppressed as it had been previously. The rule of law began to regain lost ground. In his universal *Chronicon,* or list of significant events in history, Jerome records only this trial and Cicero's departure from Rome as entries for the year 80 B.C.E.[26]

CHAPTER SEVEN

Defense against a Lover's Malice

Otacilia vs. Gaius Visellius Varro

Circa 65 B.C.E.

THE STORY

Gaius Visellius Varro had an illicit affair with Otacilia for many years. Varro was a well-known advocate, Cicero's maternal cousin, and in his later thirties at the time of our case. Otacilia was one or two years older than he and married to Juventius Laterensis, fifteen years her senior. One day, Varro fell so ill that one could assume he was dying. In ancient Rome, every head of household kept a household account record. To enable his lover to surreptitiously inherit some of his estate and with his approval, she wrote in her household account record that he owed her 300,000 sesterces (IIS). The intention was to allow Otacilia to claim this sum from Varro's heirs after his death. Of course, Otacilia had not loaned him any money, but she had generously bestowed other favors upon him over the years.

Otacilia became eager to pocket the money: she vowed to make special sacrifices to the gods if they fulfilled her desire and allowed Varro to die. But Varro regained his health. Extremely upset that her hopes for riches had been dashed, she underwent a sudden transformation from a compliant mistress into a bitter lender. She sued him for the 300,000 IIS, to which she believed she had a legal claim. The judge in this case was Gaius Aquilius Gallus. He enjoyed great authority, was distinguished in his knowledge of civil law, and regularly consulted with the most prestigious men in the empire. Being as wise and conscientious as he was, he dismissed Otacilia's suit.

The only record we possess of this trial comes from the aforementioned series of short, instructional narratives by Valerius Maximus, including the trials in chapters 3 and 4 of this book. Maximus appended the following moralizing commentary to our sordid tale: he had no doubt that had it been possible, Gallus, who protected Varro from his persecutor, would also have convicted him for his shameful behavior; but having no legal alternative, Gallus was limited to rejecting Otacilia's legal chicanery in this private case (*privatae actionis calumniam compescuit*), leaving the punishment for criminal adultery to the respective court.[1]

THE PARTICIPANTS, AND DATING THIS TRIAL

The three parties involved in this case all belong to the same social class as members of the lower nobility with hopes of rising higher. Both Laterensis and Varro had taken the first steps of the senatorial *cursus honorum*. Varro, at this time already a successful advocate with some legal experience, would eventually attain the rank of aedile, which was similar to a modern chief of police in prestige and duties.[2] It is doubtful whether Otacilia's husband ever attained that rank. Otacilia also belonged to a family of some political influence: her relatives included several ranking military officers who served under Pompey, the famous Roman general and politician.[3] She and her husband had a son about twenty-five at the time and poised to embark on his own career path leading to the senate.[4]

The judge, Aquilius Gallus, was of much higher political and social rank. Already a senior senator, Gallus was probably no younger than Otacilia and thus somewhat older than Varro. Gallus was praetor in 66 B.C.E. and thus presided over the standing jury court, which heard cases involving electoral corruption. Evidence of his social standing was his residence in Rome, which was considered the most beautiful in the city. Gallus also spent many years on the island of Kerkena (in the Gulf of Syrta in present-day Tunisia), where he owned a marvelous villa and offered instruction in Roman law.[5] Gallus not only stood head and shoulders above the other three socially; he was also one of the most famous of Rome's jurists at the time. His creativity is still greatly admired, although he left no written records. What we know about him is thanks to his students, who perpetuated his knowledge, as was often the case in antiquity.[6]

Our trial can be dated from what we know or can infer about the persons involved. Otacilia was born no later than 105 B.C.E.; Varro lived between circa 104 and 58; Laterensis's life can be dated to about 120–55 B.C.E.; Gallus lived between circa 105 and 45 B.C.E. When the latter held the praetorship in 66 B.C.E., he had to have been in Rome; we also know that he was in Rome in 55 B.C.E.[7] The particulars of this case occurred in Rome, and the trial was held there. Therefore, the hearings can most likely be dated in the period during or soon after Gallus's praetorship.[8]

THE COURSE OF EVENTS IN DETAIL

Otacilia was married to the much-older Laterensis, apparently without ever being under his marital authority, and she bore him a son soon after their marriage. When she was in her very late thirties and no longer subject to paternal authority either, she entered a sexual liaison with Varro, who was some years her junior and publicly more successful than her husband. Then Varro became so seriously ill that both assumed he would die.

At this point, Otacilia took stock of her material future. After all, she had to consider that Laterensis might learn of their affair, that he would then divorce her, and that her family would disinherit her. She succeeded in convincing the terminally ill Varro to agree that she make an entry into her household account record stating that he owed her 300,000 IIS. This was a fortune at the time, albeit a smaller one. For example, to achieve equestrian status (the lower nobility) one had to possess assets worth 400,000 IIS, and to belong to the senatorial ranks (the upper nobility) one had to own land valued at 1 million IIS. If we were to compare the price of land in Rome to today's values, 300,000 IIS would be the approximate equivalent of $750,000.[9]

Varro intended that this sum be used to satisfy his "debt" to Otacilia for her services, that is, the sexual favors that she had given him, but without publicly revealing the actual purpose of the payment. For this reason, there must have been a tacit agreement between the two at the conclusion of this portion of their "business." Entries in household account records could be formalized, making reference to an allegedly existing claim but not requiring further specification. The intent was thus ultimately a gift from a lover and not a repayment. Sexual relations, especially when adulterous, could not be considered a "service" legally speaking, and thus did not fall within the scope of legal activities qualifying for payment either as an advance or for services rendered. Otacilia and Varro must have known that their agreement was legally impossible. They both must also have understood that this payment would be made only if Varro actually died from his illness. It was thus a *donatio mortis causa* for this specific, impending death, and only in this instance; it did not generally apply if Varro died before Otacilia at any other point.

Valerius Maximus further qualified Varro's intent, implying that he wanted to give his mistress a benefit similar to a bequest (*legati genus esse voluit*). Varro's heirs were supposed to pay Otacilia 300,000 IIS from their inheritance, without an (apparent) *quid pro quo*, as if Varro had willed this sum to her. However, a bequest is free of a *quid pro quo*, as it is legally a gift, but the circumstances behind this "legacy" had to remain secret. For this reason, the participants made the benefit look as if it were a repayment for a debt Varro had previously contracted with Otacilia (*debiti nomine colorando*), perhaps for a loan she had given him.

Otacilia made several vows (*vota*) to the gods, which she naturally kept secret from others. Avowals of this type involved a common formula: if the god fulfilled the request, the supplicant would do something for that god, such as making a special offering or regular sacrifices, financing an altar or the building of even a small temple. Otacilia begged the gods to let Varro die. Luckily for her, she did not have to keep her bargain with the gods, as her wish was not fulfilled. Varro recovered. He must have assumed (perhaps she led him to believe) that she would be happy about his recovery and that their intimate relationship would resume. However, the very opposite transpired. Otacilia, refusing to forget about the money she had believed was within her grasp, now demanded it. When Varro refused to pay her voluntarily, she sued him for the money, using the entry in her account book without referring to the real reason for Varro's debt.

To achieve her goal, Otacilia had to summon Varro before the Roman city magistrate, the *praetor urbanus,* before whom she had to file the appropriate legal writ, in this case a plea for a specific sum of money owed (*actio certae creditae pecuniae,* also called a *condictio*). Varro refused to recognize her demand and indeed disputed its legitimacy; he must have filed an objection (*exceptio*) in response to the writ. The praetor conceded the validity of Otacilia's writ, but he must also have granted the *exceptio* as filed.[10] He then transferred the case, as was the legal custom, to an honorary lay judge (*judex,* a position for which high-ranking citizens volunteered). It was the role of the *judex* to request and evaluate the legally relevant facts about the case. In this case, our *judex* was Gaius Aquilius Gallus, the most famous jurist of his time. According to Roman law, if the parties in a civil suit did not agree on a specific *judex* among themselves, the judge was chosen from a list of possible judges.[11] In our case, it is thus highly doubtful that Gallus's designation was random; it is more likely that the praetor or one of the parties suggested him, and that his nomination was accepted by the other party, or if it was the praetor's suggestion, by both parties. Gallus could take advice from leading statesmen (*adhibitis in consilium principibus civitatis*). There was, however, little to discuss. In the end, Gallus dismissed Otacilia's lawsuit.

In his conclusion, Valerius Maximus indulges in a moralizing observation based on an anachronistic speculation, namely that Gallus was not satisfied with dismissing Otacilia's suit but wanted to reprimand Varro as well for having committed adultery. However, because of the aforementioned writ, Gallus was not in a position to denounce Varro, as the lawsuit concerned only the monetary claim. To punish adultery, Gallus left the case to the criminal court responsible for adultery (*adulterii crimen publicae quaestioni vindicandum reliquit*). Maximus disgresses into criminal law here. The penal code valid in his time punished adulterers by confiscating half of all the man's assets and a third of the woman's, including half her dowry, banishing them both from Rome and Italy and depriving them of Roman citizenship. But the law on adultery was enacted later by Augustus in 18 B.C.E. Before then, each adulterer was punished by his and her respective *pater familias,* and each was banished from within a two-hundred-mile radius of Rome.[12] Maximus, writing for his contemporaries, especially the aging emperor Tiberius, believed he owed his audience a strong statement about this particular case of adultery. Both Varro and Otacilia were guilty of an extramarital affair, and he felt both should also have been punished according to the law at that time.

EVALUATION ACCORDING TO CIVIL LAW

At this point, we should first clarify the legal nature of the household account entries. Every Roman head of household kept a household account record, the *codex accepti et expensi* (book of receipts and expenses). Thus every independent man no longer under paternal authority, and every independent woman who had not been transferred from paternal authority to the marital authority of her husband (seldom done since the late Republic), kept a household account book. Revenues, expenses, claims, debts, and inventory were entered into the household account in chronological order.[13]

Claims (*nomina*) fell into one of two basic categories: they were recorded or constitutive. Recorded entries (*nomina arcaria*) had a legal basis, such as a loan that had been paid out, a payment for a purchase, or something similar—that is, only actual cash claims having a declaratory effect could be entered as *nomina arcaria*. Constitutive entries (*nomina transscripticia*) established an obligation to pay a debt; they could refer to an existing claim or (as a constitutive entry) establish a new claim solely on the basis of an approved entry in the creditor's household account record, which is why the latter is called a written (*litteris*) contract. Such entries (*nomina transscripticia*) were considered legally valid only if the debtor had given his specific approval, which could also be informal in nature, that is, with no written entry in the borrower's household account record. The claim referred to could also be fictitious, as in our case.

A *nomen transscripticium* is similar to a promissory note nowadays. A buyer who cannot immediately pay cash for a product signs a promissory note containing the amount due, and he gives the note to the seller. The promissory note is a contract obliging the signer to pay the funds in full to the promissory note holder upon demand or on a specific date in the future. No defects or other complaints regarding the object of sale are respected in this contract.

To return to our case, Otacilia would not have made a declaratory entry (*nomen arcarium*) in her household account record because she would then have had to prove a basis for the entry to Varro's heirs. Indeed, when Valerius Maximus depicts Otacilia's position once more at the end of his narrative, he states retrospectively that she ensured her claim *inani stipulatione* (by an empty stipulation). A *stipulatio* was actually a spoken contract expressing a debt that, when agreed upon by both parties using specific wording, was considered legally binding, regardless of the actual reasons leading to the debt; therefore it was called a verbal obligation (*verbis obligatio*).

Valerius Maximus's wording here led two legal historians, Ulrich von Lübtow[14] and Max Kaser,[15] to conclude that Otacilia actually supported her claim based on a *stipulatio,* and that the entry in the household account book was merely declaratory, and thus a simple *nomen arcarium.* However, both authors also maintain that Varro agreed to this entry himself and probably even did so in writing. They seem to suppose that a deathly ill man was able to participate in a *stipulatio,* a laborious procedure that usually had to be performed before several witnesses. Furthermore, they claim that our Varro must have provided written confirmation about a household account entry that would have been valid without any formalities. Ultimately, my objection to von Lübtow's and Kaser's arguments is that an entry in the household account record proved nothing in and of itself. For a constitutive entry, or *nomen transscripticium,* the debtor's agreement must be proved. If the entry was disputed by the debtor or his heirs, the proof could be just one trustworthy witness. For this reason, the reader should give the term Maximus uses in the main body of his narrative when describing the reasoning behind the debt more weight than in his later review of the case, in which he may have used the term *stipulatio* improperly as a short description of an abstract debt obligation.[16]

This line of argument is, however, beside the point. Whether Varro had entered into a verbal obligation with a *stipulatio,* or, as is more likely, a constitutive entry, or *nomen transscripticium* entered into Otacilia's household account record, the only pertinent action in this case was the aforementioned *actio certae creditae pecuniae,* Otacilia's claim for a certain sum of money owed. This was abstractly but concisely formulated. As applied to our case, it read: "If it is proven that Visellius Varro is obliged to pay Otacilia 300,000 IIS, you, *judex* Aquilius Gallus, are to condemn Varro to pay Otacilia 300,000 IIS; if it is not proven, then acquit him."[17] According to this tautological plea formulation, Gallus merely had to determine whether Varro actually owed Otacilia 300,000 IIS. If Varro had approved a *nomen transscripticium* or had entered into a verbal *stipulatio,* then he did indeed owe her the money.

The execution of such a formal act was sufficient to generate a payment obligation. The *actio certae creditae pecuniae* or *condictio* was the primary example of a *stricti juris judicium,* a trial in which the *judex* was strictly limited in his actions and thus had no leeway to consider good faith (*bona fides*), to determine what was most equitable (*aequius melius*), or to use his discretion in deciding (*arbitrio tuo*). Otacilia was apparently counting on this restriction of judicial ability. However, the *judex* decided against her. How did this happen?

Beginning in the late Republic, extenuating circumstances could be considered even in a case of *stricti juris judicium.* The person being sued had to claim such circumstances at a specific point in the course of the proceedings, namely at the confrontation with the accuser before the praetor. A provision (*praescriptio*) could be inserted at the beginning of the formal plea at this time, or an objection (*exceptio*) could be inserted at an appropriate point in the plea. If the person being sued had innocently omitted this step, he might be able to move the *judex* hearing the case to bring the matter back before the praetor, who would then be able to insert the desired provision or objection into the formal plea.

According to the better-documented Roman law of the imperial period, two centuries later, there were three possible objections in our case: the objection according to the *Lex Cincia* against excessive gifts (*exceptio legis Cinciae*); the objection of an informal, deviating agreement (*exceptio pacti*); and the objection due to fraud (*exceptio doli*). Maximus describes Otacilia's *actio* quite exactly: a presumed loan of money. However, he does not mention the legal means by which the case was dismissed. Rather, he makes judgments in anticipation of the outcome: Otacilia made her claim with "false mind" (*fronte inverecunda*) and an "empty stipulation" (*inani stipulatione*). At the end, Maximus says that Gallus let his *prudentia* and *religio* prevail, that is, his wisdom and conscientiousness, and rebuffed her frivolous complaint (*calumnia*).

The *Lex Cincia,* enacted about 200 B.C.E., prohibited excessive gifts to persons outside the immediate family circle. Anyone who effectively promised such a gift, as was the case here, could ward off a suit by invoking the *Lex Cincia.* But this legal and less-dramatic means of fending off the lawsuit would have revealed that Otacilia was not claiming repayment for a loan, but that Varro just wanted her to receive this sum of money. Anyone in the audience at this public trial[18] could easily have deduced the reason behind this substantial gift. The *Lex Cincia,* while helpful in this case, would have nullified any discretion the parties had left.[19] Yet the greatest argument against Varro's invocation of the *Lex Cincia* lies in the point raised by Gallus that Maximus stresses: the accusation against Otacilia, that she had knowingly submitted a spurious claim. The option to raise an objection based on the *Lex Cincia* was up to the person being sued, in this case Varro; the plaintiff, Otacilia, could not know if he would do it, but had to await his decision.

Maximus condemns Otacilia right from the start. He found her false mind (*frons inverecunda*) particularly offensive, for had she not secretly speculated on Varro's death? Later, opposing Varro's recovery, she was unwilling to abide by their tacit agreement: to claim the money only from Varro's heirs if he were to die from this illness. For Maximus, the original contract should have been void on the grounds that it was an offense against public morality (*contra bonos mores*). This, however, would be a misreading of the applicable laws. Max Kaser has clearly demonstrated that it was much later that transactions began to be considered automatically void when they violated public morality. Even if the layman Maximus had imagined this already in the first century C.E. because of his advanced sense of justice, in fact, precursor rulings did not appear until the third century, and clear laws did not come into force until the fifth. During the late Republic, this legal argument would have been inconceivable.[20]

Varro might have considered a second possible objection, based on rules governing an informal agreement (*exceptio pacti*). But this idea lies outside of what Maximus in fact reports. It is true that Otacilia no longer followed the terms of the contract—she claimed the money even though Varro had recovered. But what Maximus focuses on is her greed even as her lover was knocking on death's door. And he reports that Gallus's judgment was narrowly focused on a defense based on fraud (*exceptio doli*).

During the imperial period, this defense would have turned on these words: "if in this matter nothing occurred [in the past] and nothing does occur at present due to Otacilia's fraud" (*si in ea re nihil dolo malo Otaciliae factum sit neque fiat*). At that time, one distinguished between two kinds of fraudulent behavior: past fraud, committed at the conclusion of the contract (*dolus praeteritus*, also known as *dolus specialis*), and present fraud (*dolus praesens* or *dolus generalis*), or intentional deceit when filing the lawsuit. Otacilia would obviously have satisfied the criteria for both types of fraud; Gallus's primary accusation was that she was filing a frivolous lawsuit, thus committing present (general) fraud.

We do not know how Varro's objection read at the time of the trial; in particular, we do not know if it already referred explicitly to present fraud. As stated earlier, Gallus's jurisprudence teacher, Quintus Mucius Scaevola the Pontifex, was the first to introduce a very general objection based on behavior in bad faith on the part of the accuser—more exactly, an offense against good faith (the opposite of fraud). This defense could be used to counter any suit, indeed as a provision (*praescriptio*) to be placed at the beginning of the formal plea.

Scaevola initiated this objection in 94 B.C.E. after the senate had sent him to the wealthy province of Asia (western Asia Minor), a region so shamelessly looted by Roman merchants that the native inhabitants were fomenting rebellion. The new Roman authority, Scaevola, invoked this *praescriptio* to protect the locals, especially the Greek city-states, from Roman capitalists, who had forced the Greeks into taking out loans at outrageous interest. Having taken the Greeks' wealth, the Roman entrepreneurs now planned to take possession of the family silver; the legal limitations on interest rates applied only to Roman citizens. The *praescriptio* still reads rather circuitously and was limited to transactions involving previous fraud: "This matter will be heard: if that agreement was made in a manner inconsistent with good faith, it must not be kept."[21]

A further point should be made about Aquilius Gallus, the judge who ruled against Otacilia. He went on to develop the general plea concerning fraud (*actio de dolo*) as a tool for attack, not just a defense mechanism against frivolous suits. At Gallus's suggestion, the urban praetor integrated this judgment into his perpetual edict (*edictum perpetuum*), an edict that stayed in force during his entire term of office. According to Cicero, it was around 76 B.C.E. that the statesman Gaius Aurelius Cotta concluded his list of private law pleas by praising "finally the broom by which means all wickedness shall be swept out, the procedure concerning fraud, which my good friend Gaius Aquilius developed."[22] The development and legal enactment of this argument thus took place not long before 76 B.C.E. In 44 B.C.E., Cicero noted that such a remedy was not available in earlier cases, because "my colleague in office and friend, Aquilius Gallus, had not yet developed the formulas on fraud."[23]

Here Cicero is speaking about legal remedies against fraud in the plural (*de dolo malo formulas*), and thus not only about that specific plea. If one interprets this statement literally (and there is no reason not to do so), then Aquilius Gallus must have developed at least one second legal remedy against fraud between 76 and 44 B.C.E. This suggests the conjecture that Gallus also reformulated the objection (*exceptio*) based on fraud, in particular that he appended the possibility of fraud just committed in the present (*dolus praesens, generalis*) to the well-known possibility of fraud during the conclusion of a transaction. Perhaps Otacilia's case served as the catalyst.[24] Once Gallus had taken on the role of *judex* in her case, he may have seen this case as a means of considering Varro's objection, should it prove to be true, within the context of the formal plea cited above, and of formulating broader principles against fraud. Gallus could have legally implemented this by convincingly formulating the objection based on fraud, namely by discerning two provisions therein, and recommending to the acting *praetor urbanus* that he incorporate this bipartite objection into Otacilia's legal writ.

People appear to have been satisfied with the solution this defense made possible. Otacilia was left with nothing, and public sympathy for her was out of the question. After all, it was she who had drawn her devious machinations into the public arena in the first place. The authority of Aquilius Gallus led to incorporation of the now validly formulated objection into the standing edicts issued from that year on by the two praetors responsible for private law, the *praetor urbanus* and the *praetor peregrinus.* We then find them in the edict from the second century C.E.

EFFECT

Valerius Maximus began his report on this trial with the words "The case I am going to speak of was not consigned to silence"; in other words, it remained within living memory. We even have a witness from the Augustan period. The most famous jurist from that period, Marcus Antistius Labeo, then advising on a similar trial, declared the objection based on fraud as relevant in a case involving a *stipulatio,* again most likely the *actio certae creditae pecuniae.*

That trial involved a man who became, like Varro, deathly ill. He promised (stipulated) a specific sum to his wife's cousin, money that should actually go to the wife. But according to Roman law all spousal gifts were invalid. Obviously, our defendant was attempting to circumvent the laws preventing him from making a spousal gift; gifts to a surviving spouse, *donationes mortis causa,* were then also invalid. Like Varro, our defendant recovered his health, and, like Otacilia, his cousin sued for the money. Labeo informed the husband that he could base his defense on fraud. In the second century C.E., Julian approved this approach, as did Ulpian in the third.[25] Their opinions also stressed present or general fraud (*dolus praesens* or *generalis*). However, the objection's scope had been expanded in the meantime, and it was now granted even if the lawsuit was considered to be merely grossly unfair by an impartial authority. Moreover, it no longer mattered whether the plaintiff was cognizant of this unfairness and could himself be accused of fraudulent behavior.

Two examples serve well to demonstrate the objection's new scope concerning unfairness. Suppose a man makes a contract with a clause that offers damages if he does not appear at the market at noon on Friday. On the Friday in question he is stuck at home with a communicable disease. Under the expanded rules, he could ward off a lawsuit using the objection based on fraud, regardless of whether or not the accuser had been adequately informed about his illness at the start of that trial.[26] Or suppose I had a young horse in my stable, too young to work, and this horse escaped. A stranger caught it and sold it to you, who in turn bought in good faith, believing the seller to be the owner. A while later I recognize my horse and demand that you return it to me. While keeping the animal, you had paid for its upkeep. If I am unwilling to compensate you for those expenses, you can reject my suit using the objection based on general fraud (*exceptio doli generalis*).[27]

From this point forward, the objection based on fraud was a fixed feature in civil law jurisprudence, limited in that present, impartial "fraud" on the part of the accuser had become apparent as the proceedings began, and of which there was sufficient evidence of "gross unfairness" in the meantime. There are records of many examples of its use as special provisions over time that were adopted as specific standards in the inventory of civil jurisprudence opinions.[28] The general objection based on fraud was even expanded further to include a general remedy for the abusive exercise of rights.

If Otacilia were to sue over a promissory note today, she

would have no chance of success as soon as Varro revealed the exact circumstances, in particular that he had signed the note to be used only in the case of his death from the illness from which he had just recovered. Indeed, Varro could even take the initiative immediately after his recovery and demand the promissory note back because it would have unjustifiably enriched Otacilia. The right to demand return of a promissory note was developed by jurists during the Roman imperial period: two hundred years after our case, the recovered Varro would have been able to demand an annulment from Otacilia of her claim based on her household account entry with a *condictio* as well. A *condictio* would also have been granted in the meantime if someone had provided something to someone, and both agreed that it had been provided for a specific purpose. In this case, Varro had provided Otacilia with a claim, but the intended result of that provision failed to occur.

CHAPTER EIGHT

Corrupter of Morals through Poetry, or Accessory to a Conspiracy?

Ovid's Banishment

8 C.E.

THE EVENTS

In 8 C.E. the renowned poet Ovid suffered a calamity that would cloud the rest of his life. He was then fifty years old, scion of a respected equestrian family from Sulmona in Abruzzo, and a celebrity in Rome. But the emperor Augustus suddenly exiled him to Tomis (present-day Constanta), a place far away on the Black Sea where hardly any of the inhabitants spoke Latin. Our knowledge about what led to his banishment stems primarily from Ovid himself. He wrote several works in exile, including "Sorrows" (*Tristia*), "Letters from the Black Sea" (*Epistulae ex Ponto*), and the diatribe "Ibis" (*In Ibin*), in which he also referred to his trial. In addition to explicit statements, which the reader should not simply accept as historical facts, these works contain insinuations and pregnant silences. Scholars have long argued

83

over how this information should be interpreted, and numerous theories have been presented.[1] The most common conclusion has been that Ovid was guilty of sexual misconduct,[2] and of its incitement in his "Art of Love" (*Ars amatoria*), a doubtlessly incriminating work in that regard. Yet more exacting analysis and proper consideration of the tension between poetic fiction and historical events have laid many of the hypotheses to rest while supporting the following.[3]

Augustus himself pronounced the sentence, announcing it publicly by way of imperial edict,[4] a highly unusual format for a judicial decision. This edict stated that the condemned had incited others to adultery by means of his poem,[5] the *Ars amatoria,* even though it had been published seven or eight years previously, in 1 B.C.E. or 1 C.E.[6] The particular act of adultery for which Ovid was punished must have been the recently exposed affair between the emperor's granddaughter, Julia, and Decimus Junius Silan.[7] Julia was married at the time to Lucius Aemilius Paulus.[8] Given the numerous and sumptuous banquets that Julia and Paulus hosted, as well as Ovid's popularity in their social circles, it is very likely that Ovid was a welcome guest at their house,[9] and that his young hosts would have become familiar with his love poetry. In addition to the *Ars amatoria,* these include the *Amores,* the *Remedia amoris,* and the *Heroides,* the last being a series of fictitious love letters from famous mythological women addressed to their absent lovers.

As we have learned, the punishment for adultery was banishment from Rome and Italy, combined with the loss of Roman citizenship. The exiled person was allowed to keep half of his assets, the other half being forfeited to the state; but loss of citizenship also entailed annulment of his marriage. At the time, Ovid was married to his third wife, this time happily.[10] In writing about the verdict, Ovid reiterates that he could have been condemned to death,[11] and that the emperor had spoken to him directly. Both of these statements imply that there was a second, far more important reason for his banishment than his poems. But Ovid believed it wiser to say nothing more of this if he hoped to eventually gain a pardon.[12] Nevertheless, we can identify this reason.

Others involved in this case were punished even more severely. Julia was punished for adultery and exiled to the island of Tremiti, north of the Gargano Peninsula in the Adriatic.[13] Silan's son, whom she bore in exile, was killed on Augustus's orders.[14] Silan, surprisingly, was not punished right away. He was informally advised that the emperor never wanted to see him again, and thus considered it prudent to leave Italy. After Augustus's death, his successor, Tiberius, allowed Silan to return.[15] In contrast, Julia's husband, Paulus, was convicted of treason and executed.[16] By examining the relative punishments meted out, we can conclude that plans forged in Julia's house for a different succession after Augustus amounted to treason.

Augustus had no son, but he wanted a successor as emperor. He had named two promising grandsons, his daughter's children and Julia's brothers, as his heirs, but the boys died in 2 and 4 C.E. under mysterious circumstances. The aging Augustus therefore adopted his stepson Tiberius, the elder son of his second wife, Livia, from her first marriage and thus not related to Augustus or Julia by blood. He also adopted his last remaining grandson, Agrippa Postumus, Julia's remaining brother, who was barely fifteen years old at the time. And he prevailed upon Tiberius to adopt his nephew Germanicus, the son of Tiberius's dead brother. In the years that followed, Livia's influence grew. Agrippa Postumus fell out of her favor, and then out of Augustus's. The emperor, having adopted paternal authority, banished

Postumus in 7 C.E.[17] His exile directed the succession definitively away from Augustus's family line to Livia's; they had no children together. And with Tiberius's adoption of Germanicus, this new imperial line was fixed for two future generations.

Julia must have felt that she and her close relatives had been demoted. The Augustan family line ran through her exiled brother, now nineteen years old, and her own legitimate children with her patrician husband Paulus included a son who could claim lineage as noble as that of the Julians and the Claudians, Livia's sons.[18] Ovid may have learned in Julia's house of alternative plans for the succession even if he did not actively participate in the discussions himself; at any rate, he lost no opportunity to remind his readers that he had only seen or heard of something terrible.[19] Yet he also claimed that he had in no way agitated against the emperor. From a legal standpoint, however, he would have been required to inform the authorities about any such plans, or even mere intellectual games of this nature. The latter also fulfill the definition of treason, since they can serve as preliminary steps toward the deed itself.

THE TRIAL

Ovid states that he was condemned neither by the senate, the body that passed judgment mainly on misdeeds by senators,[20] nor by a jury; thus the proceedings were not conducted as an ordinary trial, but by the emperor himself.[21] However, the most unusual aspect of this trial is that the verdict and sentence against Ovid were delivered behind closed doors when Augustus angrily confronted Ovid with the second, main charge, which he was to keep forever secret.[22] The trial procedures involving adultery were highly regulated down to the last detail, but here Augustus reduced them to a bare minimum. Apparently he wanted to reproach Ovid with the main charge, which had become quite well known;[23] but he feared that if it became part of the official record, it might stir up further controversy about his succession. Therefore, he published the verdict in the form of an imperial edict, attested to in this and just one other case,[24] and simply declared that Ovid was banished by reason of incitement to commit adultery through his *Ars amatoria*.

THE OFFICIAL JUSTIFICATION

Ovid declares himself to be innocent, at least as concerns sexual misconduct.[25] In pre-Christian periods, and in several countries up to the twentieth century, adultery was legally understood to mean only sexual intercourse with a married woman. In contrast, sexual misbehavior by married men with unmarried women was something completely different. In the first two books of his *Ars amatoria,* Ovid describes how a man can seduce a woman, and in the third book, how a woman can seduce a man. It is conceivable that his text might have contributed to an extramarital affair. From a legal standpoint, Ovid may have inspired a reader to commit adultery or may have aided and abetted in its commission.[26] Yet the poet insists that he himself has no idea how to seduce a married woman. He further claims that it never occurred to him that a married woman could be induced to commit adultery through his poetry.[27] Of course, these lines of Ovid's poetry cannot be taken at face value. If the poet had made these claims during a legal hearing, they would have been regarded as mere self-justifying assertions.

In addition, Ovid argued that the incriminating texts were already several years old when he was banished for writing them.[28] That fact, however, is legally irrelevant. Literary works can easily trigger an act several years after publication or lead to the commission of adultery, to return specifically to our case. Instigation to commit a crime or aiding and abetting are punishable only if a crime is actually committed as a result. A crime of this type had indeed recently occurred, and both Silan and Julia must have been familiar with Ovid's *Ars amatoria*. Being then about thirty years old, Julia could certainly have read the poems and been influenced by them.

Adultery had become punishable only in 18 B.C.E. At that time, twenty-five years before our case, members of the senate had openly sneered in the emperor's presence because of his numerous affairs, some of which involved married women.[29] Thus Augustus, at their insistence, enacted the *Lex Julia de adulteriis coercendis* (Julian law for punishing adultery). This law, as stated previously, defined the punishment for adultery and regulated the legal procedures by instituting a public trial before a jury.

We have to ask whether Augustus received legal advice during all of this, and if so, from whom. Ovid accuses a certain enemy of discrediting him with the emperor by quoting individual lines from the *Ars amatoria* out of context.[30] In 1971, Raoul Verdière revealed the name Ateius Capito, found in telestics and acrostics (the last letters and first letters of poetic lines, respectively, read from above to below or backward) in Ovid's *Tristia*.[31] In 1981, L. Janssens found similar acrostics in Ovid's diatribe *In Ibin*, which was also written in his exile; the title refers to the ibis, an unclean bird.[32] Capito was court jurist for Augustus, and Tacitus and Suetonius characterize him as a career civil servant. He had already advised the emperor in a number of delicate situations.[33] He seems to have been engaged in this legal conundrum as well, because the official rationale for Ovid's banishment was legally creative indeed. But Janssens surely goes too far when he claims that Capito is the model for the reviled villain in Ovid's poem *In Ibin:* a man who had been Ovid's friend but now conspired against his return, harassing Ovid's wife still in Rome, and coveting Ovid's fortune. The telestics and acrostics in the diatribe *In Ibin,* which Janssens so readily accepts,[34] are overly construed and thus appear less than convincing.

THE SECOND OFFENSE

Ovid was ordered not to name the second charge against him, for which the emperor reproached him only verbally, yet angrily and with sharp words;[35] the poet acquiesced to the emperor's desire for discretion.[36] Yet he cannot resist dropping hints about it in his poems. He states repeatedly that his transgression was much less grievous than taking up arms against the emperor. He also claims that he would never have gone so far as to threaten the emperor's life,[37] nor would he have delivered speeches directed against Augustus,[38] nor pursued an agenda injurious to him.[39] These actions would have constituted treason without a doubt, but it could also have been committed in other ways. Ovid states that he was guilty only of seeing something criminal, and completely by chance at that.[40] He was guilty only of an error or an aberration,[41] a criminal naïveté, folly, anxiety.[42] He agreed that his behavior certainly deserved punishment, but felt that it was also ultimately excusable.[43]

The law concerning treason (*Lex Julia maiestatis*) was enacted about 45 B.C.E.; Julius Caesar had proposed it.[44] It defined crimes of treason and outlined them in detail. But it also contained the general clause "by whose deceit or oath anyone is forced to act in a way against the Roman state" (*cuius dolo malo iureiurando quis adactus est, quo adversus rem publicam faciat).*[45] Ovid appears to have observed treasonous deliberations and then to have believed, rather naively, that by not participating he was not truly involved. He likewise seems not to have considered that whoever knew of such plans and failed to disclose them to the proper authorities could also be acting against the Roman state. Ovid's failure to betray such activities could have been interpreted as deceit, though he himself called it a forgivable mistake. That this was indeed the offense that Augustus held against him as being most important is demonstrated by the punishments of Aemilius Paulus and Silan.

The type of treasonous considerations that may have been discussed can be determined by considering the time frame in which the authorities acted against Julia, her husband, and Ovid: against him only in late 8 C.E., but as early as late 7 C.E. against Julia and Paulus. In 7 C.E., the question of Augustus's succession, which had long been uncertain, was finally clarified. Through the definitive removal of Julia's remaining brother, her relatives, Augustus's descendants, were ultimately excluded from the line of succession in favor of Livia's son and grandson.[46] To understand these events, Julia's interests ought to be considered: she was the wife of a patrician from a highly regarded family and mother to a great-grandson of Augustus. It is also worth noting that after Augustus's death and the ascension of Tiberius, Ovid apparently gave up all hopes of a pardon.[47] This all leads us to conclude that Julia's circle had argued about replacing Tiberius, or at least weakening his prospects, in favor of Julia's brother Agrippa Postumus or even her husband Paulus or their son. It may also be true that Livia and Augustus felt themselves to have been attacked by Ovid's drama *Medea* (now lost), in which the eponymous main character kills her children.[48]

THE PUNISHMENT

Ovid was indeed banished to a distant locale. He had understand-able reasons for exaggerating how dull and dreary his life there was, lacking all Roman culture. Nevertheless, he retained his freedom and even his citizenship, and thus his marriage. More-over, he kept his assets,[49] apparently all of them.[50] Yet Augustus had all of Ovid's works removed from the public libraries,[51] and the *Ars amatoria* was blacklisted.[52] But that was only an indirect result of the published verdict. Ovid was deeply grateful to the emperor for having mitigated his sentence.[53]

We know that Augustus had introduced specific punish-ments for adultery a quarter century earlier, in the law he him-self enacted to fight this crime. Aside from banishment, the condemned man forfeited half of his assets, the woman a third, including half of her dowry, both lost citizenship, and women convicted of adultery were prohibited from remarrying.[54] Con-tributors to a crime, especially instigators and accessories, were generally punished identically to the primary actors.[55] Accord-ing to those stipulations, Ovid should have lost his citizenship, which would have voided his marriage, and he should have been forced to give up half of his estate, yet neither occurred. The reason for the emperor's clemency may well have been the rec-ognition that Ovid the writer had only indirectly instigated the actions of others, though Ovid the observer had failed to report and prevent them.

PETITIONS FOR MERCY

As long as Augustus lived, Ovid went to great lengths to secure a pardon. He wrote numerous quasi-sincere poetic letters intended for publication and addressed to influential friends in Rome, his wife, and Augustus.[56] These include the five books of the *Tristia,* begun on his journey into exile in the fall of 8 C.E. and concluded in 12 C.E., and from 12 to 14 C.E. *Epistulae ex Ponto.*[57] Ovid writes that his love poetry was meant to be harmless, a mere poetic dalliance,[58] and that his error was likewise excusable, arising as it did out of naïveté and not malice. He had not acted to gain advantage for himself.[59] Augustus had indeed already pardoned men who had openly opposed him.[60] It is true that Augustus, especially toward the end of his life, tended to show mercy,[61] and he had reconciled with Agrippa behind Livia's back (though the evidence for this is questionable). The sudden death of Augustus also meant the end of Agrippa.[62]

Ovid then focused his attentions on Germanicus, who was married to Julia's younger sister Agrippina. The first six books of Ovid's "On the Roman Calendar" (*Fasti*), which were to be completed in Rome, were dedicated to him.[63] However, all of these efforts came to nothing. Ovid finally settled into his new surroundings, learned Getish, and even wrote poetry in that language. Appropriately, he composed a poem in praise of Augustus.[64] In time, the city of Constanta and neighboring towns came to honor him.[65]

IDIOSYNCRASIES OF THIS CASE

As unusual as this legal procedure was, if one can call it that,[66] the aspect that later periods considered important was that it was conducted before the emperor in person, and in private, not publicly. The word "private" here does not mean that Ovid and Augustus were alone; at least one accuser and the emperor's advisers, his *consilium,* would have been present as well. It should

be understood that when the emperor chaired a military tribunal in the field or acted as a *judex extraordinarius* in the provinces,
he could do away with general criminal procedures, especially
with the public criminal procedure. In Rome, however, the
emperor regularly held public court, especially in criminal matters.[67] In this trial, he decided to deviate from one of the central
procedural rules, that of being open to the public. As mentioned
earlier, the verdict was also announced in an idiosyncratic manner, namely as an edict. Augustus orally reproached the accused
with a second charge, but it was not really heard, at least it was
not included in the public verdict.

The constitutional basis for all of Augustus's liberties is not
clear. He seems to have summarily ignored the standard procedures in this case, because raison d'état seemed to require it. Nor
did he follow the legal guidelines in punishing Ovid. Instead, he
employed his own discretion here as well by not claiming half
of Ovid's estate as mandated by the law, nor did Ovid lose his
citizenship. We are dealing here with the genesis of the imperial court, whose legal basis remains unknown,[68] and which later
emperors, especially Claudius, used more vigorously.[69]

This case is instructive for another reason, too. Today we still
observe politicians who, seeing their power threatened, accuse
their political opponents and whistleblowers of having committed moral misdeeds, and, if possible, criminal offenses.[70] This
occurred in Germany in the early 1950s. The conservative Catholic politician Alois Hundhammer had been strongly criticized in
the *Süddeutsche Zeitung* for allowing his religious beliefs to influence his political decisions. The newspaper's founder and editor
in chief, Werner Friedmann, was sent to prison for illicit sexual
relations with an economic dependent. In fact, the woman, whom
Friedmann later married (the marriage lasted until his death),

had worked briefly at the newspaper in a position quite removed from his supervisory capacity. Politicians, especially authoritarian ones wanting to eliminate popular rivals, often grasp at such means, researching or even inventing scandals from their opponents' private lives to publicly discredit them.

CHAPTER NINE

A Precautionary Crucifixion

The Trial of Jesus

7 April 30 C.E.

THE EVENTS

When Jesus was living in Palestine, the region was divided into four territories. Let us begin with Judea including Jerusalem, a special part of the Roman province of Syria, but governed by its own prefect from the equestrian class. This prefect generally resided in Caesarea Maritima, but he also made use of a palace in Jerusalem that had been built by Herod the Great, a client king until his death in 4 B.C.E. Herod's palace continued to serve as the primary seat of the now Roman authority whenever the prefect felt it necessary, especially during large Jewish festivals. Those events filled the city with celebrants from Palestine and many surrounding regions. The second territory was Galilee, located north of Judea and west of Lake Gennesaret (Sea of Galilee); the village of Nazareth lay within its borders. This region was ruled by Herod Antipas, a Jewish client prince who enjoyed going to Jerusalem during the high Jewish holidays and had his own palace in the old capital. The third territory lay to the north and east of the same lake and included the Golan Heights; Herod Antipas's half brother Philip ruled these areas as tetrarch. Finally, the fourth territory belonged to the large province of Syria, governed by a senator whose province stretched from Syria proper to Phoenicia and as far south as Haifa including the Decapolis, a politically and culturally united league of ten cities, to the south and southeast of Lake Gennesaret. This senator's residence was in Antioch in the northwest of the province, and four legions were assigned to his command. He also held supreme authority over Judea and its prefect.[1]

In early April in 30 (or 33) C.E., the itinerant preacher Jesus of Nazareth was escorted into Jerusalem by a large throng of followers. Historians believe that Jesus was probably born in Nazareth, actually in 1 B.C.E., so that the year 1 C.E. really began a few days after his birth.[2] He came to celebrate Passover in the Holy City with his closest followers, in particular the twelve disciples.[3] In 30, Passover fell on what the Romans reckoned as 8 April, the Sabbath. Almost immediately after Jesus's arrival, tension rose in the city, and the members of the Jewish high priesthood reacted. The priests served on the most important of the Jewish self-governing bodies, the Sanhedrin, or High Council. This body had seventy-one members who served under a high priest appointed by Rome and were responsible for maintaining order. The position of high priest had remained in one family for several decades; Annas, the former high priest, had served for several years before retiring in favor of his son-in-law Caiaphas. The elders of the leading families served on the Sanhedrin. They counted among their members the old, conservative priestly caste of the Sadducees. Other members of the Sanhedrin were the "scribes," a biblical term used to denote the Pharisees. They were known for their charity and strict observation of religious laws, including those more recent than the Torah.

The Sanhedrin decided that Jesus deserved the death penalty, yet it was obvious that they would have to move unobtrusively against him so as to avoid unrest among the people. At any rate, as it was imperative not to take action against Jesus during Passover, they agreed that the affair should be settled before that. The Sanhedrin's cause was made easier by a fortuitous happenstance. One of Jesus's disciples, Judas Iscariot, was willing to work with them. He had left the group and offered to show Caiphas's men where Jesus would be spending the night.

It was in the Garden of Gethsemane in East Jerusalem, on the Mount of Olives, land that belonged to one of Jesus's followers. Caiphas sent a troop of temple police with Judas, and they arrested Jesus there. Once the disciples saw that he did not want them to put up futile resistance, they scattered to the four winds. The temple police took Jesus across Jerusalem to the house of the high priest, Caiphas, which lay in the west of Jerusalem, in the upper city south of Herod's palace. The Sanhedrin had assembled there to pass judgment. Peter had followed them from afar. When startled by a servant in the courtyard of the high priest's house, however, he denied being one of the prisoner's followers.

Jesus was accused before the High Council of blasphemy, and witnesses were summoned to testify against him. As they contradicted each other, their testimony was considered invalid under Jewish law. Meanwhile, Jesus's response was indeed blasphemous, and they found he deserved the death penalty. He was spat upon, ridiculed, and consigned once again to the custody of the temple police. They detained him overnight, during which time they beat him.

Early the next morning, on Friday, 7 April, the Sanhedrin met again and passed a resolution to bring Jesus before the Roman prefect, Pontius Pilate, where he would be accused of treason for claiming to be king of the Jews, and of fomenting unrest. He was brought in fetters before the prefect, who was holding public court in the square in front of the palace. When Pilate asked Jesus if he was king of the Jews, he answered with a short affirmative. Without seriously examining whether the accused posed a true danger to the Roman hierarchy, Pilate condemned him to death by crucifixion, which always included flagellation beforehand, for presuming to be king of the Jewish people. Jesus was remanded to the execution squad, whose soldiers first took him to a courtyard in the palace where they flagellated and mocked him. They scornfully dressed him in a robe of imperial purple, placed a crown of thorns upon his head, and gave him a stout reed for a scepter. They knelt before him mockingly, spat in his face, and beat him with the reed. Afterward, they removed the robe and led him to the place of execution, Golgotha, or "place of the skull," outside the city walls. Jesus was forced to carry his own cross, but he had become too weak to do so. The soldiers forced Simon of Cyrene, a town in North Africa, to carry the cross; he had journeyed to Jerusalem to celebrate the Passover. At Golgotha, Jesus was nailed to the cross in the third hour (about eight to nine in the morning), and an inscription was placed over his head that included the name of the crucified as Jesus of Nazareth and the reason for his condemnation, his claim to be king of the Jews. The inscription was multilingual to guarantee broad comprehension: in Aramaic, the local vernacular; in Greek, the language of the educated; and in Latin, that of the Roman authorities. Two thieves who had committed murder were crucified with him.

Jesus was mocked and ridiculed by passersby and his accusers. He died about 3:00 p.m., so that just enough time remained to obtain a favor from Pilate, who allowed him to be taken down that same day and buried. Joseph of Arimathia, a respected Jewish citizen and follower of Jesus, had secured that favor and made his own burial chamber available for this purpose. Normally the crucified were not removed this soon. They were instead left to hang for a long time to serve as a warning to others. In this case, Pilate seems to have disregarded the deterrent aspects of a crucifixion. Jesus's followers were forced to hurry, as they had to be finished before sundown because the Sabbath began at shortly after six in the evening. They succeeded, and the body was wrapped in a linen cloth and laid in the grave.

OUR SOURCES

Although Jesus's case is the most extensively reported trial from antiquity, many of its details are contested. This is because the most detailed reports are the four Gospels, as well as several other biblical texts rejected by the Christian Church as apocryphal.[4] It was less important to their authors to record historical events objectively than to emphasize the "good news." For them, the story of Jesus's suffering was just the prologue to the announcement of his resurrection. Through his suffering, he released all humanity from the bondage in which they lay, remote from God. This was the message that his followers intended to preach, initially to the Jews, and later to all humanity. Their words were meant to convert or reinforce them in their belief in Jesus as the Christ, the salvation-bringing Redeemer. It was important for the authors to demonstrate that the Redeemer was not a mythical figure, but a man who had actually lived among the people in the Roman Empire and under specific emperors and governors.[5] All of these historical details were provided to serve a higher goal, that of their mission.

The factual reliability of the Gospels as objective sources is further diminished because they were written down many decades after the events they report. In addition, and perhaps more importantly, the mental environment essential to the early Christian mission's success had changed fundamentally. Before the Jewish Rebellion (66–73 C.E.), the followers of Jesus had already progressed from proselytizing solely among Jews to preaching to all peoples. The Jewish Rebellion was quashed, and the spiritual center of the Jews, the Temple in Jerusalem, and the city itself were demolished. To fulfill their duty to spread the word of Jesus to all peoples while retaining the goodwill of the Roman authorities and the Romanized populace, Jesus's followers as Jews, which they and their Savior all were by heritage and upbringing, had to clearly distance themselves from their fellow Jews, who had just fought a bitter, seven-year-long war against the global empire that was Rome.

The oldest extant Gospel is that of Mark. It is also the shortest. We presume that it was written about shortly after 70 C.E. during the Jewish Rebellion, probably in Roman Syria. Scholars believe it to be based on a fundamental text written in the 40s or 50s, whereas in the 30s, just after the crucifixion, it is likely that only small narrative scraps were circulating among the earliest Christians.[6] The Gospel according to Matthew is based on Mark's and includes additional detailed information. Many of its details, however, seem to be legendary embellishments to the history of salvation, many of them conciliatory toward the Romans and therefore anti-Jewish. Luke's Gospel can be evaluated similarly in that the history of salvation is likewise still narrated from a Jewish tradition and also reveals pro-Roman and anti-Jewish sentiment. Luke heightens the tale's plausibility for Roman citizens by adding more involvement on the part of the Roman legal and administrative branches than could have occurred.[7] One example is Luke's depiction of the Nativity, in particular its details about the contemporary governorship of Cyrenius (Quirinius, Luke 2:1–2). Because the first three Gospels have so much narrative in common, they are called the Synoptic Gospels and are often printed in parallel columns. The Gospel of John, written about 100 C.E. or early in the second century, departs quite markedly from the first three. His Gospel provides a philosophical dimension to the salvation story yet also contains particularly aggressive anti-Semitic statements. However, even this much later record gives us additional facts about Jesus's story.

In addition to the Gospels, there are also brief references to Jesus in works by Tacitus[8] and Flavius Josephus,[9] though the Josephus passage was interpolated by a later Christian writer. Josephus was a Jewish prisoner of war from the Jewish Rebellion who had been brought as a slave to Rome, where he was freed by Emperor Flavius Vespasian. He thus became a Roman citizen and continued to live in the city, earning his living as an author while receiving an annual salary from the emperor. He had his own reasons for wanting reconciliation.

We have further records attesting to the existence of Caiphas and Simon of Cyrene in the Gospels.[10] The same is true for Pontius Pilate. He is described in the writings both of Flavius Josephus and of Philo of Alexandria, the latter also a Jew and a contemporary of Pilate. Indeed, scholars have collected so many details about Pilate that his character has been widely established as ruthless, corrupt, and power-hungry, yet flinching when afraid that his superiors in Rome might receive an unflattering report about his activities in the province.[11]

ROMAN CRIMINAL JURISDICTION
IN THE PROVINCES

The governor of a Roman province was usually from the senatorial class. He held supreme authority over the legions stationed in his region and functioned as the representative of Roman authority and final judge. He exercised direct jurisdiction in criminal cases and could even impose the death penalty upon provincial criminals who were not Roman citizens; citizens were entitled to appeal to Rome. Most of the more exacting and controversial civil cases the governor handed over to a senator from his entourage who had expertise in civil law.

In smaller regions such as Judea a prefect from the equestrian class was considered sufficient. Rome had taken Judea from an indigenous prince despised by the local population, and annexed it to the province of Syria. The local prefect originally had no authority to impose the death penalty (*jus gladii*). But if the circumstances required it, for example if the region was particularly restless, such authority could be specifically conceded to him. This power had been given to Pilate's predecessors and to him as well.[12] Local courts generally held jurisdiction only in minor cases, including minor infractions; the harshest punishment they could impose was severe flogging.[13]

In Rome, trials of noncitizens were bound by detailed rules and regulations. But Roman officials were not so restricted in the provinces. Only minimum requirements had to be met. The accuser had to submit an accusation in writing to the governor in which a specific person was accused of having committed a specific crime. This effectively prevented spurious law-suits by establishing responsibility. The accused had to be able to adequately defend himself, but he did not have the right to an advocate, a public defender. If the defendant challenged the incriminating facts, the accuser had to prove that his assertions as submitted were indeed accurate. Lastly, the sentence had to be justified, and its essential content announced publicly, while the judge could decide whether the hearing would be held in public or in a closed courtroom (*in secretario*).[14] The provincial governor was also generally required to respect Rome's defini-tion of which crimes were punishable; however, he was given some leeway to prosecute and punish an act that was novel or specific to his province, and which he, as Rome's representative authority, considered detrimental to society.[15]

ARREST OF JESUS OF NAZARETH

The primary controversy concerning the arrest of Jesus has to do with which authority took him into custody. Was it the Jew-ish temple police, or were Roman forces involved as well? While the Synoptic Gospels provide a coherent report in which only the Jewish temple police were active, the Gospel of John states that a Roman cohort under the command of a chiliarch (tribune) made the arrest. A Roman cohort usually counted five hundred auxiliary troops—the total number stationed in Jerusalem at that time.[16] What is more, if Romans were involved, they must have been sent by Pilate as the Roman authority, they would have brought the prisoner directly before him, and the prisoner would have spent the night in Roman custody. But in all the Gospel accounts, including John's, Jesus was brought before the Jewish High Council, first before the former high priest, Annas, and then before Caiphas, the high priest serving at that time, and he spent the night in Jewish custody. Scholars have concluded that the participation of the Romans, in particular in such high numbers, cannot be accurate. In contrast, the betrayal by Judas Iscariot remains plausible, although he may have received more or less than the reported thirty silver coins.[17]

THE ROLE OF THE JEWS

According to the Gospels of Mark and Matthew, Jesus was first condemned to death for blasphemy by the Jewish elders during a night session of the Sanhedrin, or High Council, immediately after his arrest. Luke and John report only a nocturnal interrogation conducted by Annas, who then transferred Jesus to the custody of the reigning high priest, Caiphas. According to all four evangelists, the high priests accused Jesus in the morning before the prefect on charges of treason and fomenting unrest against Rome, but Pilate initially declared Jesus to be innocent. Then the high priests roused the people to such intensity that they shouted for Jesus to be crucified. Pilate ultimately bowed to the will of the crowd, but, according to John, not until he had been threatened with an unfavorable report before the emperor. According to the Gospels, Pilate was a benevolent ruler in Judea who showed weakness when confronted with Jewish fanaticism. The driving force behind and primary responsibility for the crucifixion of Jesus fell upon the Jews, both their authorities and the common people.

After the Holocaust, Jewish scholars, initially Paul Winter working in London and publishing in Berlin, and later Chaim Cohn, senior prosecutor in Israel, began to more thoroughly investigate the subject of the Jews' collective guilt in the crucifixion of Jesus.[18] In this process, they came to the conclusion that the High Council could not have litigated against Jesus, nor could the Jewish people have influenced the course of the trial, especially not as described by John, or as in the somewhat more concise versions by Matthew, Luke, and Mark. Jewish procedural law expressly forbade nocturnal hearings as well as trials on the Preparation Day before Passover. In addition, it required that at least one day had to elapse following the hearing of evidence before a sentence could be rendered. Although these regulations are first documented in the Mishnah, written about 200 C.E., they also appear in older records. On the other hand, Catholic scholars have maintained that the Jews might have made an exception when confronted with false prophets and corrupters who preached insurrection against God. They also posit that haste was required in the case against Jesus to keep his many followers from being mobilized.[19]

The objections of Catholic scholars appear just as unconvincing as the complete denial of Jewish involvement. Jesus's arrest by the temple police, the decision by the High Council early on Friday morning to accuse him of a capital crime before the prefect, and above all the accusation itself remain difficult to argue away. The earliest Gospels describe a court procedure before the High Council. According to Jewish law, this could have been a preliminary investigation including the examination of witnesses and the accused. It did not end in a sentence, but rather with the conclusion that Jesus merited the death penalty according to Jewish law. He was therefore accused before the Roman prefect of a crime that called for the death penalty according to Roman law. This version of events includes direct participation by the Jewish authorities in Jesus's arrest, trial, and crucifixion. At the very least, a bare majority of the Sanhedrin agreed to bring him before the Roman prefect and charge him with a capital crime punishable by crucifixion. Therefore, the result of this decision is still associated with the Jewish authorities.

Participation by the Jewish people remains more problematic. According to the Gospels, the role of the Jews is closely interwoven with the pardoning of a prisoner as an amnesty during the festival, and when Pilate offered Jesus, the crowd shouted to have the notorious criminal Barabbas released instead. In fact, a Roman governor would not have agreed to releasing any criminal, particularly without consulting the emperor. Now, this man's full name was Jesus Barabbas, and his second name, Barabbas, actually means "son of the father." Jesus was a common name at that time, and our Jesus could also have been named or called "son of the father." Therefore, the hypothesis has been offered that the Jewish people in fact demanded that Pilate release Jesus of Nazareth, but that the Roman governor refused to do so. This episode might have been revised after the Jewish Rebellion, to make it flattering to the Romans and critical of the Jews.[20] A modern example of such rewriting of history in order to appeal to popular sentiment at that time can be found in the popular German historian Felix Dahn's *Ein Kampf um Rom* (A Struggle for Rome). This long historical novel on the war between the Goths and Byzantines, who had invaded Italy in the sixth century C.E., was written shortly after Bismarck's founding of the German Empire in 1871. Dahn sometimes closely followed the narrative of the Byzantine historian Procopius but replaced Goths with Greeks in order to transfer Procopius's negative evaluation of the Germanic tribe as perfidious and disloyal to the Byzantines.

It is hard to ignore the consistent reports of the Gospels and of Flavius Josephus that Jews contributed to the death of Jesus and were, in fact, instrumental in his demise, in spite of new research by Jewish scholars and others.[21] But actions against Jesus must have been limited to the few Jewish leaders in Jerusalem, those in authority who collaborated with the Roman occupation when it was convenient to do so. That there were crowds demanding Jesus's crucifixion, indeed crying out: "Let his blood be on us and on our children!" as used later to tar all Jews and fuel the flames of anti-Semitism throughout Christendom, is not only unlikely but directly contrary to the ways Roman laws were observed and enforced. The very opposite is more probable.

THE TRIAL BEFORE PONTIUS PILATE

Early in the morning on that Friday, 7 April,[22] the representatives of the Sanhedrin brought Jesus before the only Roman representative who could sentence him to death and who happened to be holding court. At that time, the length of an hour depended on the season, as the time from sunrise to sundown was divided into twelve equal parts. Because 7 April falls close to the equinox, that day lasted from about 6:00 a.m. to 6:00 p.m. in modern reckoning. This means that the hours recorded at this trial do not deviate substantially from ours, whose inflexibility has more to do with coordinating schedules across long distances than with daylight.

Thus it was probably about 7:00 a.m. when the Jewish elders appeared in Pilate's court. Since their accusation involved a capital offense, the case had precedence and was obviously heard immediately. According to the Synoptic Gospels, the trial took place in public in front of the palace. John has Pilate hearing the case inside the palace, yet he also writes that the prefect turned repeatedly to the public for their opinion. However, it is highly unlikely that a Roman governor would change positions repeatedly during a hearing. The trial cannot have lasted very long, as Jesus was afterward forced to walk, carrying the cross, to the execution grounds, where he was crucified between 8:00 and 9:00 a.m. Even if Simon of Cyrene helped him for part of the way, it was still a slow journey.

According to Mark, Simon was the father of Alexander and Rufus. In 1941, an ossuary dating to the first century C.E. was found near Jerusalem in the Cedron (Kidron) Valley in a Cyrenian family tomb. According to the inscription, it held the bones of Alexander, son of Simon. Although the names Simon and Alexander were not uncommon at that time, this particular combination of names was unusual, and the additional link with Cyrene suggests that those archaeological artifacts indeed refer to the Simon of Cyrene from the Gospels.[23]

Pontius Pilate may well have hesitated to condemn this man, Jesus, whose guilt was more than a little doubtful. However, the accusation that the Jewish people were being incited to rebel against Roman authority was a matter Pilate had to take seriously. Civil disturbances were, after all, a daily occurrence in his province. Jesus entered Jerusalem to nearly riotous acclaim and created a stir in the forecourt of the temple when he sought to drive out the merchants and the money changers, overturning tables and whipping out the livestock. The accusers may actually have boosted Pilate's decisiveness by threatening to send a delegation to Rome. Such an embassy could easily allege other grievances,[24] and Pilate was known for the brutality and corruption of his associates. Even if he himself was not involved in their plots, he could still be held responsible for their actions. He might well have believed that his best course of action was to make a display of Roman power. Perhaps he thought that this minor itinerant preacher would soon be forgotten. After all, the Romans had already crucified hundreds, and this one would be no different.[25]

According to Luke, Pilate initially tried to pass the problem off to Herod Antipas, the client prince of Galilee, Jesus's home province, who was spending the festival in Jerusalem at a palace not far from that of Herod the Great, where Pilate was holding court. However, Herod Antipas sent Jesus back to Pilate. The jurisdiction in a criminal trial was—and is—not determined by the origin of the accused, but by where the crime took place.[26] Moreover, this delay, which would have added at least an hour or more to our timeline, does not fit the time frame of the crucifixion, the descent from the cross, and the entombment.[27] The entire trial cannot have lasted very long, as stated above, and yet it was a standard criminal trial according to Roman law. It was not, as some historians have claimed, merely a coercive measure—that is, it cannot have been just a police action, nor one taken under martial law.[28] At that time, Jerusalem was neither under a state of emergency nor subject to military rule. Pilate sat upon the judicial bench holding a court of law. The above-mentioned minimum requirements for a trial were fulfilled. And if the prefect, in contrast to the liberal embellishments of the later Gospels, did not go to great length to arrive at a fair verdict, that might have had to do with the social status of the accused. Jesus of Nazareth was neither a Roman citizen nor even a member of one of the local families represented in the different city councils. Philosophers and itinerant preachers mattered little to the Romans at that time.

THE JUDGMENT AND ITS EXECUTION

The trial ended with a sentence, which had to be formally pronounced, even if the Gospels do not mention this point specifically. They do tell us that the convict's name and the reason for his execution were posted on the cross itself and expressed in all three languages. This fact alone presupposes a formal sentence.[29] The flagellation carried out before the actual execution was the standard concomitant punishment for crucifixion,[30] not exceptional brutality added to this conviction. The additional details supplied in Mark—the mocking by Pilate's soldiers in his palace, the need to find a bystander to carry the cross so that the procession could continue, the offering of vinegar, the division of Jesus's clothing among the execution squad, the simultaneous crucifixion of two criminals, the insults from passersby, in particular from high priests, and the presence of the women and one disciple from among Jesus's followers—all these are quite believable. Equally likely is the postmortem involvement of a quiet follower of Jesus, Joseph of Arimathia, whose name indicates an origin in Rama in Judea, as is Pilate's act of mercy.[31]

PONTIUS PILATE'S MOTIVES

According to the historical evidence, Pontius Pilate was not the benevolent but overcharged governor who appears in the later Gospels, whose opinions were overridden by the Jewish people, the upper class, and the populace as a whole. Instead, he was a strict representative of Roman might who would rather kill one too many of the natives than one too few. That he questioned the danger that Jesus represented to the Roman authority can be read from the reports. Once the man had been eliminated as a risk, Pilate granted one last, modest appeal for mercy. If he had any doubts whatever, they could have been quickly suppressed by thoughts of political exigence according to the motto "It is better to have condemned one too many rather than one too few." He was probably also motivated by the danger of a conflict with the accusers and their retinue, who could denounce him in Rome. Execution was his safest option, whereas an acquittal or even mere corporal punishment would have antagonized some very determined groups in the native population, which could have jeopardized his entire future career. He had already had conflicts with the Jews in which he had ultimately been forced to concede.[32]

After six further years of service in Judea, Pilate was accused of extreme acts of violence not by the Jews, but by the Samaritans, who had lost many of their own to his verdicts. This accusation was made to the senatorial governor of Syria, and Pilate was relieved of his duties in 37 C.E. He was sent to Rome to answer for his crimes before the emperor Tiberius (14–37 C.E.). However, by the time Pilate arrived in Rome, Tiberius had died[33] and been succeeded by the youthful Caligula (37–41 C.E.). To celebrate his accession, Caligula declared an amnesty for crimes that had been committed but not yet expiated under Tiberius.[34] Pilate seems to have emerged unscathed by this fortuitous change in government, although we have no further historical evidence about him. Eusebius of Caesarea and Orosius, church historians from the fourth and fifth centuries respectively,[35] state that Pilate committed suicide to avoid the trial that Caligula instigated against him, but this story seems to be a later Christian tale of his getting what he deserved.

SIGNIFICANCE

Jesus's sentence set a negative precedent that lasted for the next three centuries in the Roman Empire. Later emperors and their officials had the notion that Christians were merely the followers of an ignominious criminal and likewise deserved to be executed as agitators against the empire, without further investigation as to whether they actually represented a danger. This attitude is addressed in the next two chapters.

The trial of Jesus can be considered exemplary in a more general sense. To those who strive for humane justice it is a striking reminder that legitimate courts and meticulous officials can nonetheless pass outrageous sentences, even the epitome of an unjust sentence. It happens time and again. Plato had already generated awareness about such injustice in the educated public in his *Apology* about the death of Socrates. Granted, Socrates was condemned by his fellow citizens in Athens, whereas Jerusalem was ruled by an occupying power; Jesus was put to death by being subjected to humiliating and painful torture, whereas Socrates calmly accepted what Plato describes as a mild death by poison.

Let us take the more recent case of Stanley "Tookie" Williams and the lack of mercy shown by a governor as an example. In 1969, at the age of fifteen years, Williams founded a gang in Los Angeles that eventually became notorious for many crimes, including murder. Williams was found guilty and condemned to death for four murders in 1981, although the evidence of his direct involvement in those crimes was not entirely reliable. Because he insisted on being innocent of the crimes until the end, thus keeping his case tied up in the courts, his execution was delayed. However, after twenty-four years on death row, his conviction remained legally binding, and his appeals ran out. During his incarceration, Williams experienced a personal sea change, becoming a man who wholeheartedly rejected violence. He expressed this in several publications and wrote more than ten books. In particular, he influenced members of his old gang and other gangsters to seek a nonviolent resolution to their conflicts. Many listened to him and took his nonviolent message to heart. Once his appeals ran out, only the governor could pardon him.

The governor was supported by groups vehemently in favor of the death penalty, and he felt he could not afford to appear "soft on crime" in their eyes. He said that he was unconvinced that Williams's transformation was genuine, and it is true that there have been other cases in the United States in which seemingly reformed criminals were pardoned and then went on to commit heinous crimes. But in Tookie Williams's case, the governor's reasoning was probably just an excuse. Of course, his overriding motive was to get reelected. He thus did not oppose the execution of a man who had spent twenty-four years on death row; only his direct and public intervention could prevent it. Instead, like Pilate, he preferred to let things run their course rather than allow his constituents to paint him as weak. Williams was executed. If the governor had truly been interested in containing violence, he should have granted him clemency to spend the rest of his life in prison, where he would have continued to work patiently promoting nonviolence.

CHAPTER TEN

"They Hate Mankind"

Nero Prosecutes Christians

64 C.E.

THE EVENTS

In 64 C.E. a terrible fire destroyed vast areas of Rome,[1] including much of the Caelian and the Palatine hills and as far as the
Esquiline. After the fire, Nero (54–68 C.E.) planned to build his
extensive palace, the Domus Aurea (Golden House), and gardens on this vast ruined area of Rome. The suspicion that Nero
himself arranged the act of arson in order to create the space for
his building plans arose immediately after the fire and contin-
ues to this day. At the very least, it was odd that the fire brigades
controlled by the emperor failed; the *vigiles* numbered around
seven thousand men stationed at seven locations around the city
at that time, and they proved spectacularly incapable of fighting this fire. To effectively counter this suspicion, Nero sought a
scapegoat and accused the Christians.

A short time before this, under the leadership of Peter and
Paul, the Christians had founded a community in Rome, which
had grown meanwhile to several hundred members. They kept

aloof from public life. In particular, they did not participate in traditional Roman cultic rituals, carrying out their own rituals in complete seclusion. This perceived aloofness and secrecy, along with elements of the Christmas celebration and the Communion rituals, led Romans to believe that Christians killed small children, drank their blood and ate their flesh, and organized orgies promoting adultery and incest.

The Christians were accused of arson, and those who openly professed their belief were detained and interrogated. After being questioned about arson, they were forced under torture to name other Christians, who were then arrested in great numbers, accused with the others, and condemned. The evidence for arson was weak, but Nero and his judges distrusted the Christians' resolute withdrawal from all Roman society and saw it as an indication of their general hatred of mankind. The arson convictions grew out of this prejudice.

The usual methods of executing lower-class arsonists included unarmed "combat" with wild animals in the arena during festivals (*bestiis subicere*), crucifixion (*crux*), and death by fire (*vivi exurere*). But Nero wanted more elaborate and exemplary ways of punishing those who had burned Rome. For the executions, he opened his gardens on the Vatican Hills, which contained a hippodrome, to the public. He also modified the punishments. The condemned were forced to wear the hides of wild animals, obviously game animals, and were set upon by hunting dogs, who tore them apart. Others were crucified, and still others were used as living torches to light these gardens at night. That is, they were probably covered in pitch and ignited, perhaps even chased around. Christian women were costumed as Danaides or as Dirce and subjected to the torments that those historical women suffered (more on this later). To these punishments, he added chariot races on the track that Caligula had begun around the Vatican and that he, Nero, had completed, the Circus Neronianus. He himself drove a chariot in these races, disguising himself as a charioteer to mingle among the people incognito.

About two hundred Christians were sacrificed in this single wave of persecution. At that time Peter, who had founded the Roman community together with Paul and was now their sole leader (Paul had already been executed), was also arrested and condemned, even if he was not immediately executed. Although the Christians were widely hated and suspected of committing every act of depravity, these exceptional torments, arising as they did from an almost artistic delight in watching the victims suffer, aroused sympathy in many onlookers.

OUR SOURCES

Tacitus reports Nero's measures in these cases in his *Annales*,[2] of which large fragments have been preserved by chance. Tacitus was a well-placed Roman historian, writing his *Annales* around 118 C.E. or a bit later. The imperial biographer Suetonius, a man of letters in service to the emperors, writing a little later, records these events in passing, including them among Nero's good deeds.[3] Early Christian writers mention these persecutions briefly: Clement of Rome, head of the Roman community of Christians in the late first century, includes a few remarks;[4] and Tertullian, one of the early fathers, also mentions them in passing, around 200.[5] It is not until the fourth and fifth centuries that we have extensive reports from the Christian viewpoint, as recorded in texts by Lactantius, Eusebius of Caesarea, and Sulpicius Severus. These figures were fathers of the church who wrote with the aim of propagating the Christian message.[6] Insofar as worldly events were referred to, as in the case of Severus, they were merely copied from Tacitus.[7]

Even the Tacitus text is problematic. For example, the early editors of his *Annales* (and the most modern) correct *Chrestianos*, the term as it appears in the most reliable manuscript, to *Christianos* because Tacitus himself explains that it derives from *Christus*. But Tacitus might also have used *Chrestianos* on purpose. In the vernacular, Χρηστός (*chreestos*) means "the useful one, the honest one" and was a common slave name; Tacitus may have used this malapropism intentionally to sneer at Christians as followers of a slave.

The same manuscript of the *Annales* has another reading that refers to the Christians: *odio generis humani coniuncti* [sic] *sunt* (They are united in hatred of mankind, §4), but editors have generally corrected this to *convicti sunt*... (They are convicted of...). Karl Büchner has justifiably criticized this widespread correction, though his correction does not decisively alter the text's meaning.[8] Whether the Christians were convicted not of arson but of hatred of mankind, or whether they were united less in arson than in that hatred, is immaterial. In both readings the participles *coniuncti* and *convicti* refer not only, as Büchner thought, to hatred of mankind, which Tacitus found obvious, but to the arson as well, which he was not convinced the Christians had indeed committed. Evidently Tacitus wanted to state here that the Christians had not committed this specific crime, meaning that he implicitly sustained the suspicions against Nero.[9] Nevertheless, Tacitus maintained that the usual capital punishments were justified because in his opinion the Christians were genuinely dangerous criminals.

Concerning the aggravated death penalty, especially punishment by burning, our old manuscript reads: *ut ... laniatu canum interirent aut crucibus affixi* (scil. *interirent*) *aut flammandi* (scil. *interirent*) *atque ubi defecisset dies in usum nocturni luminis urerentur* (so that they died by ... being mangled by dogs or fixed on crosses or were to be burned, ignited once daylight had faded to produce nocturnal light). Philologists take offense at *aut flammandi atque,* so some prefer the reading of a copy of this manuscript from the sixteenth century made by an erudite humanist. Instead of *aut flammandi* (or to be burned), the copy reads *et flammati* (and burned); thus the crucified were burned. Other philologists more radically eliminate *aut crucibus affixi aut flammandi* as not belonging in the original text. Neither group understands sufficiently the three kinds of aggravated death penalty in Roman law, namely beasts, cross, and flames. Tacitus relates how Nero refined the first and the third, in the Christians' case using their flames to illuminate the night. This latter punishment could not be carried out immediately after the sentence, which had to be pronounced during the day. These Christians were not condemned to be crucified and burned immediately (*crucibus affixi et flammati*), but a second group was crucified, and a third (another *aut*) to be burned (*flammandi*) later in the darkness to brighten the evening entertainments (*ubi defecisset dies in usum nocturni luminis urerentur*). Tacitus differentiates, as do the pertinent legal texts, three types of the aggravated death penalty.[10] Reducing these to two, which would happen if we assume that it was the crucified who were ignited, would be gratuitous. In the late fourth century, Sulpicius Severus,[11] who based his report on Tacitus, clearly distinguishes death by animals, cross, and burning alive, as does the old Tacitus manuscript.

THE TRIAL

Tacitus writes that the Christians were exterminated to satisfy one man's cruelty (*tamquam . . . in saevitiam unius absumerentur*), that is, his lust for the suffering of others. He thus implies that Nero himself presided at this trial and pronounced the verdicts. If so, then the entire trial took place before the imperial court. This court was usually held in public; at the very least, the verdict had to be pronounced publicly. This arrangement would have suited Nero's desire to influence public opinion via this trial. Thus it must have taken place in public. In addition, private accusers must have stepped forward. They were required to bring the case before the court,[12] and there would have been plenty of willing volunteers for the emperor's case. The emperor acted as judge together with his advisers, the *consilium*,[13] and he could freely determine the trial's location. In general, he presided over court in the Forum in Rome; when away from Rome, he held court in a portico (*porticus*) or in an imperial villa, which was then opened to the public.[14] Nero may have made the Vatican gardens available, which he had inherited from his mother, not just for the executions, but for the trial beforehand as well.[15] This display of generosity—allowing public access to privately held gardens—made him especially beloved by the common people, even after his death.[16]

THE CHARGE AND CONFESSIONS

According to Suetonius and Christian authors such as Tertullian, Nero accused the Christians of believing in a new, malicious superstition. Modern historians have interpreted his accusation as religious outrage, sacrilege, or even treason. But these charges would not have enabled Nero to blame these culprits for the devastating fires. Tacitus reports in more detail, though without all the legal specifics, that the Christians were accused of arson. By this he must mean all Christians, including those who were arrested later after having been named by others under torture. His grammar alone may lead us to suppose that Tacitus believed that the first Christians were arrested because the public knew they were Christians, that they had been forced to divulge the names of their fellow Christians, and that the latter were then only accused of religious outrage and the like.

But what would the Christians arrested first have confessed? They certainly must have confessed their Christian belief and thus their affiliation with the Christian community. However, they would have undergone further interrogation and would probably have been tortured to provide more information and reveal the names of their accomplices. Some in this first group probably broke under torture and confessed to arson, although most of the Christians were surprisingly resilient, especially when dealing with pagan authorities. At this point, the wheels of police power could have squeezed out ever more names to be condemned for arson. With such confessions at hand, the accusers had no need to provide details of how and why the fires were set. And of course Nero was not interested in such detailed investigation.

In other words, all the Christians were probably convicted of arson, even those who merely admitted to being Christians. We often encounter this type of flimsy argumentation during times of mass hysteria; for instance with regard to the activities of the Baader-Meinhof gang in West Germany during the 1970s,

as those merely acquainted with convicted or suspected terrorists or "enemies of the constitution" were quickly labeled by the
authorities as friends of terrorists and, as such, enemies of the
constitution themselves. And while they were not convicted of
crimes, many lost their jobs, offices, and reputations.

THE PUNISHMENTS

According to the Twelve Tables (ca. 450 B.C.E.) and the Corne-
lian homicide law enacted by Cornelius Sulla (81 B.C.E.), arson
was punishable by death, that is, beheading, crucifixion, or burning alive. In addition, the condemned person's fortune was forfeited to the state. As a further kind of aggravated death penalty,
Caligula (37–41 C.E.) introduced fighting with wild beasts in the
arena.[17] The penalties were graduated in scale according to social
class. Upper-class convicts were beheaded, whereas commoners,
which the Christians were, were to be punished by being burned
alive, crucifixion, or fighting with wild beasts.[18]

.Nero, however, embellished these traditional executions
through his own inventiveness, openly playing with familiar myths. When he clothed the Christians in the skins of wild
animals and set the hounds on them, they were obviously supposed to reenact the tale of Actaeon. According to myth, he was
transformed into a stag and ripped to pieces for daring to boast
that he was a better hunter than the goddess Diana; likewise the
Christians were slain for claiming to worship more devoutly
than the most pious pagans. When Nero made them into living
torches for nocturnal illumination of his park on the Vatican, the
punishment could be understood as atonement for burning down
the Palatine temple of *Luna noctiluca,* the lunar goddess who lit
the nights. Finally, Nero dressed some Christian women as Dan-

aides, who stabbed their suitors on their wedding night and were therefore gruesomely killed by the sole survivor. He also costumed them as Dirce, who, according to legend, tied her rival to the horns of a steer by her hair; the beast then trampled the woman to death; later, Dirce suffered the same fate at the hands of her enemies.[19] Through these costumes, Nero wanted to display the supposed depravity of the often foreign-born Christian women and to satirize their prized virginity.[20]

Nero personally entered the chariot races that were held in connection with this orgy of death. But these events involved no direct use of the Christians. Tacitus mentions the races as part of the great spectacle that Nero created to entertain the public and divert attention from any adverse rumors. By mingling among the people incognito, he was probably spying to observe the effects of his staging.

COMPASSION FOR THE CHRISTIANS

Tacitus did not censure Nero's excesses because he himself felt any compassion for the Christians. He considered any empathy with the condemned to be misplaced. They clung to an ill-fated superstition (*excitiabilis superstitio*), and by committing atrocities (*atrocia*) and disgraceful deeds they proved themselves guilty (*sontes*) and deserving of the newest, most exemplary punishments (*novissima exempla meriti*). Even Suetonius considered the severe punishments of the Christians to be among Nero's meritorious deeds. In his opinion, Christianity was a malicious superstition (*superstitio malefica*).

Tacitus rebuked Nero because his approach failed. His novel punishments achieved the very opposite of a "reasoned attitude" toward the Christians; many Romans felt compassion for them instead (*misericordia oriebatur*). We do not know who or which social class empathized with the Christians, whether this was the *plebs Romana* or subgroups of the plebs, as Büchner claims.[21] In any case, Christians were no longer just hated (*invisi*) in Rome, as Tacitus asserted at the outset of his report; they also had sympathizers, although this only arose because of Nero's excessively cruel treatment of the Christians.

EFFECT

Nero's approach toward the Christians affected the representatives of Roman law, particularly those involved in criminal justice, as a precedent. His dubious conclusion, that the confession of Christian belief evidently caused them to commit the most heinous misdeeds, took on a life of its own. From this point on, affiliation with this religion carried with it a death sentence; to be Christian became a crime in and of itself.

Nero did not enact anything like a formal legal statement, an edict, an imperial rescript, or even a mandate to the magistrates, although this has been hastily assumed on the basis of the words of some Christians.[22] The trial for arson, or, more probably, the series of trials, was sufficient in and of itself to label confession of Christian belief alone as a criminal act.[23] All imperial statements had by this time assumed an exemplary function if not absolute authority in legal matters. Thus even a tyrant such as Nero gained from this tradition, so long as sentences complied with general legal sensibilities and were not revealed as the product of tyrannical behavior. The latter happened only in response to Nero's excesses in persecuting the Christians.

THE FATES OF PETER AND PAUL

Just because Peter was executed later does not necessarily mean that he was not involved in Nero's persecutions after the fire. As the leading figure in the community, he must have been arrested like the others and condemned to death, and presumably only his execution was postponed; after all, he was an especially important witness from whom the authorities must have hoped to gain additional information, especially the names of other members of his community. He even might have been granted leave to continue to lead the Roman Christian community from prison,[24] which would have enabled the authorities to observe and record his contacts. In the end, he was crucified.[25]

Paul, on the other hand, was beheaded.[26] He was a Roman citizen and may have belonged to the upper class in his hometown of Tarsus (southeastern Asia Minor); there he was probably a member of the *honestiores* (distinguished families),[27] even though during his missionary travels he practiced as a craftsman. At any rate, he was not condemned with the other Christians, as he had already been executed a year earlier in 63 C.E. He was arrested in 58 in Jerusalem, accused of fomenting rebellion,[28] and brought before the court in Caesarea,[29] where, as was his right as a citizen, he appealed to be heard in Rome, where he finally arrived in the fall of 60 C.E.[30] There, he was placed under house arrest, meaning that he had his own home from which he could have continued his missionizing efforts, even while under constant surveillance by soldiers.[31] After two years, that is, in 63 at the latest, this came to an end. He was probably condemned to death at this point, presumably still for having fomented rebellion, and executed.[32]

CHAPTER ELEVEN

A Criminal Organization?

Pliny the Younger Judges Christians

Circa 110 C.E.

THE EVENTS

Around 109 C.E.,[1] Emperor Trajan (98–117 C.E.) learned that something was amiss in the province of Pontus et Bithynia, which lay along the southern coast of the Black Sea, extending from the Straits of Bosporus to the east almost as far as Trapezus (present-day Trabzon). This was a senatorial province to which the senate appointed a proconsul to rule as governor for one year. The Roman authority thus changed annually, and in this province it was represented only by a second-tier proconsul, a former praetor. The current crop of trouble in the province took many forms. Cities had overextended themselves financially with poorly thought-out building programs. Unrest was rampant among the populace; groups (*factiones*) had sprung up everywhere; in particular, clubs (*hetaeriae*) that demonstrated political ambitions were formed.[3] To create order, the emperor, in accord with the senate, sent the trusted and highly respected former consul Pliny the Younger to serve as a commissioner *extraordina-*

rius in the province for an undetermined length of time. Among other instructions, Pliny was ordered to disband all associations. He therefore published a corresponding edict as soon as he arrived in the province.[4]

Once on the scene, Pliny discovered that Christianity had spread among all social strata of the populace, particularly in Pontus, along the Black Sea coast;[5] it had also spread beyond urban areas into the countryside. The Christians distanced themselves from traditional cultic practices, and temple visitations and honoring the gods had declined severely. This also meant (Pliny may be exaggerating here) that scarcely any animals were being purchased for sacrifice.[6] But a more crucial point was that the Christians shunned pagan festivals and refused to pay homage to the emperor's statue. Correcting this situation was obviously part of his mandate.

From this point forward, whenever Pliny encountered Christians, he tried them in his court. He asked them personally whether they were indeed Christians, not leaving that role to the accuser. If the accused professed to Christianity, he persisted by asking yet a second and indeed a third time whether they wished to adhere to this belief even under penalty of death. Those of unwavering faith were sentenced to death, and, if not Roman citizens, they were executed immediately. Citizens were transferred to Rome.[7]

In one of the coastal cities,[8] Pliny received an anonymous booklet containing a comprehensive list of Christians. They all were brought before him. Several claimed to have had nothing to do with Christianity, that they were not Christians and never had been. Pliny subjected these individuals to a sacrificial test by bringing several cultic images and a statue of the emperor for this very purpose. Those who sacrificed incense and wine according to the proper religious rites and vilified Christ were acquitted. Several others admitted to having been Christians but claimed they had abandoned the belief, some a mere three years, but others as much as twenty years earlier. They, too, were subjected to the same sacrificial test. Everyone in those groups passed and was pardoned.[9] Thanks to Pliny's cautious approach, the cults of the gods began to revive.[10]

Gradually, however, Pliny began to have doubts as to whether his sentences were indeed right. He particularly wanted to learn what specific crimes these avowed Christians had actually committed. Public opinion and long-standing belief held that Christians were wicked, capable of every misdeed imaginable, and even constantly committing crimes. Pliny considered the defectors to be reliable witnesses, and they were willing to testify. However, they merely revealed that the Christians regularly met on a certain day (which probably meant Sunday) before sunrise in order to praise Christ, whom they worshipped like a god. They sang antiphonies together and solemnly vowed to commit no misdeeds: not to commit theft, fraud, or adultery, not to break a vow, and not to defraud funds entrusted to them. At this point, they would go their separate ways and meet again later to share a common simple meal, where everyone behaved harmlessly. Once Pliny forbade all private associations, they stopped meeting. This causality appears to be a not entirely consistent bit of self-praise for the imperial commissioner. He had not yet been in the province for three years; however, as he had stated earlier, these informants had left the Christian community between three and twenty years previously. Pliny wanted to know if Christian practices were really this innocuous, so he ordered two female Christian slaves to be interrogated under torture. They revealed nothing but what

Pliny called absurd and extravagant superstition (*superstitio prava, immodica*).

In view of the large number of offenders, he decided to report all of this to the emperor and await his decision. In the meantime, Pliny suspended all cases. In particular, he wanted to know whether the emperor believed that Christian children should be executed like the elders; whether the emperor approved of his practice of granting clemency to penitents, a solution of which he was rather proud; and whether the mere profession of Christianity justified punishment, regardless of whether or not it had led to criminal activity.

The emperor's response was short and failed to explicitly answer Pliny's primary question as to whether it was right to put Christians to death simply for isolating themselves and attending their separate religious services. In his reply, Trajan first praised his loyal servant, especially for investigating just what deeds had been committed by those accused of Christianity (*in excutiendis causis eorum qui Christiani ad te delati fuerant*). He then drew three inferences from Pliny's report. First, Trajan emphasized that judges in cases involving Christians were given quite a bit of leeway in their judgments, meaning that very young or otherwise "weak" Christians could be punished less severely. Next, there were to be no searches targeting Christians; they could be punished only if they had been accused in the usual way by a private individual; however, the method and severity of punishment were not mentioned. Third, he approved the clemency practices Pliny had established and on which he had advised the emperor.

While it remains true that Trajan did not specifically state whether Christians deserved the death penalty simply as Christians, he did respond insofar as he mandated two ways to show leniency, which is still quite unusual when dealing with capital offenses today. He forbade the search for Christians and urged clemency when the convicts publicly expressed remorse. Trajan also made an unambiguous directive, namely that Pliny completely disregard any anonymous accusations.

OUR SOURCE

The only documentation we have of these events is in two letters exchanged by Pliny and Trajan,[11] thus written by those directly involved therein. Both the emperor and his commissioner held positions of authority. They are likely sources we can trust, being famous men of integrity.

Pliny was born in the Alpine town of Como to a wealthy family in 61 or 62 C.E.; his career followed the expected *cursus honorum* to the senate with considerable success. His assignment to Pontus et Bithynia as imperial commissioner *extraordinarius* was apparently his last official duty,[12] which he executed between the autumn of 109 and 110. He died while still in office or shortly afterward.[13] The collection of letters from Pliny that we have includes his correspondence with Trajan. The straightforward exchange with the emperor, organized chronologically and containing a total of 124 texts, relates the history of his governorship in the East starting with letter 15. Pliny is often somewhat dismissed nowadays as a man of many words with little self-confidence to take responsibility. But his critics fail to consider the tenor appropriate in letters addressed to the emperor. Language that sounds overly fussy to modern ears should be interpreted in light of Pliny's desire to steer his ruler carefully, so that Trajan would approve of his more humane treatment of the provincials.[14] Thus Pliny, at their request, sometimes defied legal requirements to accommodate the people and was actually directly rebuked by the emperor as a result.[15]

Trajan, who was born in Seville probably in 53 C.E., ruled from 98 to 117 C.E. and had an excellent reputation in the senate and among the populace in Rome. In later centuries, he was considered the best of all Roman emperors. The fifty-one extant letters to Pliny reveal a benevolent ruler who praised his associates as often as possible, whenever it seemed justified. Trajan respected both the authority of his commissioner and the rights of the provincial inhabitants; he occasionally reminded Pliny of specific laws in his province while emphasizing the responsibility of both the imperial commissioner and the provincials in the exercise of the latter's legal rights. His guiding principle was maintaining peace and order in the province and a flourishing economy throughout the realm, an integral part of which was based on solid finances and the thrifty management of resources belonging to the empire and its provinces.

THE LEGAL BASIS FOR THE INITIAL PROCEDURES AGAINST THE CHRISTIANS

At the beginning of his tenure, Pliny proceeded decisively against the Christians according to set rules, condemning to death Christians who confessed and having them executed forthwith. His preliminary assertion in his letter to Trajan is that he did not know to what extent they were usually punished or whether their deeds should be investigated (*quid et quatenus aut puniri soleat aut quaeri*). This assertion is obviously mere courtly etiquette, an example of Pliny downplaying his actual knowledge in order to get the emperor to agree to his new suggestions. Through his investigations, Pliny had actually become better informed about

Christians than Trajan was. But when Pliny initially executed the Christians as a matter of course, he must have taken for granted that practicing Christians were guilty of a capital offense.[16]

Yet how did this come about? Both Suetonius[17] and Tertullian[18] describe Nero as the emperor who began to persecute Christians as such. Suetonius was a pagan author somewhat younger than Pliny, and his protégé, who apparently accompanied him to Pontus et Bithynia. Tertullian, writing eighty-five years later, was a practicing jurist and lawyer in Rome before converting to Christianity. Oddly enough, neither mentions the burning of Rome and Nero's accusation of the Christians, yet these facts and the persecution of Christians must be connected. Nero, as we have seen, had convicted the Christians living in Rome of arson according to the official version, regardless of how arbitrarily this decision was reached, and had them executed for that explicit crime. Their numbers were so great that the judiciary, over time, simply began to inquire whether the present accused were involved with the Christians. If they answered yes, they were condemned—as arsonists—without further ado.

Gradually, courts began to regard Christianity itself as a crime, and precedents throughout the empire solidified into a new legal doctrine. Nero cannot have personally passed judgment on all of the Christians, roughly estimated at two hundred, who appeared before his court. After the first cases, the trials may well have been overseen by others, probably prefects, who must have received specific instructions about the defendants. These instructions, perhaps in conjunction with Nero's own convictions, were then regarded as binding precedents, and they may have led others to infer later that Christianity was formally culpable in and of itself.

There is a widely disseminated opinion that throughout the

two centuries between Nero and Emperor Decius, Christians were not put on trial but were executed as a mere police action to restore public safety and order.[19] This opinion is an example of the uncritical adoption of Theodor Mommsen's theory of *coercitio* (police justice), which has too little basis in our sources.[20] In fact, we learn from Pliny's letters that Christians had to be accused in formal indictments—(*nominis*) *delationes*—and then convicted and executed, and that Trajan insisted on such formal indictments.[21]

WHY DID PLINY SUDDENLY SUSPEND ALL TRIALS AGAINST CHRISTIANS?

From the beginning of his tenure in Pontus et Bithynia, Pliny's attempt to solve the problem of the Christians was not insensitive. When it came to the traditional severity, which even he believed necessary to counter this new superstition, he deviated from the usual routine regarding the subject in two important ways. As an intellectual, he was interested in the specific criminal acts that these people might have committed; that is why he as the magistrate became personally involved in the inquiries into whether the accused were confirmed Christians, and why he did not relinquish argumentation in the trial to the accusers or perhaps the defense. Second, his initial goal was not the immediate extermination of his opponents, or the eradication of Christianity by killing a substantial number of the provincial inhabitants. Instead, he sought to win as many as possible back to belief in the traditional gods, in which worshipping the reigning emperor as a god was essential. He must have known or at least learned very quickly that true Christians would refuse to offer sacrifices to the gods or to mock Christ. He knew they would be ostracized by their fellow Christians for doing so, which they would have found devastating. Thus he instituted the rule of repentance. Those who renounced the superstition in the future were pardoned without consideration of how zealously they had participated in the community in the past. In order to achieve this, Pliny pressured the accused Christians relentlessly. He threatened them with the death penalty if they did not recant, and gave them many chances. Apparently, his tactic worked in many cases. Christian sources do not make this clear, maintaining that only a handful showed weakness.

Following these successes, Pliny delved further and, out of intellectual curiosity, questioned the defectors about the actual practices of Christianity to discover its appeal. In particular, he wanted to know which of the many sinister tales associated with Christianity were true. To Pliny's surprise, none of the evil rumors were confirmed. On the contrary, the Christians seemed to live quite virtuously except for their excessively superstitious beliefs, which required them to distance themselves from all festivals that the other provincials celebrated because at some point they entailed honoring the pagan gods. The imperial commissioner was not content with the defectors' answers and sought a means to test their statements. After all, they were made by the pardoned, who had every reason to downplay or extenuate their past actions. He therefore detained two deaconesses, significant Christian women, and because they were also slaves he was allowed to question them under torture. At that time, people believed that those who were tortured invariably told the truth. Even under torture, however, these women, obviously refusing to renounce their faith, revealed nothing other than those harmless Christian practices.

At this point, Pliny should have had the two women executed as avowed Christians, but he was no longer certain they deserved the death penalty. He thus suspended all procedures against the Christians until the emperor could relieve his doubts by answering his specific questions. To this end, Pliny adroitly presented his superior with his procedures for pardon,[22] which he had developed on his own initiative. His behavior might be considered an usurpation of the emperor's power, so he described the steps he had taken in the best light in order to win imperial approval. Thus we should not interpret his initial statements literally in which he emphasizes that the Christians' mere belief in their superstitions sufficed to justify the death penalty (end of §3). This differs too fundamentally from his most recent understanding of Christians and their practices. Instead, he probably made those statements to ensure his arguments against this sentence would be heard at all. Also, by provisionally aligning himself with the prevailing law of the empire, he made certain that he would not be accused of judiciary incompetence.

WHAT DID TRAJAN CHANGE?

Some maintain that Trajan answered only one of Pliny's questions, that is, whether he had been correct in his handling of the Christian defectors.[23] In fact, Trajan's reply contains several sweeping statements on the matter, even though he left, as was customary at the time,[24] much to his emissary's discretion. After some opening, habitual praise of Pliny, Trajan's letter emphasized the considerable discretionary power that magistrates already had, also in dealing with Christians. Pliny therefore had the option to punish Christian children less severely, to consider mitigating circumstances, and even to abstain from the capital punishment of adults, which was otherwise routine. However, Trajan's advice was not a renunciation of previous legal practices; rather, he was simply reminding Pliny of the flexibility he could exercise as a governor.

Responding to his commissioner's basic doubt, Trajan issued just one firm guideline, but it is a strikingly novel one. From this point on, Trajan prohibited Pliny from seeking out Christians: *conquirendi non sunt* (they must not be hunted). From now on, no more Christians were to be targeted, no informers were to be appointed to identify them, Pliny should not travel within his province seeking out locations with many Christians for punishment, and, finally, no accusers should be encouraged to bring cases against them. Furthermore, Trajan approved of Pliny's amnesty procedures in their entirety, with the final amnesty as a kind of pardon (*venia*).[25] Apparently, Pliny had convinced the emperor that the level of recidivism among the defectors was low because the intractable Christian communities, unlike the pagans, would not take those back who had renounced their faith even once.

The prohibition on accepting anonymous accusations was not really new, but one that Trajan needed to reiterate. It is not actually a consequence of the principle of accusation, according to which a frivolous or false accuser was made accountable for his actions. Even in the case of anonymous denunciations, if the charges were actually substantiated, accusers may have appeared. Yet this prohibition is a necessary consequence of the ban on ferreting out suspects. Trajan placed special emphasis on his rejection of anonymous denunciations, stating that it applied to all offenses, not only as regarded Christianity; however, because anonymous denunciations were widely practiced and there was ambiguity about the deleterious effects of such cowardly denunciations, the faithful were especially vulnerable to them. Today, anonymous accusations are investigated as a matter of course, as we have full-time state attorneys; without whistle-blowers, many crimes nowadays would remain secret.

WHAT WAS CRIMINAL
ABOUT CHRISTIANITY?

Where modern penal provisions are concerned, there is always a question about the legally protected interest that laws are meant to address. Pliny's investigations showed that Christians did not really threaten society with serious criminal acts. Yet both Pliny and Trajan continued to feel that Christians deserved the most severe punishment just for being Christian. How could this be? In Pliny's letter, this position may be just rhetorical; perhaps he was offering only a verbal concession to common prejudices while actually implying that severe punishment was no longer necessary. Disobedience of his prohibition against forming associations would not require such severe punishment. Moreover, all associations had been forbidden only recently and only in his province, not throughout the empire. This prohibition was mentioned only in passing in both men's letters.

Did the Christians' stubborn and inflexible obstinacy (*pertinacia et inflexibilis obstinatio*), which at the beginning of his letter Pliny used to justify his initial executions before disclosing his newly acquired knowledge,[26] truly deserve the death penalty? The emperor apparently thought so, and Pliny apparently agreed. Because the Christians withheld themselves from the centuries-old communion, from the religious rites and festivals, and rejected long-standing traditions, they were unreliable, even if they had committed no specific crime for a long period of time. The Christians' rejection of traditions threatened the very fabric of Roman society. One cannot say that these two men were completely wrong, for when Christians finally gained power over the empire, they did indeed change society completely, irrevocably, for thousands of years, often showing little mercy.

CONTINUED APPLICATION

While it would be absurd to prohibit the search for common criminals, the prohibition against searching for Christians was respected by all future emperors into the third century. This restraint on the part of the state has been criticized for leaving Christians vulnerable to the whims of private accusers, who usually disapproved of the new religion.[27] Nevertheless, it was private accusers who initiated all trials well into the medieval period; only individual exceptions existed, for example in cases of treason or crimes against the crown. There were no state prosecutors in antiquity or the Middle Ages. This situation remained unchanged until the rise of inquisitorial proceedings in the twelfth and thirteenth centuries under the influence of the church, when the initiative for criminal investigation rested with the judge, carrying with it the risk of amalgamating the role of the criminal judge with that of the criminal prosecutor. The "delivery" of Christians for private prosecution was therefore unavoidable in antiquity, whether or not the state actively participated as investigator and instigator of accusations. As long as the state refrained from targeting Christians, they were generally left in more peace than 140 years later when the state began to actively pursue them.

The pardoning of recanting Christians, which did not apply to common criminals either, remained an option for a longer period. Such pardons did not appeal to fervent Christians but did prove to be a great temptation for those whose belief in their faith was less solid; the possibility of pardon induced many Christians to return to pagan society. It was thus a cunning policy on the part of the pagans. When the Christians began to punish unbelievers and, even more harshly, heretics, they, too, adopted this practice of pardoning defectors. During the later Middle Ages, and particularly in the fourteenth and fifteenth centuries, this practice led to the forced baptism of Jews and Moors, primarily in Spain and Portugal. And during the Counter-Reformation in the sixteenth and seventeenth centuries, it precipitated simulated conversions and forced observances of state-sanctioned rituals.

There are more or less comparable situations involving the pardoning of repentant offenders today. If we look for a parallel in our time, abstaining from completing a criminal act combined with trying to undo the offense because of genuine remorse does not quite fit the bill, since those are mitigating factors only when the crime has not gone beyond the attempt, but genuine remorse is a factor judges consider in sentencing for actual crimes. A closer parallel to Pliny's practice of pardoning repentant Christians is the suspension of a sentence through probation, but this is always only conditional—that is, the pardon is revoked in the case of recidivism. In the latter case, that is, if the repentant offends again, the original punishment is imposed, as well as a more severe penalty for relapsing and committing an additional offense. Yet this also fails to provide a complete parallel to the Roman practice: those who reverted to Christianity in antiquity expected to be penalized only for their renewed practice of the faith; no additional penalties were imposed. However, the relapse and previously awarded clemency, which proved to have been granted in vain, would be considered when determining the punishment, and Christianity remained a capital offense for another two centuries after Trajan and Pliny.

CHAPTER TWELVE

Brutal Slave Owners

Umbricia, Julius Sabinus, and Alfius Julius on Trial

Circa 130–152 C.E.

This chapter does not begin with the story of a particular law case but examines some important rules issued by emperors of the second century C.E. and reported by compilers who wrote many years later. The compilers, Ulpian and Gaius, tried to collect what was known about some limits of masters' power over their slaves and the procedures that should be used to call abusive owners to account. Ulpian's reports contain texts called rescripts. These were legally binding opinions that an emperor issued directly to a subordinate or a private person who sought his advice on a legal question.

THE REPORTS

Ulpian reports as follows:[1]

> When a master has treated his slave cruelly or forces him into a life of shame and vice, the provincial governor's duty is clearly described

in the rescript of Emperor Antoninus Pius (138–161 C.E.) to Aurelius Marcianus, proconsul of Baetica (southern Spain). The terms of the rescript are

The power of masters over their slaves should remain unimpaired, nor should any man's rights be taken from him; but it is in the masters' interest that relief from cruelty, hunger, or intolerable outrage not be refused to those who justly implore. Be cognizant, therefore, of the complaints of those members of Julius Sabinus's household who have fled for protection to my statue. [Each new emperor had his portrait bust erected in all of the larger cities.] *And if you find that they have been treated with undue harshness or subjected to an infamous outrage, order them to be sold with the stipulation that they must never return to their master's power. If he evades my ordinance, he will learn how severely I will deal with the offense.*

Emperor Hadrian had already sentenced a certain lady called Umbricia to five years' relegation [exile from her province and Italy] because she had, for trivial reasons, treated her maids with great brutality. Emperor Antoninus Pius likewise sent a rescript in the following terms in reply to a petition by Alfius Julius:

The obedience of slaves must be maintained not just by exercising authority, but also by reasonable treatment, fulfilling their needs, and the fair apportionment of tasks. You should, on your part, therefore, take care to treat your slaves fairly and with moderation, so that you may be able to give them orders without difficulty. Otherwise, if it appears that maintaining them is beyond your means, or that you exercise authority with revolting cruelty, the proconsul may be required to prevent the mischief of a possible outbreak by forcing you, with my sanction, to sell your slaves. Dated . . . 152 C.E.

Gaius reported:[2]

At the present time, neither Roman citizens nor any other persons who are under the command of the Roman people are permitted to employ excessive or groundless severity toward their slaves. For, by a provision of Emperor Antoninus Pius, anyone who kills his slave without good reason is not less liable than one who kills the slave of another. [He was thus not only obliged to compensate for damages; see below.] The excessive harshness of masters is restrained by another provision by the same emperor. Having been consulted by certain governors of provinces referring to slaves seeking refuge at the sanctuaries of the gods or the statues of the emperors, he ordered that if the masters' cruelty appeared intolerable, they be compelled to sell their slaves. In both cases he acted justly, for (note that this is a rule) we should not make bad use of our rights. For example, spendthrifts are thus also forbidden to manage their property.

OUR SOURCES

The author of the first report, Domitius Ulpian, was born a Roman citizen around 170 C.E. in Tyre, now Soûr in southern Lebanon, at that time part of the Roman province of Syria. He probably began his education in Syria[3] and went on to study law in Rome, where he made his career. Ulpian began working in the office of imperial petitions in April 203 C.E. Anyone could submit a petition during imperial audiences, which was decided from a legal point of view; if a written version of the legal reasoning was required, it was drafted by this office.[4] From early 205 until May 209, Ulpian served as the head of this department as the *a libellis* or *magister libellorum*. After the death of Emperor Septimius Severus in February 211, Ulpian remained loyal to Caracalla, Severus's elder son and successor. In December 212, probably at Ulpian's suggestion, Caracalla granted Roman citizenship to all free inhabitants of the empire who did not yet enjoy this privilege. Immediately after Caracalla's edict, Ulpian began writing book after book, apparently hoping to demonstrate that Roman law was flexible enough to apply to the many new citizens.[5] Among these works is *De officio proconsulis libri X* (On the Duties of the Proconsul in Ten Books), written probably in 213. This text was widely read in the later empire. It also described the criminal law applied in the provinces. The chapter from which our text originates is entitled "On the Cruelty of Masters" (*De dominorum saevitia*).

We have access to this text in a later work entitled "The Law of God That the Lord Gave to Moses" (*Lex Dei quam praecepit Dominus ad Moysen*), now commonly known as the *Collatio legum Mosaicarum et Romanarum* (Collation of Mosaic and Roman Laws). It is a slender, incomplete book written by a Christian during the late fourth century and addressed to Roman jurists. The anonymous author, probably from the circle of Ambrosius, bishop of Milan, obviously wanted to demonstrate to Roman jurists, most of whom were still pagan, that concepts of Christian law found in the Old Testament resembled the Roman law concepts and were even older. His ultimate intent was to prove that current Roman laws reiterated the laws of Moses. With this goal in mind, our anonymous author juxtaposed texts from the second to fourth books of Moses (Exodus, Leviticus, Numbers) with excerpts from classical Roman jurists' writings and imperial decrees having similar contents. He fulfilled his aim up through criminal law, but his courage must have failed him at the laws of inheritance, which he began next but did not finish.[6] His criminal law begins with homicide and severe bodily harm, with which the section "On the Rights and Cruelty of Masters" (*De jure et saevitia dominorum*) is affiliated. This is followed by sexual crimes, theft, and so on, according to the organization of commandments 5 to 10.

Our second report is from Gaius.[7] We know only his first name, as was common in the Greek-speaking regions of the empire. In fact, he was not only born in the empire's Hellenistic East; he spent his life there as well. Born around 120 C.E., he enjoyed Roman citizenship and considered himself a Roman. He thus studied Roman law in the capital, where he associated with representatives of the leading law school at that time. Afterward, he returned to the East and presumably settled in Beirut, a Roman colony with Italian property law, where he became a teacher of legal studies and a prolific author. His introductory classes were so popular that students in the academic year 160–161 took notes that they redacted and disseminated under the title "Instructions in Four Books" (*Institutionum libri IV*), now commonly called "The Institutes of Gaius," a text that circulated in several versions.

EXTRALEGAL PRECEDENTS

The just treatment of slaves was actually not a new idea.[8] Cicero had already emphasized it in his *De officiis:*[9] "But let us remember that we must have regard for justice even toward the humblest [slaves]. . . . They [the moral authorities] do not direct us badly who would have us treat our slaves as we would our employees: they must be required to work the same; they must be given their dues." The philosopher Seneca the Younger (ca. 4–65 C.E.) wrote his essay "On Clemency" circa 55 C.E., when he practically ruled the Roman Empire in the name of his pupil Nero. In this essay, which he dedicated to the young emperor, he stated:[10] "It is commendable to exercise authority over slaves with moderation. Even in the case of human chattel you should consider not how much he can be made to suffer without retaliating, but how much you can inflict while adhering to the principles of equity and right, which require that mercy be shown even to captives and purchased slaves." Seneca expresses himself in a similar manner in the somewhat later essay "On Benefits":[11] "There are certain things, for instance food and clothing, which the master must supply to the slave. . . . Whoever hears of injuries inflicted by masters upon their slaves may restrain their cruelty and lust and dampen their stinginess in supplying them with the necessities of life." After Nero removed Seneca from his position, the latter dedicated a long letter to his friend Lucilius describing how a master should treat his slaves.[12]

Around the same time, shortly after the year 60, Columella wrote in his textbook "On Agriculture":[13] "Investigation of the householder should be even more painstaking in the interest of slaves of this sort, that they not be treated unjustly in the matter of clothing or other allowances [by managers]. . . . And again, when they suffer from cruelty and greed [on the part of the manager], they are more to be feared. Accordingly, a careful master inquires . . . also of those not in bonds as more credible, whether they [the slaves] are receiving what is due to them under his instructions; he also tests the quality of their food and drink by tasting it himself, and examines their clothing, coats, and footwear. In addition, he should give them frequent opportunities for making complaints against those who treat them cruelly or dishonestly."

OLDER LEGAL PROVISIONS
TO PROTECT SLAVES

Legal provisions to protect slaves from their masters first appear in the first century C.E. Around the year 45, Emperor Claudius arraigned slaveholders who had killed their sick slaves on counts of malicious homicide.[14] In 61 C.E., the Petronian Law Concerning Slaves[15] was enacted by the consul Petronius Turpilianus, a loyal adherent of Nero.[16] It prohibited compelling slaves to fight with wild animals in the arena, and also selling them for that purpose, which brought especially high prices. From this point onward, those who dealt in slaves for such purposes, both sellers and buyers, were subject to severe penalties. A short time later, the senate addressed this subject and passed several resolutions that supplemented the law. If a slave committed a crime, the master as paterfamilias could no longer condemn the slave to fight for his life in the arena; a magistrate, however, could hear the criminal case and allow the slaveholder to punish the slave in this way. In 97 C.E. (some say in 83), the senate passed the anti-castration law,[17] which specified that anyone who had his slave castrated, which greatly increased his value, had to forfeit half of his estate.

HADRIAN'S RESCRIPT

In the second quotation from Ulpian, he reports that Emperor Hadrian had condemned a certain *matrona,* a woman of respectable reputation named Umbricia, to five years' exile because she had treated her female slaves so cruelly. This meant that Umbricia was forbidden to remain in her home province or in Italy for that duration. It is true that some scholars consider this to be a one-off decision in an isolated case from which we cannot infer any later influence.[18] In fact, we do not have any unambiguous reports of actual punishments in similar cases, although such cruelty must have occurred often. In another text, Ulpian actually informs his readers that the emperor occasionally made decisions, and in particular imposed penalties, that applied in only one case, specifically addressing one offender, and that were unsuitable for use as precedents for disciplinary actions in similar cases.[19]

On the other hand, Ulpian also incorporated this very decision by Hadrian into his guidelines for provincial governors and reported it in his discussion of a new statutory offense called "cruelty of masters" (*saevitia dominorum*).[20] He characterized this decision as a precedent that ought to be exemplary. Two universally applicable decisions by Hadrian point in the same direction. He forbade both explicitly and generally the killing of slaves by their masters and ordered that if, by committing a crime, the slaves earned capital punishment, they were to be condemned by state courts.[21] He also banned the sale of male and female slaves to brothel owners and gladiator schools if the slaves had not already indicated their willingness to serve in such a manner—that is, if they had not previously prostituted themselves or fought as gladiators.[22]

THE FIRST RESCRIPT BY ANTONINUS PIUS

Ulpian quotes a rescript written by Antoninus Pius[23] to his proconsul in Baetica, a highly civilized and urbanized Roman province occupying southern Spain,[24] and stresses its importance by presenting it verbatim and placing it as the first of his authorities. Pius (138–161 C.E.) was Hadrian's successor to the imperial throne and rendered outstanding service to the empire in his conscientious extensions and explanations of Roman law.

The rescript begins with a prologue in which the emperor attempts to quell any misgivings on the part of slave owners. The government's conservative position is clear from the outset: slavery will continue unabated, and the authority of slave owners will not be compromised. No man, be he a Roman citizen or not, may be deprived of his rights, and that includes his rights over certain other human beings. That is, Pius highlights both the personal power of slave owners[25] and the general inviolability of ownership. Thereafter, he appends the concept that it is in the personal interest of the slave owners to have their slaves work without causing problems. Thus masters should refrain from inflicting intolerable injury (*intolerabilis injuria*) on their slaves. Pius's use of language implies that even those who lack legal rights, can suffer *in-juria,* that is, denial of their *jura,* or rights. What is novel is that Pius implies that slaves have certain fundamental rights. Thus as long as their appeals are justified, they should be able to appeal to the emperor for redress for cruelty, hunger, and insufferable wrongs. Whether their pleas for help are justified can be determined only if they can appeal to the emperor. The ubiquitous statues of the emperor provided asylum to those who could reach them, and they could not be forcibly removed from them.

It is only at this point that Pius prescribes the consequences for specific cases: the Roman representative—in the case of a province, the governor—should lead an inquiry (*cognoscere*), and thus initiate a somewhat legal procedure against any slave owner whose slaves have fled to the emperor's statue. The slaves in question, while not standard accusers, should play a significant role in the trial by appearing as appellants (*querellae eorum, qui ad statuam confugerunt*). The procedure should, as in other law cases, end with a verdict by the magistrate and the determination of legal consequence (*si cognoveris*). If cruel or otherwise unjust treatment is proved, the slaves are to be separated forever from the master but not rewarded with freedom, nor is the master to be put at an unnecessary disadvantage, nor is his social position to be diminished more than inevitably. That is, the master should not suffer any more financial loss than necessary by leaving the injured slaves to be sold on his behalf. In this process, the slaves might command a price below their value, and expenses for the slaves' upkeep could be deducted from the net proceeds from the sale. Pius's threat to punish the slave owner was to be implemented only if he attempted to thwart the emperor's dictates. However, Ulpian employs the term *etiam* ("also"; literally, "and already") when then discussing Hadrian's punishment of Umbricia, which implies that the forced sale was not the only conceivable punishment.

According to these guidelines, slaves were no longer completely without legal rights, neither substantively nor procedurally.

THE SECOND RESCRIPT
BY ANTONINUS PIUS

As the third and final portion of the extant text, Ulpian incorporates a second verbatim rescript from Antoninus Pius that includes the date 152 C.E. This directive was sent to a private person, named Alfius Julius. It also begins with a prologue, a general admonition targeting all slave owners. Pius imposes three obligations on those who possess other human beings: namely moderation, that is, the avoidance of cruelty and brutality; the guarantee of necessities, meaning adequate nourishment,[26] clothing, and housing; and the fair apportionment of labor. This last obligation specifies the concept of just treatment, highlighting its most important aspect. The "fair apportionment" clause also covered daily rewards and punishments.

Initially, Pius reminds Alfius of the positive aspects of treating slaves well, namely that which makes them more apt to follow orders. This is followed by a sudden and drastic change in tone: should these three obligations not be fulfilled, serious consequences would ensue, up to and including a slave revolt. This was to be prevented at all costs; therefore, the emperor's representative must intervene and order a compulsory sale in order to protect all slave owners.

ADDITIONAL IMPERIAL DIRECTIVES

In another, procedural context, Ulpian cites a decision made by Marcus Aurelius (161–180 C.E.) and sent to Quintus Voconius Saxa.[27] Marcus Aurelius was successor to Antoninus Pius and initially reigned together with his adoptive brother, Lucius Verus (161–169 C.E.). Saxa was then serving as proconsul in Africa Minor, which then covered present-day Tunisia and northwestern Libya. Primitivus, a slave, had been unjustly accused of a homicide but had nevertheless confessed. All slaves had to be interrogated under torture, and Primitivus eventually admitted that he had lied in his confession to avoid being returned to his legal master. That is, he had preferred suicide with the help of the criminal justice system to life under his master. Again, the coemperors recommended as redress that the slave be officially sold on his master's account, under the stipulation that the slave never be returned to him.

This limitation on the object being sold, in this case Primitivus, would affect every future owner, as we would say today, *in rem;* that is, if Primitivus were returned to the ownership of his old master, he would be freed *ipso jure,* automatically. This provision might lower his sales price somewhat. But if a subsequent owner unwittingly sold Primitivus back to his current master, who, if he made the purchase himself, knew about the prohibition, that seller could scarcely be accused of breaking the law, and thus no redress would be exacted from any predecessor. The loss would fall on the abusive slave owner, and he was expected to bear a certain degree of property loss. The imperial brothers appended another comment to this directive, namely that they were doing the slave owner a favor in protecting him from more serious consequences.

Around 170 C.E., Emperor Marcus Aurelius wanted to relieve the financial burden on the cities that organized entertainment for the people. Although gladiatorial combats and fights with wild animals were particularly popular, they were also expensive. Marcus Aurelius therefore determined that criminals convicted of serious crimes and the leaders of enemy troops captured in battle, both of whom were automatically slaves of the state, could be sold to the cities for a modest fee.[28] These slaves would then participate in games of this type. An unintended outcome of this decree increased suffering among faithful Christians, for unrepentant allegiance to their faith remained a capital crime, even though they were prosecuted only if an accuser appeared, and they refused to recant.[29] Anyone prepared to act as an accuser could easily make state slaves out of those Christians who did not hide their faith. Those convicted were then condemned to unarmed combat against wild animals in the amphitheaters.[30] This funding benefit to the cities thus dramatically worsened the plight of all criminals whose verdict meant state slavery. The efforts to humanize the slaves' conditions, which Marcus Aurelius also supported, did not extend to these state slaves.

Ulpian also concerned himself with the official duties of the urban prefect in Rome, who was the highest imperial representative to the city and its environs. In this regard, he insisted that the prefect listen to any slave who accused his master of brutality, undue severity, insufficient food, or coercion to perform obscene acts. To this end, he cited an instruction from Emperor Septimius Severus written around 200 C.E., which ordered the urban prefect to protect slaves from being prostituted.[31] Prostitution was a profitable business for the owners of female slaves and young males.[32] Running brothels was also profitable for some members of the upper classes,[33] so much so that it took the Christian emperors over a century to establish effective laws prohibiting coercion into prostitution at the very least.[34] Severus is also considering just the coercion of slaves into prostitution here; those willing to engage in it were not affected by his instruction. In any case, Ulpian mentions no specific sanctions, which may have included only the sale of the affected slaves on the master's account with the aforementioned stipulations.

GAIUS'S LEGAL CONCEPT

In the second text quoted above, from Gaius, there is a universal rationale governing the obligations of slave owners to their slaves. In the extant text it is introduced by *regula,* a term added later, meaning "This is a rule": "We should not make bad use of our rights; thus also spendthrifts are forbidden to manage their property." This is a generalization that applies to all owners, which is why some scholars believe that the whole sentence was also added later. According to their theory, this statement does not fit in this context, because Gaius, in the first book of his "Institutes," where the sentence appears, does not discuss property rights, but rather the master's power understood as a personal right.[35]

If the entire sentence was added, this would presuppose a later glossator who sought to amplify Gaius's thoughts on the matter. But the concept behind this sentence, the justifying generalization, and the parallel idea of depriving spendthrifts these rights were all conceivable to Gaius; he could well have arrived there himself. We cannot assume that Gaius, when writing on personal rights, might not also make a reference to property rights.[36] At any rate, it is clear that Gaius understood that this restriction of the master's power, as highlighted by the emperor, was to be taken seriously. In fact, he dealt with this in rather lengthy fashion in a text for those just beginning to study Roman law. No later jurist seems to have considered these restrictions of the master's power in detail, aside from Ulpian.

EFFECT

Ulpian was not a mere compiler of these regulations.[37] Sixty to eighty years after Hadrian and Pius he issued their directives for the more humane treatment of slaves in an instructional text for provincial governors.[38] In the section on penal law in which he instructed governors on the punishment of serious crimes, he produced his own chapter entitled "On the Cruelty of Masters" (*De saevitia dominorum*). In so doing, he defined a statutory offense.[39] Ulpian's writings were widely disseminated, exerting strong influence on criminal justice in the provinces. Lactantius, one of the fathers of the church from the early fourth century, was appalled by Ulpian's severe treatment of Christians.[40] We can therefore assume that provincial justice must have followed these guidelines insofar as the authorities had any interest in the law.

We do possess two pieces of information on the treatment of slaves from the end of the third century, however, which check our optimism. The first incident is recorded in December 285, that is, just a few months after Diocletian established his rule throughout the empire. The soldier-emperor told one of his fellow soldiers in convoluted speech that he should not fear being accused of immoderate punishment (*propter immoderatam castigationem*). That is to say, the slave-owning soldier would not be accused of grievously unjust exercise of his rights. The soldier had apparently beaten his slave—perhaps with good reason, perhaps severely and unjustly, perhaps aggravating the condition of a man already sick, at any rate enough to leave the impression that the legionary had been immoderate. Whatever happened, the slave had died.

A particular influential compendium on law was produced around the end of the third century after this decision by Diocletian. In it, this decision is briefly summarized in the chapter "On Homicide," which stated that the death of a slave resulting from a beating by his master would have penal consequences only if the intent was to kill the slave. In that case, the penalties would be those applied for manslaughter.[42] A dubious clause was appended: the duration of the criminal liability of a beating, intending to cause death, would still imply a limitation of the right to apply corporal punishment at the appropriate level. Yet how does one prove the intent to kill?

We thus doubt whether the attempts by Hadrian, Pius, Marcus Aurelius, and later Ulpian to limit the severity of masters met with long-term success. In the end, it appears that Ulpian did not succeed in establishing rules of law, criminal sanctions, and individual trials. Ulpian sought to implement these decisions as laws, and he may even have had some success over a short time, at least with governors who had an interest in legal matters. But over the long term his efforts were undermined by the bleak reality of the third century. In the above-mentioned compendium, lip service was paid to the ideas of this humanitarian approach; in effect, the older indifference of the authorities carried more weight. Ulpian's new statutory offense did not find its way into any later legal text or into any collection of imperial decisions. Only the *Lex Dei,* inspired as it was by Christian beliefs, included a corresponding section.[43] At any rate this Christian text was widely disseminated in the early Middle Ages,[44] when slavery had by no means been abolished but had, at least in the countryside, adopted somewhat gentler features.

CHAPTER THIRTEEN

Self-Help Is Punished

Marcianus before Marcus Aurelius

Circa 170 C.E.

THE STORY

Emperor Marcus Aurelius, who reigned from 161 to 180 C.E., passed judgment on a certain Marcianus, an otherwise unknown but apparently highly respected Roman.[1] Marcianus had taken specific items belonging to someone not named, claiming this man owed them to him. The case came before the imperial court, and the emperor patiently instructed the accused Marcianus that if he believed he had a claim to something, he must bring the matter before the court, leaving his opponent in possession. Marcianus objected that he had not employed force, but the emperor maintained that force does not just consist of inflicting wounds on other men but is also employed when a man simply takes what he believes is owed him without going to the courts. The emperor dealt sternly with Marcianus, stating that his actions were contrary to the law and did not conform to his honesty, dignity, and sense of duty. Marcus Aurelius appended a general statement as well: that any creditor proved to be in possession of his debtor's property, who had not given that property to the creditor, would forfeit his claim to said property for having taken it without court authorization. Such actions were considered devious; Marcianus had taken the law into his own hands.[2]

THE REPORT IN ITS ORIGINAL CONTEXT

Our source for this trial is Callistratus, a little-known, late-classical Roman jurist. He was active around 200 C.E. in the Hellenistic eastern part of the empire where he published five small legal works.[3] The text of interest here is taken from his work describing the judicial activities of the provincial governors, in which the emperor's input in developing Roman law was discussed at length. Book 4, part 2, through book 6 of this work concerns the law of criminal procedure and substantive criminal law for serious offenses, whereas libel, minor bodily harm, bare theft, and similar crimes were settled by punitive damages. Our text, at least according to the transmission,[4] refers to private violence (*vis privata*), which was described in detail in one of the laws enacted by Augustus, the *Lex Julia de vi privata* (Julian law on private violence). This *Lex Julia* specifies which actions were punishable as *vis privata,* and the penalties to be imposed.

SPECIFIC CASE DETAILS

We can be reasonably certain that for some unknown reason Marcianus had a contractual claim to some piece of property still belonging to his debtor. Thus the case did not involve a claim *in rem,* that is, for restitution of property already belonging to Marcianus but in the possession of his opponent. There is some confusion in the language of the report, due to the repeated use of both *reposcere* (demand back) and *petitiones* or *petitor* (petitions or applicant), which are typical terms found in *in rem* claims. However, the use in the introductory sentence of *creditores, debitores,* and *deberi* (to be owed), as well as *jus crediti* (right to collect a credit), the latter appearing in both the introductory and the concluding sentences, clearly indicates that a contractual claim (*in personam*) is being discussed. Finally, the words *rem ullam debitoris* (any possession of the debtor) in the concluding summary phrase also indicate a mere contractual claim, which raises the question, was the claim for monetary payment or for particular objects—and if the latter, then were they specific objects, that is, specific apples, or just any apples? In this context, the repeated use of *reposcere* indicates a noncash benefit, and indeed a specific article.

A sales contract should be considered the primary basis for a claim to a specific object, especially when the buyer has paid for an article he has not yet received. In this case, *jus crediti* (right to collect a credit) would be understandable. The buyer, who paid in advance without getting the article immediately, had given the seller a certain credit in the broad sense of the word, which is how the Romans would have understood it.

DETAILS OF THE LEGAL POSITION

If one accepts a claim for delivery of specific articles already purchased, or otherwise owed, then the following legal points should help modern readers understand why Marcianus, a man of some standing, would stoop to procure these items on his own initiative, that is, outside of the law during the Roman imperial period. According to the Roman law of civil procedure, debtors, no matter what they owed, were never condemned by the court to settle a debt nonmonetarily. If they owed benefits in-kind (articles), they were required to deliver only the appraised value of the object; they were never required to provide the actual item owed. Legally, therefore, Marcianus could only have had his debtor condemned to pay the cash value of the articles owed to him. In addition, he could not have had the judgment executed immediately. Instead, he would have had to wait another thirty days to see whether the debtor, or another in his place, would voluntarily pay the sum determined by the court. Should the debtor fail to pay the sum, a further court date would be set in order to verify that the debtor had failed to pay and to examine whether any other objections had arisen following the judgment.

Admittedly, once all of the delaying tactics that a debtor could employ were exhausted, things became very serious, very fast. The creditor could and, indeed, was required to seize all of the debtor's assets and send them to the auction block (principle of collective execution against his property) in order to satisfy the creditor's claim to the value of the amount owed from the proceeds; and the debts of anyone who reached this phase of the legal proceeding were automatically doubled. Meanwhile, however, the debtor had many opportunities to make articles "disappear," or to damage them. Marcianus may have had a highly personal interest in these specific items not represented in the appraised value. Our text unfortunately reveals nothing about the nature of the items in this case. But let us suppose, for example, that Marcianus purchased heirlooms from a relative, or that he had fathered children with someone else's slave and then purchased and paid for the children before taking delivery.

Only the most serious matters came before the emperor, and

when they did, it was almost always by way of appeals from lower courts. Marcianus most likely first appeared in a lower court with a provincial governor serving as magistrate, and there are some indications that he was acquitted, namely his certainty that he was innocent, his thorough instruction by the emperor, and not least the extraordinarily gentle punishment he was given for a criminal offense. After all, the *Lex Julia de vi privata* called for a fine of a third of the convicted man's assets, and he was made *infamis* (disreputable),[5] though this law originally applied only to violent criminal acts committed with the aid of a gang (*manu facta*) or with physical violence. A mob or a violent assault was necessary to invoke this law.[6] Marcianus's case contained no hint of either.

Until then, individuals were allowed and even expected to exercise their rights without recourse to a legal writ or court order in more circumstances than we would approve today. Such practices were often considered necessary; the legal process then relied far more on the active participation of an individual exercising his rights than nowadays. Roman law still empowered individuals to take the law into their own hands,[7] even after the state became more and more involved in enforcing civil judgments, and state involvement grew quite gradually. In the early imperial period, creditors for outstanding monetary debts were allowed to seize objects belonging to the debtor on their own initiative as long as they showed restraint.[8] In the mid-second century, they were still allowed to extort (*extorquere*) money from debtors as well.[9] If this was the case for monetary debts, it stands to reason that it was even more likely that creditors were allowed to seize objects they were owed so long as the claim was not disputed, and the creditor kept within legal limitations; that is, he took only the object that would fulfill his claim, and the seizure involve no mobs, physical violence, or blows. It was clearly not prohibited, or at least not prosecutable for a creditor to save himself time at court by instead exerting pressure on his debtor (within the legal limitations), so that the latter would make good on his debts.

It was also in the debtor's interest to avoid a judgment that would require his having to pay a sum of money he could not afford and that might necessitate subsequent seizure of all his property. For this reason, a creditor's visit regarding an undisputed debt could easily lead to his simply taking the money owed him, or taking the specific object or the owed number of articles from an inventory. The debtor's resistance should be overcome without resorting to violence as the Julian law then understood the term.

MARCUS AURELIUS'S INNOVATION

It was not until the philosopher Marcus Aurelius occupied the imperial throne and addressed Marcianus's case that self-help, or taking the law into one's own hands, was forbidden in this regard. Such action was declared to be illegal private violence (*vis*) and punishable by loss of the claim. In his concluding summary, the emperor stated that if no judge was involved in the dispute, all items that a creditor might hold, though they belonged to his debtor, were to be considered illicit possessions, and that they had been taken *vi* (by force). His ruling included those assets owed to the creditor that might have ended up in the creditor's possession by chance. The only exception involved items the debtor had voluntarily given to his creditor. By interpreting this law so broadly, the emperor hoped to outsmart the strategies employed by aggressive creditors. To that end, he defined every type of self-help with the intent of debt recovery as an illicit use of private violence under the Julian law.

The scope of application of the *Lex Julia* had already been expanded many times. For example, Julian sanctions had been applied to those who illegally plundered a shipwreck. They were also used to prosecute those who misused the courts by dishonestly persecuting a third party together with secret conspirators using civil procedures; the successful accuser then divided whatever he had gained from the conviction with his coconspirators.[10] In Marcianus's case, however, the punishment was far below what the law dictated. The creditor only lost his claim. He also seems to have kept his good reputation, nor was he subjected to the Julian law's main feature by forfeiting a third of his assets.[11] From this point onward, the unauthorized recovery of debts, no matter how gently executed, was considered a form of private violence but with a reduced penalty.

According to modern conceptions of good governance, such alterations of penal laws should be enacted by the legislature. Before the decision by Marcus Aurelius, rules concerning an individual's debt-collecting procedures were rather vague. There was no threat of punishment as long as one proceeded with enough restraint to avoid the Julian law against private violence. Marcianus must have been deeply affected by the emperor's new clarification. While the emperor did not consider that Marcianus had acted illegally (*non jure*), he did lecture him that from now on such behavior was incorrect, and that he expected him to follow the new law. Apparently, Marcianus was the first person affected by this new interpretation, which he could not have predicted. But in that era it went without saying that the emperor could change the law at any point during a trial, even when acting as judge,[12] and even if he had asked the legislature to change the law in a similar case.[13] The emperor's new ruling did not affect Marcianus as severely as it might have.

EFFECT

We have numerous statements from the judiciary and by jurists on the unauthorized recovery of claims after this case. In 205 Emperor Septimius Severus (193–211) decided in favor of someone named Maximus, who had stipulated with his lender that if the money were not paid back on schedule, the lender would be allowed to trespass onto his property. The emperor determined that the lender still had to obtain legal permission to access Maximus's property, in this case from the provincial governor, even if the lender had committed no violent act while trespassing.[14] Shrewd lenders seem to have reacted to Marcus Aurelius's restriction by adding the right of self-help in their contracts with borrowers. By this ruling, Severus or his government (Ulpian? see below) declared such a clause invalid. The clause still protected lenders for the time being from criminal liability, and thus against loss of claim.[15] Statutory prohibitions having the only consequence that a contravening contract clause was invalid but without penalty were not unusual in Roman law; they were called *leges minus quam perfectae* (laws less than perfect).

At that time, Ulpian presided over the office of imperial petitions and was formulating the imperial rescripts to private individuals, thus also the one just mentioned.[16] His own writings contain a brief excursus about Marcianus's case. Ulpian outlines the new legal situation regarding the recovery of monetary debt, including the mild but still effective sanction as loss of claim.[17] But that gentler sanction was short-lived and later disappeared, while the private, unauthorized recovery of claims remained covered by the *vis privata* law. Ulpian's student Modestinus records that the *occupatio* (occupation) of a borrower's property by the lender without judicial authorization called for the usual punishment for *vis privata*, namely the confiscation of a third of the lender's assets and stigmatization as *infamis*.[18] In a decision outlined by the jurist Hermogenianus, Emperor Diocletian declared that private violence occurred if a lender trespassed by force onto the borrower's estate and took posssession of it.[19] In addition, a short legal compendium written about 300 C.E. summarily declares that a lender's unauthorized seizure of his debtor's property was considered private violence requiring even more serious punishment at that time: persons of rank lost a third of their assets and were subject to relegation, that is, limited exile, while people from the lower classes, usually with no assets of value, were condemned to forced labor in the imperial mines.[20] These punishments were included in the Visigoths' codification of Roman law in 506 C.E., and their code endured in the Iberian Peninsula and especially Gaul. However, they are absent in the legal codification in the Eastern Empire under Justinian in 529 to 533, which preserved all the contradictions of the various rulings and remarks of Marcus Aurelius, Callistratus, Severus, and Ulpian, on the one hand, and Modestinus and Diocletian, on the other.[21]

Today we take it for granted that a creditor must go to court to satisfy a claim if a debtor fails to fulfill his or her obligation voluntarily. Creditors who take the law into their own hands commit criminal coercion and are guilty of trespassing as well. Nevertheless, the tendency to attempt the recovery of monetary debt without involving courts remains, although much of this unpleasant business is left to professional collection agencies nowadays. For their part, such agencies may indeed be tempted to challenge the boundaries of the legally acceptable, even if intimidating company names, such as Russian Repo and Sicilian Persuasion Collection Agency, can scarcely be prosecuted in and of themselves.

CHAPTER FOURTEEN

Protecting a Ward Prevails over Standard Payment Practices

The Dispute over the Rutilian Country Estate

Circa 200 C.E.

THE STORY

In 197–198 C.E., a lot of private land in Italy was put on sale after a civil war. Many senators and members of the equestrian class had been executed as traitors for having affiliated with the losing side,[1] and their assets were confiscated and auctioned off. A certain Ovinius, perhaps a wholesale dealer in confiscated assets, sold a country estate called the *fundus Rutilianus* to one Aemilius Larianus. This buyer did not pay for the estate immediately but made a deposit and agreed to pay the balance in two equal installments at two-month intervals, thus in two months and again in four months from the date of purchase. According to a forfeiture clause (*lex commissoria*) in the purchase agreement, if he did not make one of these payments on time, the contract would be voided; however, jurists at that time did not interpret this clause literally. Such contracts would not be voided automatically, but the seller (Ovinius in this case) would have the option of withdrawing from the contract if he chose to do so. Nowadays this would be rescinding a sales contract.

Larianus died unexpectedly before paying the first installment. His only heir and successor was Rutiliana, apparently his daughter. She was certainly under the age of twelve and could even have been an infant. Her guardians proved to be delinquent in their duties to her and her property,[2] for which they were eventually convicted and replaced by others. Ovinius had informed the original guardians about the contract and its binding provisions and had emphasized the payments' due dates. He had frequently (*saepe*) admonished the guardians, but they had not paid. After a year, Ovinius gave up and sold the property to Claudius Telemachus, a rich Greek from the city of Xanthus in southwestern Asia Minor. His family had held Roman citizenship for generations,[3] and the emperor had recently elevated him to senator—one of many chosen to replenish the senate's numbers. As a senator, Telemachus was required to invest a fourth of his assets in Italian land, and he probably paid a higher price for the *fundus Rutilianus* than Larianus had done.

Rutiliana's guardians filed a plea on her behalf; she was still under twelve and apparently remained so throughout the proceedings. The plea was filed with the urban praetor in Rome, the elected magistrate who adjudicated civil cases among citizens. Her guardians asked that she be reinstated to the previous status with regard to the purchase agreement. This reinstatement (*in integrum restitutio*) gave minors (i.e., all persons under the age of twenty-five), among others, the right of legal compensation for losses in business dealings. Rutiliana lost her case. Her guardians, however, appealed to the urban prefect, the representative of the emperor in Rome and its environs, normally an outstanding older senator. He, too, ruled against her.

Finally, the guardians appealed to the emperor, Septimius Severus, who discussed the case with his advisers (the *consilium principis*). The jurist Paul, the first to comment, was also one of the youngest. He agreed that Rutiliana's claim should be denied, on the grounds that neither she nor her guardians had drawn up the original sales contract. The emperor thought differently: for him the deciding points were that the due dates for the payments had fallen during the girl's period of immaturity, that she needed special protection when assuming the role of the buyer, and that her guardians at that time had failed her. Ovinius's option to rescind the contract could be traced back to this very specific failure on the part of the guardians.

At this point, Paul changed his view to agree with the emperor's ruling, but he based his decision on other factors. Ovinius had continued to demand payment of the remaining installments once the due date had passed. By doing so, he no longer insisted on his right to rescind the contract, and in effect he thereby waived this right.[4] The crucial issue here seems to be whether Ovinius was entitled to make a substantial profit by canceling the old contract and selling the estate to Telemachus, or whether Rutilia could still complete the purchase at the original, lower price. The emperor clearly felt that the child had been cheated by her first guardians, and both he and Paul tried to justify ruling in her favor, but on different legal grounds. Paul maintained that the fact that the payment date had only come due once Rutiliana had become heir was immaterial. This circumstance played just as insignificant a role as when a lender liquidated collateral, even though the due date passed only after the borrower's death. Paul continued that it was the forfeiture clause (*lex commissoria*) that had so displeased the emperor, who therefore decided in favor of the girl. The fact that her guardians at the time had neglected to look after her interests and had ultimately been dismissed as delinquent also played a significant role in the emperor's decision.

THE AUTHOR OF THE REPORT

Our information about this case stems from Paul himself. He was probably around thirty-five years old at the time,[5] thus one of the youngest members of the emperor's *consilium,* and yet he appears to have spoken first. During sessions of the imperial court, Emperor Septimius Severus (and probably most of his predecessors) usually encouraged jurists to state their opinions on a case before he expressed the final opinion and delivered judgment.[6] This protocol was very different from that in the official advisory council, the Roman senate, where the highest-ranking member spoke first, and all the others were expected to agree with him.

Paul probably came from one of the eastern provinces, studied law in Rome under the famous jurist Cervidius Scaevola, then worked as an advocate, author of legal texts, teacher of Roman law, and legal consultant. He was appointed to the emperor's *consilium* around 200 c.e., and by 207 he had become the legal adviser to Papinian, a close friend of the emperor's. Papinian had also studied with Scaevola, was a senior member of the *consilium,* and in 207 held the post of civil praetorian prefect. There were two praetorian prefects, the one the commander of the imperial guard in Rome, the other the highest civil servant. Paul himself became the civil praetorian prefect in 219. A year later he was banished by the teenage emperor Elagabalus. However, Elagabalus was soon assassinated, and Paul was summoned back to Rome to serve as an adviser to the new emperor, Severus Alexander (222–235).

Paul was a prolific writer in all literary genres of Roman law. His works filled nearly three hundred scrolls (*libri*), covering about ten thousand modern printed pages. His commentaries and monographs are noteworthy for their unconventional choices of legal issues. He also wrote legal textbooks and casuistic literature with numerous case histories stemming from his practice as a legal consultant, his legal instruction for advanced students, and, as in the present case, his participation in the imperial court. Our case is from a work titled "Imperial Verdicts Issued in Jurisdiction in Six Books" (*Imperialium sententiarum in cognitionibus prolatarum libri VI*),[7] where it appeared under the rubric "On the Restitution of Persons under Twenty-Five Years" (*De in integrum restitutione minorum XXV annis*).[8]

DETAILS OF THE CASE

The Rutilian country estate was initially established by a man named Rutilius, possibly an ancestor of our Rutiliana, perhaps through the maternal line.[9] Therefore her father could have had a sentimental interest in the estate, especially if she was to be his sole heir. The Apulian town of Rutigliano south of Bari draws its name from such a *fundus Rutilianus*,[10] and there may have been several estates of the same name.

Paul's text does not explicitly state that Rutiliana was Larianus's daughter. But her situation indicates that she must have been either his daughter or his granddaughter. She was the sole heir of the deceased and paternally orphaned, evidenced by her status as a child under wardship. Her original guardians proved incompetent, so it is highly unlikely that Larianus named them. Rather, it seems that he died intestate, that is, without a formal will, leaving Rutiliana as his only legitimate child (or possibly only legitimate grandchild, i.e., child of an only son who died before him). If she had been the child of another man, she would have been paternally orphaned before Larianus died; in that case, he would have had to declare her his sole heir in a formal will and provided her with competent guardians.

Paul also reveals nothing more about the history of this estate's ownership, nor about who finally took possession. Such points were immaterial to the issue of restitution of a minor,[11] the main point in Paul's discussion. But we can sketch some possible outcomes. Following the victory in this restitution case, her guardians may have sought to gain possession of the estate. But that would have been difficult if Ovinius had already transferred ownership and possession to Telemachus. Even if Ovinius still had possession, he could not be sentenced to deliver it to Rutiliana. He was required only to pay the monetary value of the estate at the time of the verdict, minus any payments still due. Probably, Telemachus had paid much more for this estate, so Ovinius had much more at stake in this case than just the opening payment Larianus had made before his death; he may even have already repaid this. On the other hand, Ovinius and Telemachus now knew of the emperor's interest in the girl's case, and they could well have felt compelled to surrender the property to her and somehow work out the terms of their mutual loss. Ovinius may have transferred the estate to Larianus, but it had not become his property before completion of the payments, remaining instead only his revocable possession (*precario*) until all payments had been made. Ovinius would have combined this revocation of the possession with revoking the sales contract, retaking possession of the estate and transferring ownership to Telemachus.

LEGAL ISSUES

According to Roman law, a person became of legal age at the time of sexual maturity, which had been codified in the imperial period: for boys at age fourteen, and girls at twelve. Until that age, any child who lost his or her father was assigned a guardian. The first choice would be the man whom the father had named in his will. If there was no will, guardianship devolved to the closest paternal relative, determined by definite legal rules. If no such relatives were living or willing, then the *praetor tutelarius,* whose sole task was assigning guardians for immature orphans, would select a suitable man. Incompetent guardians were usually found in the second group, the paternal relatives.

Those young people over the age of fourteen and twelve respectively, who had been disadvantaged by a transaction, still had legal protections up to age twenty-five (*minores XXV annis*). Younger children (boys under fourteen, girls under twelve) were already protected by guardianship laws; if they were disadvantaged, they could demand compensation damages from their guardian, from any guarantors he had named, or from the magistrate who had selected him. It is only surprising that in our case a young child should additionally enjoy the protection provided for minors under twenty-five.

As mentioned above, the forfeiture clause in Roman sales contracts was formulated very strictly but handled more leniently by the jurists. If the contract payments were not made on time, the seller had the right to revoke the sales contract in any manner, including taking repossession, for example, in this case, for the purpose of selling the property to Telemachus. In practice, the sales contract (and perhaps property transfer) was not forfeitured automatically as soon as a payment date was missed; the deal was considered void only if the seller chose to exercise this clause and made his decision known to the purchaser. Otherwise, if the buyer regretted his purchase, he could void the contract by simply not paying the next installment. Besides, automatic forfeiture would have left no leeway to forgive the buyer for small deviations from a payment plan, a flexibility that business dealings so often require. For all these reasons, the jurists interpreted the forfeiture clause as merely the seller's right to withdraw if he chose to do so.

THE MATTER UNDER DISPUTE

The initial point on which Paul and the emperor disagreed was whether or not the protection of minors under twenty-five should be invoked in Rutiliana's case. The praetor's edict concerning minors protected them if a minor was somehow deprived by the conclusion of a transaction. The edict stated: *gestum esse* (has been transacted).[12] The lower courts had rejected this line of argument; this was not a case in which a child was deprived because she or her guardians improperly concluded a transaction. It was Larianus who concluded the transaction before he died, in his sales contract with Ovinius. Still, the emperor was concerned that a minor had been adversely affected by the transaction and Ovinius's use of the forfeiture clause. It was true that the guardians were at fault for what they failed to do, namely pay Ovinius the contract amounts on the due dates. Such failure could have been considered an action on their part if they had deliberately remained idle in order to derail the contract; but no one raised that possibility. The issue therefore became whether allowing a deadline to pass, which usually happened in estates due to negligence or lack of ready cash, amounted to a deliberate business transaction. Paul said no, and he argued convincingly with the analogy of a pawnbroker. What if someone pawned a valuable item, then died, leaving a minor heir who failed to redeem it? Would the pawnbroker be barred from selling the item after the redemption date had passed? The surrender of collateral items was meant to protect pawnbrokers against just such eventualities.

But in order to support the emperor's decision,[13] Paul took a very different approach to this case. He regarded the forfeiture clause as a *quid pro quo*. The seller granted the buyer an extension in producing payment; the buyer granted the seller the right to cancel the deal if its terms were not met. The seller alone had the right to withdraw, and to choose not to exercise that right, and Paul opined that Ovinius's behavior, namely insisting for months on payment, although the due date had passed, could be interpreted as an actual renunciation of his right to withdraw from the contract. According to Paul, the seller was obliged to decide, as soon as he could withdraw from the contract, whether he wanted to exercise that right.[14] According to Paul, the seller should not be allowed to exploit his special privilege to keep both possibilities open for a longer period of time and await the development most advantageous to himself.

Paul's reasoning is ingenious, but does it fairly represent Ovinius's actions? Quite a different interpretation is also possible: that Ovinius was a patient and considerate businessman. He gave the new business managers time to become informed about the financial dealings of the deceased. In the end, he waited for a year. It does not seem right to interpret this thoughtfulness as renunciation of his rights. He could well have understood that immediate payment of his claim would force Rutiliana's initial guardians to exhaust her other resources. Paul also considered his argument to be one devised just to align himself with the emperor's ruling.

What did this decision of the emperor's imply? What would Ovinius have had to do, according to Septimius Severus, to have been in the right? The emperor encumbered Ovinius with the disadvantages that can result if a ward has incompetent guardians. This decision made any seller who had involuntarily become the partner of a ward absorb not only the drawbacks associated with the fact that a seller exploits the incompetence of a ward's guardians to his own advantage and conducts business to that ward's disadvantage, but also those that result when that ward's guardians through their inactivity simply fail to carry out an especially favorable business that the ward had inherited. If one follows this logic to its conclusion, Ovinius would have had to ensure that Rutiliana was provided with competent guardians. Paul's strictures would also put too great a burden on any seller with a forfeiture clause for extending payment of the purchase price. He could not insist on payment more than once if he wanted to exercise his right to eventually withdraw from the sales contract.

SIGNIFICANCE OF
THE EMPEROR'S DECISION

A few years before these transactions, Septimius Severus had introduced a ruling in the senate to protect the estates of immature and minor citizens, such as his own young sons. According to this ruling their rural landed properties and those near Rome (*praedia rustica vel suburbana*) were inalienable, nor could they be used for collateral.[15] Twenty years later (215 C.E.), the court jurist Ulpian drew a conclusion that could have affected our case: a minor had bought land and in return for an extension of payment had been encumbered by a mortgage; indeed, he had to pay the remaining balance, but the mortgage clause would be invalid, and he would not put him at risk of losing the property.[16] Thus Severus had strengthened the protection of wards with respect to real estate transactions in the early years of his reign; nevertheless, he also provided exceptions in two cases: that in which the father had required in his will that his child heir sell a particular piece of property, and that in which he had used his property for collateral, as in effect Larianus had done.

According to these regulations, Ovinius should have won the legal suit. But in this case the emperor was offended by the forfeiture clause (*lex commissoria displicebat ei*);[17] Paul cites this catch as the primary reason that Rutiliana won. Apparently, Severus found this clause to be too strict and deemed that buyers must be protected from this type of harshness, at least those who, because of their youth, are least able to defend themselves and do not have competent guardians. The ethics of loan repayment mattered less to the emperor than the protection of minors, whereas Paul considered loan ethics as pivotal even when siding with the emperor.

The emperor's position cannot quite be called "consumer protection," even if this case cast Ovinius as a professional asset stripper who resells auctioned goods at a tidy profit, while casting Larianus as the bucolic buyer who strains his finances to the limit. Even current consumer protection law would not apply in this case. Nor would laws concerning the protection of minors apply in a case like this today. A minor who suffers losses due to imcompetent guardians may hold the guardians liable, as the praetor, urban prefect, and Paul had done initially.

CHAPTER FIFTEEN

A Dispute among Christians

The First Trials of the Donatists

313–316 C.E.

This chapter and the next discuss disputes that arose among Christians and made their way through various courts until they were decided by an emperor. Compared to the single-trial disputes of previous chapters, these stories are complicated because of overlapping historical circumstances. For one thing, the Christian church had its own hierarchical organization and councils for imposing discipline on its members, and Roman emperors restrained themselves from intervening. Moreover, these disputes took place in turbulent eras. Regional church activists were challenging established leaders and denying their legitimacy at the same time that particular emperors were engaged in civil wars to defend, enlarge, or consolidate their power.

Crucial decisions emerged as a result. According to a famous legend, the emperor Constantine saw a mysterious sign of the cross in the sky before a crucial battle. Thereafter, he came to favor Christianity as a state religion, in fact as the preferred religion of the empire, which would be unified under a common creed that he helped to promulgate. In our later case (chapter

16), the emperor Maximus tried to leave heresy trials and punishments to church tribunals alone, but in the end he, too, intervened and approved state executions for heretics.

THE STORY

Early in the fourth century, the Roman Empire was divided into four regions and ruled by four emperors (or tetrarchs). Constantine ruled in the western regions, from Britain through Gaul to Morocco. Maxentius held the central section, which covered southern Germany, Italy, Dalmatia, and central northern Africa. Galerius and Maximinus Daia reigned in the East, over the Balkans and the eastern Mediterranean. But wars soon broke out among these rivals, and in 312 Constantine defeated Maxentius at the battle of Milvian Bridge near Rome, allying himself with a new eastern emperor, Licinius. An important outcome of this alliance was a meeting between these two leaders in Milan at the turn of the new year 312–313, where they agreed to favor the Christian religion. The era of persecution had ended already some years earlier, and toleration had been granted. Constantine and Licinius gave Christianity equal recognition with other Roman religions.

Some writers refer to this decision as the Edict of Milan or Constantine's Edict of Toleration. But it was not an edict, nor was Christianity only then granted toleration, nor can its content be traced back to Constantine alone, as some essential decrees stem from Licinius. Nevertheless, this new policy established Christianity as a recognized Roman religion and gave Christian clerics the same tax exemptions that pagan priests enjoyed. Constantine soon went even farther by granting Christians generous reparation payments for former persecutions.

Meanwhile, an angry church dispute had erupted after the sudden death of Mensurius, the bishop of Carthage and primate (chief bishop) of the Church of Africa Minor, the area covering present-day Tunisia, northeastern Algeria, and western Libya. Mensurius had favored his deacon Caecilian as his successor, and in 309 Caecilian was elected in this diocese and consecrated by several nearby bishops. But Secundus, the primate of the church province to the west, objected that he and several other leaders had been excluded from this process and that Caecilian was an unworthy candidate.[1] He convened a synod of about seventy bishops in Carthage, at the house of a rich widow named Lucilla. This synod proceeded to summon Caecilian and demoted him and excommunicated his followers when he refused to appear. Majorinus, a member of Lucilla's household, was elected and consecrated to replace him. These events took place while ship traffic between Italy and Africa was suspended because of a political revolt. In 310–311, normal communications resumed, and the Italian bishops, including the pope (the bishop of Rome), confirmed Caecilian as the only legitimate bishop of Carthage and primate of Africa.

The Milan agreement soon followed with its grants of privileges and reparations. In Africa, however, these benefits were granted only to those leaders recognized by Rome. Secundus and Majorinus promptly objected. They asked the proconsul in Carthage to forward their complaint to Constantine and insisted that the emperor set up a nonpartisan tribunal of Gallic bishops. Constantine accommodated these demands up to a point. He established a judicial council of three Gallic bishops, but the pope was to preside, and the council was to meet in Rome. The emperor himself declined to participate. This council summoned Caecilian accompanied by ten supporters, with ten of his accusers as opponents. Majorinus had died in the meantime, and a new figure named Donatus had been elected to replace him. Donatus proved to be such a charismatic leader that by the time of his death over forty years later (around 355), most Christians in North Africa were professed Donatists. Donatus now led the opposition group. The pope added fifteen Italian bishops to the council, and Caecilian's trial began on 2 October 313.

Donatus opened with a brilliant speech, but his witnesses against Caecilian proved unreliable, and after the first day of trial, Donatus sullenly withdrew. It also became apparent that Donatus himself had violated church doctrines. His complaint was rejected, and Caecilian was acquitted by all nineteen bishops. Again Donatus appealed to the emperor, claiming that too few bishops had been involved in this judgment, and that the matter had not been thoroughly examined. He did not take issue with the pope's expansion of the court, at least not directly. For the sake of Christian unity, the emperor agreed to another hearing and summoned a synod at Arles, the seat of the primate of Gaul, for 1 August 314. This synod was to involve the church of the entire Western Empire. Thirty-two bishops attended, but Africa was represented only by the feuding parties, who could not participate as judges. The bishop of Rome asked to be excused. Donatus's complaint was reexamined, and again Caecilian was unanimously acquitted and confirmed in office.

Undeterred, Donatus appealed once more to Constantine, asking that he hear the case himself. After hesitation, Constantine summoned both parties to his court in Milan in 316. Yet again, the judgment was in Caecilian's favor, and since this court had the final word, he was definitively confirmed in his office. Some bishops persisted in their opposition, Donatus among them. But they were punished with exile, either at the conclusion of the trial or soon afterward, and forbidden to return to North Africa. The Donatists there were now deprived of their leader, and they resolutely refused to rejoin the Catholic Church. The divided Christians in Africa fell into chaos as rumors and slurs spread widely, murders and assaults demanded actions by the secular authorities, and brutality produced martyrs on both sides. Constantine allowed the exiles to return home in 321, where they were tolerated, but not granted privileges. Constantine uttered the belief that divine justice would prove much more severe than anything he could enforce.

TEXTUAL TRANSMISSION

Extensive reports about this conflict were written by the fathers of the church, in particular by Eusebius, bishop of Caesarea in Palestine; Optatus, bishop of Milev in the interior of northern Africa; and Augustine, bishop of Hippo on the African coast. All three, of course, favored Caecilian, as did the courts, bishops, and emperor, who repeatedly confirmed Caecilian's legitimacy, and thus that of the ultimately victorious party, the Catholics.

Eusebius was highly regarded by Constantine and wrote a biography of him, but his main opus is *Historia ecclesiastica* (History of the Church) in ten volumes, ending in 312–313.[2] Many have considered Eusebius unreliable. He quoted many documents in his text, mostly imperial texts in Greek, which often seemed either spurious or adulterated. A recently discovered inscription, however, confirms one of his doubted passages word for word. His reports may thus be more trustworthy than formerly supposed—except for his statements about Constantine, whom he revered to the point of spinning all contrary evidence into praise.

Optatus actively opposed the Donatists.[3] In 366–367 he penned a rejoinder in six volumes to a polemic written by Parmenianus, the leader who succeeded Donatus around 355. He added documents in an appendix, some of which are disputed by modern scholars. Optatus may have been fooled by forgeries at times, but he tried hard to present an objective account in order to heal the old schism, and he added nothing that he did not find in the documents at hand.[4]

Augustine (354–430), the most prolific and famous author among the Latin fathers of the church,[5] became bishop of Hippo in 396 and a devoted preacher and writer against Donatism and other heresies. He was the leading figure at a public religious conference between the Catholics and Donatists held in Carthage in 411; the official files of this council are extant and nearly complete.[6] After this conference, Donatism began to decline.

CAECILIAN'S DISPUTED CONSECRATION

The Donatists denied Caecilian's legitimacy and sought to install their own bishop, thereby gaining possession of church properties and other exclusive material advantages in Carthage and beyond. They wanted their clergy freed from onerous taxes and financial burdens, as well as the windfall of Constantine's compensation orders. They also complained on principle, attacking malpractices by Caecilian and other leaders who had supported him, such as Mensurius, the earlier bishop of Carthage, and Felix, the bishop of Abthugni, a few miles to the south, who had led Caecilian's consecration.

Secundus, several other bishops, and their followers considered these men to have been traitors to the faith, with Caecilian as their implied accomplice. They were accused of having surrendered sacred scriptures to the Roman authorities during the times of persecution; the Latin word *traditor* means "one who hands over" and is the root of the English word *traitor.* In fact, these charges turned out to be false, having been based on forgeries by Felix's enemies. Mensurius was accused in part because he was known to have practiced restraint and moderation under the African proconsul of his time. But he had actually arranged the hiding of the scriptures and allowed Roman authorities to discover only heretical works. These were assumed to be actual Christian texts and burned in public.

Caecilian was also accused of having maltreated Christian prisoners during the time of the persecutions. Christians from all of Africa Minor were held in Carthage, and as deacon to Mensurius Caecilian was responsible for supplying their food, drink, and spiritual support. Some of these prisoners, however, had zealously surrendered themselves to the Roman authorities in the hope of becoming public martyrs. They were thus a burden on the Carthage community, which was taxed to support all the Christian prisoners from Africa Minor. Mensurius declared that such demonstrating, would-be martyrs should not be encouraged, and most of his clergy agreed. As a result, some prisoners without relatives in the capital to support them died in prison of starvation.

The charges against Caecilian were exaggerated by his opponents and embellished with baseless details. The widow Lucilla, in particular, bore a personal grudge against him. She had made a practice of kissing the reliquary of a martyr before receiving Communion. As deacon, Caecilian had publicly rebuked her for revering a bone fragment from someone whose martyrdom was dubious.

WHY DID THE EMPEROR INTERVENE?

Constantine has been reproached for intervening without cause and bringing the authority of the state to bear in what was essentially an internal church dispute. Moreover, by granting privileges and subsidies to only one of the two Christian parties, the Roman government poured fuel on a conflagration. The old Roman policy had been to tolerate various religious cults within the empire. If that had been followed in this instance, there could have been identical benefits to both organizations, the price would not have been too high, and years of armed conflict could have been diminished or prevented altogether.

But Constantine did not consider this option. To him the unity of Christianity was as fundamental as the unity of imperial power. He shared power with no one in the Western Empire, and he soon expanded into the East as well. Since his conversion at the Battle of Milvian Bridge, where the Christians' god had so spectacularly come to his aid, Constantine lost his religious toleration and was no longer willing to authorize the pluralistic exercise of religion; in fact, he had become a monotheist, intolerant in thought and later also in action. His god was the only True God, who could be worshipped only uniformly and in unity. Aside from the very real danger of turmoil and bloody conflict between the opposing bishops' supporters, such rivalry contradicted Christianity itself as well as Constantine's understanding of the religion, which he was now experiencing with personal fervor. He simply would not condone competing leaders and a variety of Christian communities in the same place.

Under these circumstances, it appears obvious that he would support the faction that retained communion with the Universal Church, and not with the special, regional community of the Donatists. They left him no alternative but coercion. They were the ones who initially asked him to have the conflict decided by nonpartisan clerics; they were also the ones who, dissatisfied with the first verdict, appealed to the emperor for a larger and more diverse judicial bench; above all, it was they who, according to all extant written records, ultimately demanded an imperial decision. When Constantine ultimately exiled the intractable Donatist bishops, it was a final, desperate attempt to enable the opposing groups to find their way back to unity by separating the rank and file from their agitating leaders. This punishment was justified because they had, as proved before two synods of bishops and before a secular court, repeatedly frivolously accused Caecilian. Constantine was, unfortunately, deluded as to the efficacy of his punishment. Without their leaders, the Donatists became even more agitated and violent.

SIGNIFICANCE OF THIS CASE

Although Constantine had not wanted to decide matters of belief and questions about the organization of the church, he ultimately relented to the Donatists and made his ruling. Thereafter, he refrained from exerting judicial authority in church matters. In 324, after defeating Licinius, who then ruled the eastern third of the empire, Constantine became sole emperor. He then faced a conflict over Christian dogma in his newly conquered region. That was important to the affected communities, and tempers were fraying. But now Constantine had become convinced that disputes of this type should be settled by appointed clerical leaders alone, and that he should supply only all conceivable means to assist church leaders in arriving at a decision.

To that end, he convened an ecumenical council in Nicaea on the northwestern coast of Asia Minor in the year 325.

The conflict concerned the divine and human nature of Jesus. Was he merely godlike, as the Alexandrian presbyter Arius and his many disciples taught? Or was he completely of one and the same substance with God the Father (consubstantial), the opinion held by the Alexandrian bishops? To support the council in Nicaea, Constantine made elaborate arrangements for the participating bishops: free transportation through the imperial postal system, accommodations on site, meeting facilities, and much, much more. He sat as the official presider, although he attended without his bodyguards or other signs of imperial authority.[7] He specifically refrained from using his influence to guide the deliberations; instead, he had the council's final creed prepared by a commission led by Bishop Ossius of Cordoba, whom he especially trusted. Ossius then presented the draft to the full assembly. Those who refused to sign were threatened with exile, an option that only Arius chose.

Since then, councils and synods have been exclusively responsible for resolving internal questions affecting the church. In the sixth century, Emperor Justinian became involved in another Christological dispute, but his actions served only to sharpen, increase, and perpetuate animosities among Christians.[8]

The trial of Caecilian reached a broader public than expected; ordinary pagans took notice and exulted in such conflicts between the Christian parties. Julian the Apostate (361–363), a nephew of Constantine, felt secure in declaring his renunciation of Christianity once he became emperor. He was convinced that no wild beasts are such enemies to mankind as most Christians are in their deadly hatred of one another.[9]

CHAPTER SIXTEEN

The Execution of Heretics

Priscillian and His Followers
before the Court of Emperor Maximus

386 C.E.

THE STORY BEHIND THE TRIAL

During the 370s an ascetic movement came out of Egypt and spread across the western part of the Iberian Peninsula. It soon found a leader in Priscillian,[1] an attractive young nobleman, well educated and charismatic. He was born around 345, probably in the southwestern Iberian Peninsula, the Roman province of Lusitania. The Priscillianists lived modestly, fasted often, performed ascetic rituals that included a variation of the Eucharist, and recited their nightly prayers while naked, males and females together; they probably wore only loincloths. They also kept aloof from other Christians in their various communities. Priscillian convinced many women to join him, as well as two bishops, Instantius and Silvanus, whose exact official sees are unknown. Hyginus, bishop of Cordoba, learned about this sect and its practices, had misgivings, and notified his primate, Hydatius, bishop of Merida, the provincial capital.

Hydatius convened a synod of bishops in Saragossa, in the northeast of the peninsula, summoning bishops from southern Gaul, too. A total of twelve bishops met in 380 C.E. and began proceedings on 4 October, with Hydatius presenting the charges. The bishops summoned Priscillian and his followers, all of whom refused to appear. Inquiries had already been made to the bishop of Rome, Pope Damasus, about similar situations in which those summoned before a court did not appear; the pope merely reminded them that no accusation could be raised against absent parties who could not defend themselves. The assembled bishops thus had to be content with condemning some of the rumored Priscillianist practices and excommunicating all the participants, including those who only shared Communion with them. Hyginus, who had initiated the proceedings, left before the final decision was made.

To mount a counteroffensive, Instantius and Silvanus then consecrated Priscillian as bishop, even though he had not even been ordained as a priest. This ordination took place in a hurry and exploited a see that had just become vacant in Ávila (between Madrid and Salamanca). Spanish Christians soon became divided between Priscillianists and anti-Priscillianists.

When Hydatius returned to Merida, he was met with fierce hostility; Priscillian's sympathizers, also those in the neighboring bishoprics, called for him to be deposed. Consequently, Hydatius joined with Ithacius, bishop of Ossonoba (in the Algarve), and addressed the young emperor Gratian in Milan through his prefect of Gaul. This prefect held authority over Britain, Gaul, Spain, and Morocco and was on their side. Through him they obtained an imperial rescript that banished the "false" bishops. It also accused them of Manichaeism, a dualistic religion that originated in Persia in the third century and was outlawed in the

Roman Empire around 300 C.E. Were a nobleman such as Priscillian to be convicted as a Manichee, he would be punished by forced labor in imperial quarries and confiscation of everything he owned.[2]

Priscillian, Instantius, and Silvanus chose to comply with the banishment from Spain by traveling to Italy and appealing to the emperor in Milan. They continued to proselytize as they passed through Aquitaine, claiming that the emperor had forbidden them only from preaching in Spain, not Gaul. Once in Italy, they tried to gain support from Ambrosius, the influential bishop of the imperial residence, and from the pope. However, they were denied entry at both ecclesiastical courts. They then turned to the head of the imperial chancellery in Milan, Macedonius, who was estranged from Ambrosius. Macedonius secured a new imperial rescript, which suspended the old one and reinstated them in their bishoprics. Moreover, Ithacius of Ossonoba was to be brought before the court for fomenting unrest, but he fled to Trier. There the prefect summoned Priscillian and his followers, yet Macedonius again came to their aid. He managed to transfer the hearing to the renowned jurist Marinianus, the civil head of the government of Spain. He demanded that Ithacius be delivered to him, and sent court officials to Trier to fetch him.

At this point, all these complicated maneuvers were interrupted by a rebellion that broke out in Britain and spread to Gaul. It was now the summer of 383, and the entire Western Empire was shaken. The young emperor Gratian had alienated professional soldiers and civil servants alike by filling positions with the relatives and in-laws of his beloved tutor, the poet Ausonius, regardless of their qualifications. The commanding general in Britain, Magnus Maximus, exploited this discontent. He had his troops hail him as emperor, won the support of the legions in Gaul, imprisoned Gratian in Lyons, and had him later strangled. He thus took over as emperor of the West, claimed guardianship of the twelve-year-old ruler of the central empire, and tried to establish himself firmly in his throne while the eastern emperor, Theodosius I, was distracted in rebuilding the eastern army after the disastrous defeat of his predecessor, who was killed in action.

Ithacius saw his chance to turn this sea change in the empire to his advantage. Maximus needed to gain and hold widespread support, and Ithacius now offered him the chance to resolve a very divisive conflict. Priscillian was attracting a great many followers in Spain, but his form of religion had been branded a heresy by a synod of bishops. Ithacius went further. In a written accusation he denounced Priscillian and his followers for Manichaeism, and for practicing magic. Magic for evil purposes (*maleficium*) was a capital crime, and such accusations were taken very seriously in the later fourth century.[3]

Maximus referred this charge to a synod of bishops in Bordeaux, where the local bishop had already rebuffed the Priscillianists. According to church custom and one of Gratian's recent laws,[4] this case should have gone to a council of Spanish bishops, the party most directly affected. But the Priscillianists were now so numerous in Spain that it was doubtful that Ithacius could win a trial there. The Bordeaux synod met in 384 and heard charges that the Priscillianists had promoted Manichaean doctrines and practiced indecent rituals. The accusers' aim was to deprive them of their bishoprics and thus the means of further proselytizing. Instantius appeared first, defending himself so incompetently that the synod unanimously removed him from his bishopric. Priscillian refused to answer to this assembly, which now seemed prejudiced against him and his teachings. He appealed to the emperor, apparently hoping for more receptive judges on a secular court. At this point, Maximus had him and his followers brought back to Trier for trial at the imperial court.

THE TRIAL IN TRIER

Once more the accusers were Ithacius and Hydatius, but they now had to prove criminal offenses against secular laws. They continued to accuse the defendants of Manichaeism, but the primary charge was *maleficium,* or black magic, an offense punishable by death. Many leading Christians opposed capital punishment; among them were two leaders who just happened to be in Trier at the time: Ambrosius and Martin, bishop of Tours, later canonized as Saint Martin. He got the emperor to promise that a death penalty would not be imposed, but after his departure several hard-line bishops badgered the emperor to ignore his plea. Maximus left this issue to his prefect, a man known to be strict but just.[5]

Hydatius and Ithacius became aware that most bishops would abhor their pleading for executions, and they withdrew as accusers, obviously with the approval of the court. The emperor named an advocate of the exchequer (*patronus fisci*) to replace them, and the trial began. In the end, Priscillian was convicted of practicing *maleficium,* and he admitted to teaching doctrines and practicing rituals considered incompatible with the official creed. The prefect rendered the verdict. But before deciding on the punishment, which according to the law had to be death, he consulted the emperor. Maximus upheld the death penalty. As a result, Priscillian and six of his followers, among them a woman, were beheaded in the fall of 386.[6] Instantius had already been deposed by the synod in Bordeaux; now he and others were exiled to the Scilly Isles, and still others were banished within

Gaul. In Bordeaux, a female Priscillianist was stoned to death by a Christian mob.[7]

TEXTUAL TRANSMISSION

Nearly all details we know about this trial are contained in 6 of the 103 pages (in modern print) of *Chronica,*[8] a history of the world since Adam, published around 403 by Sulpicius Severus.[9] He had witnessed many of these events as a young man. Severus came from an affluent family in Aquitaine and was a successful lawyer in Bordeaux. Following the death of his young wife, he turned to a monastic life of asceticism and opened his estate as a residence to fellow ascetics. He was a particular admirer of Martin of Tours and wrote a biography of the saint after his death. There is also a brief reference to this trial by Prosper Tiro. He was likewise born in Aquitaine, probably about 390. The devastations during the civil war in Gaul (406–415) drove him to lead the ascetic life of a monk. He joined a monastery in Marseille and later became secretary to Pope Leo I (440–461) in Rome. He is our only resource for the stoning in Bordeaux, which appears in his brief report on the trial of the Priscillianists in Trier.[10]

Our best resources on Priscillian's teachings are anonymous tracts currently attributed to him or his followers.[11] We also have citations from Priscillian that Orosius, a father of the church, quotes in order to refute them.[12]

WAS PRISCILLIAN'S CONFESSION OBTAINED USING TORTURE?

Sulpicius Severus reports that Priscillian was convicted of black magic, and that he denied neither the "obscene" doctrines nor the dark rituals of which he was accused. It is commonly thought that his confession was extracted through torture,[13] but that seems doubtful. Many scholars refer to a law enacted by Constantius II (337–361) in 357.[14] It reinforced the general principle that people from the upper classes—and Priscillian was certainly one of them—must not be subjected to torture, but it included a new exception. Any members of the emperor's entourage (*comitatus*) could be tortured at any time if they were suspected of black magic. This exception did not apply either, because neither Priscillian nor his disciples were members of the emperor's retine. It is also inconceivable that the prefect, Evodius, would stretch legal boundaries to that extent. Neither Augustine[15] nor Sulpicius Severus really implies that Priscillian was tortured.

Severus states that Priscillian was convicted (*convictus*) of committing *maleficium*, but his confession concerned only his religious doctrines and rituals. Moreover, his confession contains only information that could have been gleaned elsewhere, from his writings or what was already known about the rituals. In other words, there was no need to torture him. Second, Severus's description of how Priscillian responded to the accusations is carefully worded: he answered *nec diffitens* (that he did not deny [them]). This is not how someone who is being tortured responds. The conviction for black magic appears to have succeeded thanks to statements by witnesses, who may very well have been threatened with legally sanctioned torture, and indeed tortured. We know from Sulpicius Severus that three disciples from the lower classes received very light punishments for having betrayed their compatriots to avoid being tortured.[16]

REACTIONS TO THE EXECUTIONS

Maximus probably hoped that he would ingratiate himself with the Italian bishops and the eastern emperor, Theodosius, by taking drastic action against heretics. But he deceived himself. Many Italian bishops maintained that the church should never condone capital punishment. The bishops of Milan and Rome denied the Eucharist to Ithacius and his followers. As for Theodosius, he defeated and overthrew Maximus in 388 and then permitted the Priscillianists to transfer the remains of their dead to Spain, where they were ceremoniously reinterred and honored as martyrs by a large portion of the population. Theodosius refrained from persecuting the Priscillianists in Spain, where they had flourished, especially in Galicia. Maximus had hoped to destroy them, but he had been hindered by Martin of Tours. In 388, Ithacius was deposed by a synod of Spanish bishops and exiled by Emperor Theodosius; Hydatius abdicated.

Following the death of Theodosius, his successor in the West, Emperor Honorius (395–423) persecuted the movement again. Priscillianism continued nevertheless, predominantly in northwestern Spain, far into the sixth century. Patient missionary efforts, especially by Martin of Dumio, a Catholic monk and after 561 metropolitan bishop of Braga (northwestern Spain), finally spelled its end.

SIGNIFICANCE OF THE TRIAL

The imperial court judgment at Trier marked the first time that Christians were officially convicted and executed by Catholic Christians for *maleficium,* a pretext for punishing heresy. This internal development of the church, beginning in the early fourth century, presaged this extreme form of intolerance. Ithacius and his followers took an approach that reflected the laws of the church. During the reign of Emperor Constantine in 328, the Council of Antioch had determined in Canon 5 that any presbyter or deacon who organized gatherings on his own and thus engendered a schism could be relieved of his office, provided he denied he was accountable to his bishop and remained disobedient. If he continued to threaten church stability, he was to be arrested by the secular power as an insurgent.[17] Secular law allowed for capital punishment in serious cases of fomenting insurrection, or, for the upper classes, exile to an island,[18] coupled with loss of assets.[19]

The church distanced itself from Ithacius at first, but over time an undercurrent of approval developed. This case was embedded in a tacit perception among many churchmen that executed heretics got what they deserved. Pope Leo (440–461) persecuted many heresies unrelentingly, and in 447 he particularly deplored current conditions that kept Spanish Priscillianists from being duly punished according to Roman law.[20] During the High and later Middle Ages, capital punishment for heretics became entrenched as a church policy.[21] One famous example is the execution of the early reformer John Huss, who was burned at the stake in 1415 by order of the church at the Council of Constance (southern Germany).

Conclusion

Of the sixteen trials discussed in this book, five were civil procedures, and eleven were criminal trials. However, there were, in ancient times as now, at least ten times as many civil trials as criminal cases. I have focused on trials that stand out because of their lasting effects. Then as now, criminal trials have much greater repercussions in the public sphere than do civil cases, which are often too complex to be easily digested. The development of civil law is largely left to legal experts outside the public arena, whereas criminal law and its procedure attract more public attention.

All six civil trials (two in chapter 4) fostered a progress in substantive civil law. The impact of Fannia's trial (chapter 3) about her dowry was that a husband could no longer reap financial advantage from some alleged fault in his wife if he was aware of it before their marriage. The man who set this precedent was a popular politician and field commander with no legal education, the famous Marius.

After the case of the repurchased residential property (second case in chapter 4), a seller was no longer liable for a fault in the purchased goods if the buyer was aware of the fault before concluding the purchase agreement; in this case the burden of a piece of property was an easement. In contrast, a consequence of the Caelian Hill trial, also discussed in chapter 4, was that a seller is indeed liable for a fault known to him, yet concealed from the buyer. This decision was made by a conservative politician from the Cato clan who may have been a jurist.

In the trial of Curius (chapter 5), the looser of the two possible interpretations prevailed in a case before the *centum viri* (court of hundred men) over a contentious question among jurists about a last will and testament. A hypothetical will of the testator could be considered if events failed to work out as the deceased had anticipated in his testament, as long as his intentions could be determined with some degree of certainty. Still, it took several centuries for this interpretation to gain general acceptance. This lingering uncertainty may be the consequence of Cicero's skill in painting this trial as the triumph of rhetoric over jurisprudence, which he was more than happy to mock. Cicero was so successful in the long term that many jurists today are still under the spell cast by his words.

Otacilia's case (chapter 7) concerned a concealed bequest designed by a dying man for the benefit of his adulterous mistress, namely Otacilia. This case was decided by a very famous jurist, Aquilius Gallus. He extended the objection based on fraud to include present fraud (*dolus praesens*) just by suing, which meant that deceitfully raising a formally established suit could be considered fraud. And in the trial about the Rutilian estate (chapter 14), an emperor prevailed over expert jurists in his desire to protect the estate of a minor. His decision protected the minor from nonpayment of any debts she inherited, if her guardians proved grossly incompetent.

All of the criminal trials in this book are famous, but for vastly different reasons. In deciding which trials from antiquity to include, I decided their impact on the development of the law was paramount. One cannot deduce from the trial of the victorious Horatius brother (chapter 1) that murder is justified if the victim had sympathized with the enemy. But we learn that it was possible to appeal to the people's assembly in critical cases, and their decisions were considered sovereign. This right of sovereignty passed to the emperor when the monarchy was established, and then to the ruling monarchs of Europe.

In the case against Furius Cresimus about *maleficium* (chapter 2), the belief in the effectiveness of specific practices, which carried the death penalty, was shattered to such an extent that severe punishments as foreseen in the old Roman legal codification of the Twelve Tables seemed to no longer apply.

Following years of tyranny that ended with the establishment of a dictatorship, the conclusion of the trial against Sextus Roscius (chapter 6), who was defended by Cicero against a charge of patricide, led to the reestablishment of freedom of speech after years of oppression. This case effectively established a constitutional precedent. In the trial against Ovid (chapter 8), the emperor's power of discretion first became obvious, particularly in determining how a sensitive political offense could be tried and punished.

The trial of Jesus (chapter 9) illuminated the severity and hasty procedures that Roman penal justice imposed on vulnerable provincial residents lacking an advocate among the powerful. Moreover, it led everyday Romans to suspect the followers of Jesus of Nazareth of being capable of committing the most heinous crimes. We presume that Nero exploited this widespread suspicion when seeking a scapegoat for the devastating fires in

Rome in 64 C.E. (chapter 10). These trials, initiated at his instigation, branded Christians as organized criminals who deserved the death penalty. Pliny, the intellectual, examined these cases in more detail (chapter 11), but he was able to make only minor improvements in the Christians' legal situation: only a private citizen could initiate a case, and only by publicly accusing someone of being a Christian. The civil and municipal authorities were not to initiate criminal inquiries in these cases, and they were to pardon those who were truly repentant as demonstrated through sacrifices to the pagan gods. Indeed, they were supposed to urge Christians to repent.

It was not until the reign of Emperor Hadrian that the lot of a Roman slave improved. A slave owner who treated his slaves especially cruelly could be brought before courts and punished with short-term banishment, that is, five years (chapter 12). At the very least, the abused slaves were to be sold on account of the owner, with him or her picking up the costs, and with the stipulation that they were never to come under his or her ownership again. This latter punishment could also be imposed if the owner treated slaves extremely poorly or provided insufficient nourishment. However, during the later third century, these provisions lapsed.

It was Marcus Aurelius who introduced the concept that those who take personal possession of property that they are owed without engaging the courts must forfeit their claims to that property (chapter 13). Over the course of the third century, this legal innovation became less refined and those convicted of illegal self-help, or taking the law into their own hands, were subjected to the more severe punishments for *vis privata* (violence among private persons). *Vis privata* originally applied only to very specific kinds of violence: the formation of a mob (*manu facta*) to forcibly obtain goods, for instance, or assault, but around 300 C.E. it was applied more generally.

Our series ended with observations on how various emperors dealt with internal church questions. Instead of deciding by imperial fiat, Constantine initiated the custom of convening the largest possible synod of bishops to decide the matter. After thorough debate on the subject among experts and without intervention by the civil authority, the aim was for a suitably large majority of bishops to agree. The most severe sanction that the church could impose was expulsion from the Eucharistic community, or excommunication. In the Donatists' case (chapter 15), it was hard for the emperor to resist pleas from the defeated party for his intervention. In the end, he ruled against Donatists who had frivolously and falsely accused a bishop, and condemned their leaders to exile. The usurper Magnus Maximus had heretics executed for *maleficium* in 386 (chapter 16). Synods continued to judge cases of heresy and schism, but execution of the Priscillianists under Roman law had a lingering effect in the church. However, capital punishment emerged centuries later as an approved sentence against heresy.

The judges in Horatius's and Cresimus's trials (chapters 1 and 2) were the people's assemblies. The Curius and Roscius cases (chapters 5 and 6) were decided by an extensive judicial bench. In their cases, the parties and their representatives in court deserve most of the credit for far-reaching decisions, for they were able to influence large numbers of judges more easily than individuals. The judges in Fannia's, Lanarius's, and Otacilia's cases (chapters 3, 4, and 7) were distinguished nobles who served as *judex unus* (sole judge). In Otacilia's case, and perhaps in Lanarius's, these nobles happened to be jurists.

In Ovid's trial (chapter 8), the emperor himself sat in judgment. In Jesus of Nazareth's case (chapter 9), the emperor's representative had no interest in a just decision. Pilate was primarily concerned with getting the trial over with as quickly and with as few repercussions for himself as possible. Omnipotent judges still succumb to this temptation. In contrast, Pliny, Emperor Trajan's proxy in the province Pontus et Bithynia, deciding in the Christians' cases, did exactly the opposite (chapter 11): faced with a routine, mindless practice, he examined the issues on his own initiative and mitigated the treatment of Christians in an essential point. He then succeeded in gaining the approval of his emperor (Trajan) for his judicial innovation.

With respect to the seven trials heard by the emperor himself (chapters 8, 10, and 12–16), we note that he took a personal interest in the proceedings. This is obvious in the case of Augustus versus Ovid, Nero versus the Roman Christians, Marcus Aurelius versus a buyer accused of self-help, Septimius Severus in the case of protecting minors, Constantine with regard to Christian unity, and Magnus Maximus's persecution of heretics, even if he was spurred on by Catholic bishops. It is only in the decisions involving cruel slave owners, made by Hadrian, Antoninus Pius, and Marcus Aurelius, that we can observe that influential advisers, perhaps jurists, may have been significantly involved. In any case, it is because of the efforts of a jurist, Ulpian, that this series of decisions focusing on human rights was compiled and disseminated. Although the law became harsher later, it was Ulpian who attempted to give even the slaves some kind of human rights and to establish the legal ramifications for the more humane treatment of slaves in his century.[1]

NOTES

ABBREVIATIONS

CJ	*Codex Justinianus*
C. Th.	*Codex Theodosianus*
D.	*Digest* of Justinian, part 2 of the *Corpus juris civilis* (Body of Secular Law)
DKP	*Der Kleine Pauly—Lexikon der Antike,* vols. 1–5 (Stuttgart, 1964–75)
DNP	*Der Neue Pauly—Enzyklopädie der Antike,* vols. 1–16 (Stuttgart, 1996–2003)
	English translation: Brill's *New Pauly— Encyclopaedia of the Ancient World* (Stuttgart, 2002–10)
HLL	Reinhart Herzog and Peter Lebrecht Schmidt, eds., *Handbuch der lateinischen Literatur der Antike*

Vol. 1, *Die archaische Literatur von den Anfängen bis Sulla's Tod,* ed. Werner Suerbaum (Munich, 2002)

Vol. 4, *Die Literatur des Umbruchs von der römischen zur christlichen Literatur,* ed. Klaus Sallmann (Munich, 1997)

Kaser, *Privatrecht* — Max Kaser, *Das römische Privatrecht,* vol. 1, *Das altrömische, das vorklassische und das klassische Recht,* 2nd ed. (Munich, 1971)

Kaser/Hackl, *Zivilprozeßrecht* — Max Kaser, *Das römische Zivilprozeßrecht,* 2nd ed., rev. Karl Hackl (Munich, 1997)

Liebs, *Römisches Recht* — Detlef Liebs, *Römisches Recht—Ein Studienbuch,* 6th ed. (Göttingen, 2004)

Manthe/ Ungern-Sternberg, *Große Prozesse* — Ulrich Manthe and Jürgen von Ungern-Sternberg, eds., *Große Prozesse in der römischen Antike* (Munich, 1997)

MGH AA — *Monumenta Germaniae historica, Auctores antiquissimi* (Berlin, 1877–1919)

Mommsen, *Strafrecht* — Theodor Mommsen, *Römisches Strafrecht* (Leipzig, 1899)

Nogrady, *Strafrecht* — Alexander Nogrady, *Römisches Strafrecht nach Ulpian Buch 7 bis 9 De officio proconsulis* (Berlin, 2006)

PIR — *Prosopographia imperii Romani saec. I. II. III,* 2nd ed., 8 vols. (Berlin, 1933–2012)

RE — *Realencyclopädie der classischen Altertumswissenschaft, Neue Bearbeitung,* 84 vols. (Stuttgart, 1893–1980)

RH — *Revue historique de droit français et étranger, 4ème série*

Schanz, *Literatur*	Martin Schanz, *Geschichte der römischen Literatur* Vol. 2, *Die römische Literatur in der Zeit der Monarchie bis auf Hadrian*, 4th ed., rev. Carl Hosius (Munich, 1935) Vol. 4.1, *Die Literatur des vierten Jahrhunderts*, 2nd ed. (Munich, 1914) Vol. 4.2, *Die Literatur des fünften und sechsten Jahrhunderts* (Munich, 1920)
Schilling, *Poena*	Andreas Schilling, *Poena extraordinaria: Zur Strafzumessung in der frühen Kaiserzeit* (Berlin, 2010)
SDHI	*Studia et documenta historiae et iuris*
SZ	*Zeitschrift der Savigny-Stiftung für Rechtsgeschichte—Romanistische Abteilung*
ZPE	*Zeitschrift für Papyrologie und Epigraphik*

I. KILLING A SISTER FOR MOURNING A FALLEN ENEMY

1. Free translation of Livy, *Ab urbe condita* 1.22–26; the deed and the trial, chap. 26: . . . exercitus inde domos abducti. (2) Princeps Horatius ibat trigemina spolia prae se gerens; cui soror virgo, quae desponsa uni ex Curiatiis fuerat, obvia ante portam Capenam fuit, cognitoque super umeros fratris paludamento sponsi, quod ipsa confecerat, solvit crines et flebiliter nomine sponsum mortuum appellat. (3) Movet feroci iuveni animum comploratio sororis in victoria sua tantoque gaudio publico. Stricto itaque gladio simul verbis increpans transfigit puellam. (4) "Abi hinc cum immaturo amore ad sponsum" inquit, "oblita fratrum mortuorum vivique, oblita patriae. Sic eat, quaecumque Romana lugebit hostem." (5) Atrox visum id facinus patribus plebique, sed recens meritum facto obstabat. Tamen raptus in ius ad regem. Rex, ne ipse tam tristis ingratique ad vulgus iudicii ac secundum iudicium supplicii

auctor esset, concilio populi advocato "Duumviros" inquit, "qui Horatio perduellionem iudicent, secundum legem facio." (6) Lex horrendi
carminis erat: "Duumviri perduellionem iudicent; si a duumviris pro-
vocarit, provocatione certato; si vincent, caput obnubito; infelici arbori
reste suspendito; verberato vel intra pomerium vel extra pomerium."
(7) Hac lege duumviri creati. Qui se absolvere non rebantur ea lege ne
innoxium quidem posse, cum condemnassent, tum alter ex iis "Publi
Horati, tibi perduellionem iudico" inquit; "i lictor, colliga manus."
(8) Accesserat lictor iniciebatque laqueum. Tum Horatius auctore
Tullo, clemente legis interprete, "Provoco" inquit. Itaque provocatione
certatum ad populum est. (9) Moti homines sunt in eo iudicio maxime
Publio Horatio patre proclamante se filiam iure caesam iudicare; ni ita
esset, patrio iure in filium animadversurum fuisse. Orabat deinde, ne
se, quem paulo ante cum egregia stirpe conspexissent, orbum liberis
facerent. (10) Inter haec senex iuvenem amplexus, spolia Curiatiorum
fixa eo loco, qui nunc pila Horatia appellaltur, ostentans "Huncine"
aiebat, "quam modo decoratum ovantemque victoria incedentem vidis-
tis, Quirites, eum sub furca vinctum inter verbera et cruciatus videre
potestis? Quod vix Albanorum oculi tam deforme spectaculum ferre
possent. (11) I, lictor, colliga manus, quae paulo ante armatae imperium
populo Romano pepererunt. I, caput obnube liberatoris urbis huius;
arbore infelici suspende; verbera vel intra pomerium, modo inter illa
pila et spolia hostium, vel extra pomerium, modo inter sepulcra Curiatiorum. Quo enim ducere hunc iuvenem potestis, ubi non sua decora
eum a tanta foeditate supplicii vindicent?" (12) Non tulit populus nec
patris lacrimas nec ipsius parem in omni periculo animum, absolve-
runtque admiratione magis virtutis quam iure causae. Itaque, ut caedes
manifesta aliquo tamen piacolo lueretur, imperatum patri, ut filium
expiaret pecunia publica. (13) Is quibusdam piacularibus sacrificiis fac-
tis, quae deinde genti Horatiae tradita sunt, transmisso per viam tigillo
capite adoperto velut sub iugum misit iuvenem. Id hodie quoque publice semper refectum manet; sororium tigillum vocant. (14) Horatiae
sepulcrum, quo loco corruerat iacta, constructum est saxo quadrato.

   2. On this, see, most notably, Andreas Alföldi, *Das frühe Rom und die
Latiner* (Darmstadt, 1977), 95–98; also Anna Pasqualini, "I miti albani e

l'origine delle feriae Latinae," in *Alba Longa: Mito storia archeologia,* ed. A. Pasqualini, *Atti dell'Incontro di studio Roma—Albano Laziale 27–29 gennaio 1994* (Rome, 1996), 217–53, esp. 230f.

3. See the extensive presentation by Friedrich Münzer, "Horatius 2," *RE* VIII 2 (1913), 2322–27, esp. 2324–26.

4. Ennius, *Annales* 2, frag. 8, according to Johannes Vahlen, ed., *Enniani poesis reliquiae* (Leipzig, 1928), verse 129, or Otto Skutsch, ed., *The Annals of Q. Ennius* (Oxford, 1985), verse 123; Cicero, *De inventione* 2.78f.; Dionysius of Halicarnassus, *Romana archaelogia* 3.21f.; Valerius Maximus, *Facta et dicta memorabilia* 8.1.1; Florus, *Epitomae de Tito Livio* 1.1.3, 5f.; Pseudo-Aurelius Victor, *De viris illustribus urbis Romae* 4.8f.; Augustine of Hippo, *De civitate Dei* 3.14; Zonaras, *Epitomae historiarum* 7.6.

5. Cf. Christoph Brecht, "Perduellio," *RE* XIX 1 (1937), 615–39, esp. 622–6.

6. Livy 2.8.2f., and passim, a *Lex Valeria.* On the dubiousness of the transmission, see Giovanni Rotondi, *Leges publicae populi Romani* (Milan, 1912), 190; and Dieter Flach, *Die Gesetze der frühen römischen Republik* (Darmstadt, 1994), 59–62.

7. Livy 3.55.4f., and other authors, a *Lex Valeria Horatia;* see Rotondi, *Leges publicae,* 204; and Flach, *Die Gesetze,* 216–18; see also p. 203 about the so-called *lex Duilia de provocatione* according to Livy 3.55.14.

8. Livy 10.9.3–6, also a *Lex Valeria.* On the question of the historicity of this law of *provocatio* in comparison to the older ones, see, e.g., Marianne Elster, *Studien zur Gesetzgebung der frühen römischen Republik—Gesetzeshäufungen und -wiederholungen* (Frankfurt am Main, 1976), 120–75, esp. 165–70.

9. The sources are in Rotondi, *Leges publicae,* 301 (*rogatio Sempronia de provocatione* of Tiberius Sempronius Gracchus) and 313f. (*Lex Sempronia de capite civis,* enacted by his younger brother, Gaius Sempronius Gracchus).

10. On the course of the trial, see Friedrich Vonder Mühll, "Rabirius 5," *RE* IA 1 (1914), 24f.; Jürgen von Ungern-Sternberg, *Untersuchungen zum spätrepublikanischen Notstandsrecht* (Munich, 1970), 81–85; and Manfred Fuhrmann, *Marcus Tullius Cicero, Sämtliche Reden* (Zurich, 1970, 1985²), 2: 197–201, 202–19 for Fuhrmann's translation of the extant part of this speech.

11. Cicero, *De oratore* 2.199; and Livy 3.45.8; see the thorough study by Jochen Bleicken, "Ursprung und Bedeutung der Provocation," *SZ* 76 (1959): 324–77, esp. 333–37.

12. Acts 25:11f.

2. TEMPORARY END TO TRIALS INVOLVING BLACK MAGIC

1. Free paraphrase of Pliny the Elder, *Naturalis historia* 18.41–43: . . . C. Furius Cresimus e servitute liberatus, cum in parvo admodum agello largiores multo fructus perciperet, quam ex amplissimis vicinitas, in invidia erat magna, ceu fruges alienas perliceret veneficiis. (42) Quam ob rem ab Spurio Albino curuli aedile die dicta metuens damnationem, cum in suffragium tribus oporteret ire, instrumentum rusticum omne in forum attulit et adduxit familiam suam validam atque, ut ait Piso, bene curatam ac vestitam, ferramenta egregie facta, graves ligones, vomeres ponderosos, boves saturos. (43) Postea dixit: "Veneficia mea, Quirites, haec sunt; nec possum vobis ostendere aut in forum adducere lucubrationes meas vigiliasque et sudores." Omnium sententiis absolutus itaque est. Fritz Graf, *Magic in the Ancient World* (Cambridge, Mass., 1997), 62–65, places the episode within a wider context.

2. Undecided: Kurt Latte, "Der Historiker L. Calpurnius Frugi" (first published 1960), in *Kleine Schriften* (Munich, 1968), 837–47, here 840; Wolfgang Kunkel and Roland Wittmann, *Staatsordnung und Staatspraxis der römischen Republik,* vol. 2 (Munich, 1995), 502 and n. 112; see also 247 and n. 515. They all, however, regard only the people's assembly, the *comitia tributa,* as organized according to residential districts, without considering that, at the time of the trial, the larger assembly, the *comitia centuriata,* which was properly organized according to wealth in "centuries," was primarily organized according to *tribus* (districts), and only within the districts according to centuries; see, e.g., Johannes Michael Rainer, *Römisches Staatsrecht* (Darmstadt, 2006), 115f.

3. On him, see Friedrich Münzer, "Furius 52," *RE* VII 1 (1910), 351.

4. Thus esp. T. Robert S. Broughton, *The Magistrates of the Roman Republic* (New York, 1951), 1: 353, which covers the year 191 B.C.E. Münzer,

"Furius 52," had suggested 155 B.C.E., although in his article "Postumius 49," *RE* XXII 1 (1953), 931, lines 16–42, he preferred 185 B.C.E. But this Spurius Albinus, consul only in 174 B.C.E., had the additional cognomen Paululus, while his otherwise eponymously named cousin, consul in 186 B.C.E., had no additional cognomen: on the latter, see Münzer, "Postumius 44," *RE* XXII 1 (1953), 921–23.

5. Susan Treggari, *Roman Freedmen during the Late Republic* (Oxford, 1969), 87–106.

6. Treggari, *Roman Freedmen,* 108–10.

7. Cicero, *De re publica* 4.12; and Pliny, *Naturalis historia* 18.17f.; i.e., *XII Tables* 8.1.

8. Seneca, *Naturales quaestiones* 4.7.2; and Pliny, *Naturalis historia* 18.17f.; i.e., *XII Tables* 8.8a.

9. Servius, *Commentary on Virgil's Bucolics* (or *Eclogues*) 8.99; and Augustine, *De civitate Dei* 8.19, which attests the death penalty (*supplicium*); i.e., *XII Tables* 8.8b.

10. Mommsen, *Strafrecht,* 168, according to a famous provision in the Twelve Tables; see Cicero, *Pro Sestio* 65; id., *De re publica* 2.61; id., *De legibus* 3.11 and 44; i.e., *XII Tables* 9.2.

11. Rainer, *Römisches Staatsrecht,* 115f.

12. Kunkel and Wittmann, *Staatsordnung und Staatspraxis,* 2: 246–49, combine the roles of accuser and presider in the people's assembly; see esp. 247f.; Latte, *Kleine Schriften,* 840, does not even consider the role of accuser.

13. See Virgil, *Eclogues* 8.95–99; and Tibullus, *Elegies* 1.8.19.

14. Seneca, *Naturales quaestiones* 4.7.2f.; and Apuleius, *Apologia* 47.3.

15. As can be determined from Modestinus, *Pandectae* 12 (*D.* 48.8.13), in connection with Pseudo-Paul, *Sententiae* 5.23.15f.

16. This is recorded by Tacitus, *Annales* 12.59 (see also 14.46.1). On this, see Frederick H. Cramer, *Astrology in Roman Law and Politics* (Philadelphia, 1954), 262f.; Ursula Vogel-Weidemann, *Die Statthalter von Africa und Asia in den Jahren 14–68 n.Chr.* (Bonn, 1982), 155–60; and Detlef Liebs, "Strafprozesse wegen Zauberei," in Manthe/Ungern-Sternberg, *Große Prozesse,* 150f.

17. Tacitus, *Annales* 12.64.2–65.1; see also Suetonius, *De vita Caesarum,*

Nero 7.1. Concerning Lepida, see Edmund Groag, "Domitius 102," *RE* V
1 (1903), 1511–13; and Werner Eck, "Die iulisch-claudische Familie: Frauen
neben Caligula, Claudius und Nero," in *Die Kaiserinnen Roms,* ed. Hil-
degard Temporini–Gräfin Vitzthum (Munich, 2002), 103–86, here 149.

18. Apuleius's defense speech, *De magia* = *Apologia,* remains extant.
On the legal substance, see Detlef Liebs, "Römisches Recht in Africa im
2. Jh. n. Chr. nach der Apologie des Apuleius," in *Literatur und Recht,* ed.
Ulrich Mölk (Göttingen, 1996), 25–36; Graf, *Magic in the Ancient World,* 65–
88; Francesco Amarelli (and Francesco Lucrezi), *I processi contro (Archia
e) Apuleio* (Naples, 1997), 99–141; and Francesca Lamberti, "De magia
als rechtsgeschichtliches Dokument," in *Apuleius, De magia* (Darmstadt,
2002), 331–50. On Apuleius, see Klaus Sallmann, in *HLL* 4: 292–318 = §457;
Sallmann is wrong, however, in asserting that the marriage granted
Apuleius the trusteeship of the family fortune (294); and that the tangible proofs presented by the accuser were overwhelming (295).

19. About 185–190 C.E., Septimius Severus, who later became emperor, was accused before the praetorian prefects of having queried Sicilian seers (*vates*) or Chaldeans about the future emperor. Severus was
acquitted, and the accusers were crucified; *Historia Augusta,* Severus
4.3. Admittedly, this could be wishful thinking on the part of the late
fourth-century author. See also n. 20 below.

20. Cassius Dio, *Historia Romana* 76 (77).8–76.9.2; and *Historia Augusta,*
Severus 15.5f. On the proconsul Popilius Pedo Apronianus, see Klaus-
Peter Johne, *PIR* 6 (1998), 357f., no. 842.

21. Cassius Dio, *Historia Romana* 77 (78).17.2f. On this, see Arthur
Stein, "Sempronius 78," *RE* IIA 2 (1923), 1435f.; and Liebs, "Strafprozesse
wegen Zauberei," 152.

22. Ammianus, *Res gestae* 19.12; 26.3; 28.1; 29.2. On this, see Liebs,
"Strafprozesse wegen Zauberei," 152–57.

3. A DOWRY HUNTER LOSES OUT

1. Friedrich Münzer, "Titinius 17," *RE* VIA 2 (1937), 1549.

2. Münzer, "Fannius 11," *RE* VI 2 (1909), 1992; and id., "Titinius 17,"
1549.

3. Valerius Maximus, *Facta et dicta memorabilia* 8.2: De privatis iudiciis insignibus, 3: ... cum Gaius Titinius Minturnensis Fanniam uxorem, quam impudicam de industria duxerat, eo crimine repudiatam dote spoliare conaretur, sumptus inter eos iudex in conspectu habita quaestione seductum Titinium monuit ut incepto desisteret ac mulieri dotem redderet. Quod cum saepius frustra fecisset, coactus ab eo sententiam pronuntiare mulierem impudicitiae sestertio nummo uno, Titinium summa totius dotis damnavit, praefatus idcirco se hunc iudicandi modum secutum, cum liqueret sibi Titinium patrimonio Fanniae insidias struentem impudicae coniugium expetisse. (... Gaius Titinius of Minturno had divorced his wife Fannia, of whose unchastity he was aware when he married her, on that ground and was trying to strip her of her dowry. Marius was taken as arbiter between them and the hearing was held in public. Drawing Titinius aside, Marius warned him to give up his attempt and return the dowry to the woman. After he had done this several times to no effect and Titinius forced him to pronounce a decision, he ruled that the woman was guilty of unchastity and should pay one sesterce and that Titinius should pay the full amount of the dowry, prefacing that he had followed this mode of judgment because it was clear to him that Titinius had sought the hand of a loose woman with design on Fannia's property. Trans. D.R. Shackleton Bailey, *Valerius Maximus: Memorable Doings and Sayings,* Loeb Classical Library [Cambridge, Mass., 2000], 2: 209.) On Maximus, see, e.g., Peter Lebrecht Schmidt, "Valerius B 8," *DKP* 5 (1975), 1117f.; Ursula Blank-Sangmeister, *Valerius Maximus Facta et dicta memorabilia—Denkwürdige Taten und Worte* (Stuttgart, 1991), 338–45; Michael von Albrecht, *A History of Roman Literature* (Leiden and New York, 1997), 2: 1074–83; and Shackleton Bailey, *Valerius Maximus,* 1: 1–4.

4. Plutarch, *Vitae,* Marius 38.3f.: ... Fannia's husband was ... Titinius; she had divorced him and demanded her rather considerable dowry back. He, however, accused her of adultery. The judge in this matter was Marius during his sixth consulate (100 B.C.E.). Because, during the course of the trial, it was revealed that Fannia was truly ungovernable, and, on the other hand, that her husband had known that from the outset, had married her in spite of it, and had lived together with her for a

long time, Marius exposed both of them, to Titinius's displeasure. He condemned the woman, because of her dishonorable lifestyle, to a fine of four copper pieces, and ordered the man to return the dowry.

5. On this, see Rudolph Weynand, "Marius 14," *RE Suppl.* VI (1930), 1413–15.

6. On the legal guardianship necessary for women, known among jurists as "sexual guardianship," see, e.g., Erich Sachers, "Tutela 3," *RE* VIIA 2 (1948), 1588–99; and Olga E. Tellegen-Couperus, "Tutela mulierum, une institution rationelle," *RH* 84 (2006): 423–35.

7. Karl Czyhlarz, *Das römische Dotalrecht* (Gießen, 1870), 344f.; Alfred Söllner, *Zur Vorgeschichte und Funktion der actio rei uxoriae* (Cologne, 1969), 71–74; and Herwig Stiegler, "Divortium, culpa und retentio propter liberos," in *Mélanges Fritz Sturm* (Liège, 1999), 1: 431–52.

8. And not to the state; see Söllner, *Zur Vorgeschichte und Funktion,* 79f. Cf. Hans Julius Wolff, "Das iudicium de moribus und sein Verhältnis zur actio rei uxoriae," *SZ* 54 (1934): 315–21, here 318f., who dismisses a countersuit and accepts only an improper condemnation of Fannia: one sesterce was deducted from the value of her dowry, which Titinius was condemned to pay.

9. Mommsen, *Strafrecht,* 691f.

10. Cervidius Scaevola, *Quaestiones* 9 (D. 24.3.47).

4. A NAIVE BUYER

1. Cicero, *De officiis* 3.65–67: Ac de iure quidem praediorum sanctum apud nos est iure civili, ut in iis vendendis vitia dicerentur, quae nota essent venditori. Nam cum ex duodecim tabulis satis esset ea praestari, quae essent lingua nuncupata, quae qui infitiatus esset, dupli poena subiret, a iuris consultis etiam reticentiae poena est constituta. Quidquid enim esset in praedio vitii, id statuerunt, si venditor sciret, nisi nominatim dictum esset, praestari oportere. (66) Ut, cum in arce augurium augures acturi essent iussissentque Titum Claudium Centumalum, qui aedes in Caelio monte habebat, demoliri ea, quorum altitudo officeret auspiciis, Claudius proscripsit insulam, emit Publius Calpurnius Lanarius. Huic ab auguribus illud idem denuntiatum est.

Itaque Calpurnius cum demolitus esset cognossetque Claudium aedes postea proscripsisse, quam esset ab auguribus demoliri iussus, arbitrum illum adegit: "quidquid sibi dare facere oporteret ex fide bona". Marcus Cato sententiam dixit, huius nostri Catonis pater.... Is igitur iudex ita pronuntiavit, cum in vendundo rem eam scisset et non pronuntiasset, emptori damnum praestari oportere. (67) Ergo ad fidem bonam statuit pertinere notum esse emptori vitium, quod nosset venditor. Quod si recte iudicavit, non recte frumentarius ille, non recte aedium pestilentium venditor tacuit. Sed huiusmodi reticentiae iure civili comprehendi non possunt; quae autem possunt diligenter tenentur. Marcus Marius Gratidianus, propinquus noster, Gaio Sergio Oratae vendiderat aedes eas, quas ab eodem ipse paucis ante annis emerat. Eae serviebant, sed hoc in mancipio Marius non dixerat; adducta res in iudicium est. Oratam Crassus, Gratidianum defendebat Antonius. Ius Crassus urgebat, "quod vitii venditor non dixisset sciens, id oportere praestari", aequitatem Antonius, "quoniam id vitium ignotum Sergio non fuisset, qui illas aedes vendidisset, nihil fuisse necesse dici", "nec eum esse deceptum, qui id, quod emerat, quo iure esset, teneret". Quorum haec? Ut illud intellegas, non placuisse maioribus nostris astutos. ([65] In the laws pertaining to the sale of real property it is stipulated in our civil code that when a transfer of any real estate is made, all its defects shall be declared as far as they are known to the vendor. According to the laws of the Twelve Tables it used to be sufficient that such faults as had been expressly declared should be made good and that for any flaws which the vendor expressly denied, when questioned, he should be assessed double damages. A like penalty for failure to make such declaration also has now been secured by our jurisconsults: they have decided that any defect in a piece of real estate, if known to the vendor but not expressly stated, must be made good by him. [66] For example, the augurs were proposing to take observations from the citadel and they ordered Titus Claudius Centumalus, who owned a house upon the Caelian Hill, to pull down such parts of the building as obstructed the augurs' view by reason of their height. Claudius at once advertised his block for sale, and Publius Calpurnius Lanarius bought it. The same notice was served also upon him. And so, when Calpurnius had pulled down those parts of the building and discovered that Claudius had advertised it for sale only after the augurs had ordered them to be pulled down, he summoned the former owner before a court of equity to decide "what indemnity the owner was under obligation 'in good faith' to pay and deliver to him". The verdict was pronounced by Marcus Cato, the father of our Cato.... He, as I was saying, was presiding judge and pronounced the verdict that since the augurs' mandate was known to the vendor at the time of making the transfer and since he had not made it known, he was bound to make good the purchaser's loss. [67] With this verdict he established the principle that it was essential to good faith that any defect known to the vendor must be made known to the purchaser. If his decision was right, our grain-dealer [see §§50, 53, and 57] and the seller of the unsanitary house [see §§54–57] did not do right to suppress the facts in those cases. But the civil code cannot be made to include all cases where facts are thus suppressed; but those cases which it does include are summarily dealt with. Marcus Marius Gratidianus, a kinsman of ours, sold back to Gaius Sergius Orata the house which he himself had bought a few years before from that same Orata. It was subject to an encumbrance, but Marius had said nothing about this fact in stating the terms of sale. The case was carried to the courts. Crassus was counsel for Orata; Antonius was retained by Gratidianus. Crassus pleaded the letter of the law that "the vendor was bound to make good the defect, for he had not declared it, although he was aware of it"; Antonius laid stress upon the equity of the case, leading that, "inasmuch as the defect in question had not been unknown to Sergius [for it was the same house that he had sold to Marius], no declaration of it was needed", and "in purchasing it back he had not been imposed upon, for he knew to what legal liability his purchase was subject". What is the purpose of these illustrations? To let you see that our forefathers did not countenance sharp practice. Trans. Walter Miller, *Marcus Tullius Cicero, De officiis,* Loeb Classical Library [Cambridge, Mass., 1913].) In §§50–57, Cicero quoted Greek philosophers; beginning with §58, he deals with Roman legal cases.

2. Cicero, *De oratore* 1.178. The outcome of the second trial is the line of reasoning that can be found in his later report of the trial, *De*

officiis 3.67. In contrast, Natalie Häpke, "Licinius 55," *RE* XIII 1 (1926), 264, lines 65–68, argues that Crassus had probably helped his client to victory (wohl seinem Klienten zum Sieg verholfen), without regard for the fact that Crassus offers only a theoretical explanation and conceals the deciding point, for which reason the complaint was spurious, according to Cicero's deontology.

3. Valerius Maximus, *Facta et dicta memorabilia* 8.2: De privatis iudiciis insignibus, 1: Claudius Centumalus, ab auguribus iussus altitudinem domus suae, quam in Caelio monte habebat, summittere, quia iis ex arce augurium capientibus officiebat, vendidit eam Calpurnio Lanario nec indicavit quod imperatum a collegio augurum erat. A quibus Calpurnius demoliri domum coactus Marcum Catonem, incliti Catonis patrem, arbitrum cum Claudio adduxit in formulam "... quidquid sibi dare facere oporteret ex fide bona ...". Cato, ut est indoctus de industria Claudium praedictum sacerdotum suppressisse, continuo illum Calpurnio damnavit, summa quidem cum aequitate, quia bonae fidei venditorem nec commodorum spem augere nec incommodorum cognitionem obscurare oportet. (Of remarkable private trials. Claudius Centumalus had been ordered by the Augurs to lower the height of his house on the Caelian hill because it was in their way as they took auguries from the citadel. He sold it to Calpurnius Lanarius without informing him of what the College of Augurs had commanded. Obliged by them to pull the house down, Calpurnius along with Claudius took the case to Marcus Porcius Cato, father of the famous Cato, as arbiter under the legal formula " ... whatever he was obligated to give himself or do in good faith ... ". When Cato was told that Claudius had deliberately suppressed the directive of the priests, he immediately found against him in favor of Calpurnius, an eminently fair decision; for a seller in good faith should neither exaggerate prospective advantages nor conceal knowledge of disadvantages. Trans. Shackleton Bailey, *Valerius Maximus*, 2: 205, 207 [see chap. 3, n. 3].)

4. Franz Miltner, "Porcius 12," *RE* XXII 1 (1953), 166, esp. lines 36–42; genealogical tree: col. 103f.; on Cato Uticensis, see id., "Porcius 16," ibid., 168–211; on Cato the censor, see Rudolf Helm, "Porcius 9," ibid., 108–65.

5. On our Cato, see Detlef Liebs, "M. Porcius Cato Licinianus," *HLL* I: 563 = §194.3.

6. Namely Julius Salinato: Plutarch, *Vitae,* Sertorius 7.2; and Sallust, *Historiae* I, frag. 95, in *C. Sallusti Crispi historiarum reliquiae,* ed. Bertold Maurenbrecher (Leipzig, 1893).

7. This has been concluded from our case in particular; see Christian Hülsen, "Caelius mons," *RE* III 1 (1897), 1273–75, esp. 1274, lines 18–25; and Rudolf Groß, "Caelius mons," *DKP* I (1964), 995. See also Suetonius, *De vita Caesarum,* Tiberius 48.1.

8. Likewise *nuper* (recently) in §180, in which 93 B.C.E. is meant. Contra Häpke, "Licinius 55," 264, line 5, who thought, referring to her col. 259 (and not 253), lines 64–68, and Cicero's second speech against Verres from 70 B.C.E. (*In Verrem* II, 2.122), where Cicero uses *nuper* in relation to an event that occurred approximately twenty-five years previously, that one can draw no exact time frame from Cicero's use of *nuper.* Therefore, Häpke considered this trial to be among those of indeterminate chronology involving Crassus. However, in Cicero's speech against Verres, the topic is Roman legislation for a Greek city in Sicily, in which a longer period of time is quite conceivable, in addition to a partisan representation.

9. Valerius Maximus, *Facta et dicta memorabilia* 9.1.1; cf. Pliny, *Naturalis historia* 9.168f. About all this, see Friedrich Münzer, "Sergius 33," *RE* IIA 2 (1923), 1713f., who, however, incorrectly merges two trials of Orata with two distinct opponents into one.

10. Thus Ernst Fabricius, "Hypocaustum," *RE* IX 1 (1914), 335, lines 56–60, adopted without critical consideration by Münzer, "Sergius 33," 1713, lines 27–35.

11. Macrobius, *Saturnalia* 3.15.3.

12. On this Marius, see Friedrich Münzer, "Marius 42," *RE* XIV 2 (1930), 1825–27.

13. Julian, *Digesta* 15, found in Ulpian, *Ad edictum praetoris* 32 (*D.* 19.1.13 pr.).

14. Pliny, *Naturalis historia* 9.168.

15. Alfenus, *Digesta a Paulo epitomata* 4 (*D.* 21.2.45).

16. Ulpian, *Ad edictum aedilium curulium* 2 (*D.* 21.1.38.7 end).

17. Modestinus, *Responsa* 5 (D. 19.1.39).

18. Ulpian, *Ad Sabinum* 8 (D. 19.1.1.1); the first two lines of this text probably belong to Sabinus: Liebs, *Römisches Recht,* 270.

5. THE PARTY'S INTENTION VS. THE PEDANTRY OF JURISTS?

1. Cf., e.g., John A. Crook, *Legal Advocacy in the Roman World* (London, 1995), 45f. and 187–96.

2. Cicero, *De inventione* (written about 90 B.C.E.) 2.122: Paterfamilias cum liberorum haberet nihil, uxorem autem haberet, in testamento ita scripsit: "Si mihi filius genitur unus pluresve, is mihi heres esto." Deinde quae assolent. Postea: "Si filius ante moritur, quam in tutelam suam venerit, tum mihi—dicet—heres esto." Filius natus non est. Ambigent agnati cum eo, qui est heres, si filius ante quam in suam tutelam veniat, mortuus sit. (A head of a family, having a wife but no children, drew his will as follows: "If one or more sons are born to me, he or they are to inherit my estate." Then follow the usual phrases. Then comes, "If my son dies before coming of age, then So-and-So is to be my heir." No son was born. The agnates dispute with the man who was to be the subsequent heir in case the son died before coming of age. Trans. H.M. Hubbell, *Cicero, De inventione... Topica,* Loeb Classical Library [Cambridge, Mass., 1949], 291.) In 69/68 B.C.E., Cicero represented Aulus Caecina; *Pro Caecina* 53, 67, and 69: Ornate et copiose Lucius Crassus, homo longe eloquentissimus, paulo ante quam nos in forum venimus, iudicio centumvirali hanc sententiam defendit et facile, cum contra eum prudentissimus homo, Quintus Mucius, diceret, probavit omnibus, Manium Curium, qui heres institutus esset ita: "mortuo postumo filio", cum filius non modo non mortuus sed ne natus quidem esset, heredem esse oportere.... (67)... Scaevolam dixisti causam apud centumviros non tenuisse;... tametsi ille in aliqua causa faciebat,... tamen probasse nemini quod defendebat, quia verbis oppugnare aequitatem videbatur.... (69)... Crassus non ita causam apud centumviros egit ut contra iuris consultos diceret, sed ut hoc doceret, illud quod Scaevola defendebat, non esse iuris, et in eam rem

non solum rationes adferret, sed etiam Quinto Mucio, socero suo, mul-tisque peritissimis hominibus auctoribus uteretur. (This opinion was supported by the great orator, Lucius Crassus, in an elegant and ample speech before the centumviral court shortly before I was called to the bar; and although the learned Quintus Mucius was against him he proved to everyone, and with ease, that Manius Curius, who was to succeed to an estate "in the event of the death of a posthumous son", was entitled to succeed although the son was not dead—never, in fact, having been born! ... [67] ... you remarked that Scaevola lost his case in the centumviral court; ... though he had some reason for doing so ... he failed to commend his arguments to anybody because it appeared that he was using the letter to assail the spirit of the law.... [69] ... Crassus himself did not take the line he did in pleading before the cen-tumviral court, in order to disparage the authorities, but to convince the court that the point which Scaevola [the pontifex] was maintaining was not law; and in addition to the arguments he adduced to support his contention he went so far as to quote the authority of many learned men, including that of his father-in-law, Quintus Mucius [the augur]. Trans. H. Grose Hodge, *Cicero, The Speeches ... Pro Caecina,* Loeb Clas-sical Library [Cambridge, Mass., 1927], 149, 165, 167.) In 55 B.C.E., Cicero returns to the case in his dialogue *De oratore* (On the Orator) 1.180, 238, and 242–45; 2.24, 140f., and 220–22, and, more extensively, in his treat-ment of the history of Roman oratory, written in 46 B.C.E., *Brutus* 143–45, 256, and esp. 194–98, quoted here: Qua re quis ex populo, cum Quintum Scaevolam pro Marco Coponio dicentem audiret in ea causa, de qua ante dixi, quicquam politius aut elegantius aut omnino melius aut exspectaret aut posse fieri putaret? (195) Cum is hoc probare vellet, Manium Curium, cum ita heres institutus esset: "Si pupillus ante mor-tuus esset quam in suam tutelam venisset ... ", pupillo non nato here-dem esse non posse; quid ille non dixit de testamentorum iure, de antiquis formulis? Quem ad modum scribi oportuisset, si etiam filio non nato heres institueretur? (196) Quam captiosum esse populo, quod scriptum esset, neglegi et opinione quaeri voluntates et interpretatione disertorum scripta simplicium hominum pervertere? (197) Quam illi multa de auctoritate patris sui, qui semper ius illud esse defenderat?

Quam omnino multa de conservando iure civili? Quae quidem omnia cum perite et scienter, item breviter et presse et satis ornate et pereleganter diceret, quis esset in populo, qui aut exspectaret aut fieri posse quicquam melius putaret? At vero, ut contra Crassus ab adulescente delicato, qui in litore ambulans scalmum repperisset ob eamque rem aedificare navem concupivisset, exorsus est, similiter Scaevolam ex uno calmo captionis centumvirale iudicium hereditatis effecisse, hoc ille initio consecutis multis eiusdem generis sententiis delectavit animosque omnium, qui aderant, in hilaritatem a severitate traduxit.... Deinde hoc voluisse eum, qui testamentum fecisset, hoc sensisse: quoquo modo filius non esset, qui in suam tutelam veniret, sive non natus sive ante mortuus, Curius heres ut esset; ita scribere plerosque et id valere et valuisse semper. Haec et multa eius modi dicens fidem faciebat.... (198) Deinde aequum bonum, tesamentorum sententias voluntatesque tutatus est: quanta esset in verbis captio cum in ceteris rebus tum in testamentis, si neglegerentur voluntates; quantam sibi potentiam Scaevola assumeret, si nemo auderet testamentum facere postea nisi de illius sententia. (Thus, for example, what common man listening to Quintus Scaevola in behalf of Marcus Coponius, the case to which I referred before, would have expected, or indeed would have thought it possible, to hear anything more finished or more nicely expressed or in any respect better? It was Scaevola's object to prove that Manius Curius [who had been named as heir in the event that an expected posthumous son should die before said son had reached his majority] could not become heir, because in fact no posthumous son was born. How full and precise he was on testamentary law, on ancient formulas, on the manner in which the will should have been drawn if Curius were to be recognized as heir even if no son were born; [196] what a snare was set for plain people if the exact wording of the will were ignored, and if intentions were to be determined by guess-work, and if the written words of simple-minded people were to be perverted by the interpretation of clever lawyers. [197] How much he had to say about the authority of his father, who had always upheld the doctrine of strict interpretation, and in general how much concerning observance of the civil law as handed down! In saying all this with mastery and knowledge, and

again with his characteristic brevity and compactness, not without
ornament and with perfect finish, what man of the people would have
expected or thought that anything better could be said? Crassus, however, in rebuttal began, with a story of a boy's caprice, who while walking along the shore found a thole-pin, and from that chance became
infatuated with the idea of building himself a boat to it. He urged that
Scaevola in like manner, seizing upon no more than a thole-pin of fact
and captious reason, had upon it made out a case of inheritance imposing enough to come before the centumviral court. From this beginning,
and following it up with other suggestions of like character, he capti-
vated the ears of all present and diverted their minds from earnest consideration of the case to a mood of pleasantry.... Thereupon he urged
that the will, the real intention of the testator, was this: that in the event
of no son of his surviving to the age of legal competence—no matter
whether such a son was never born, or should die before that time—
Curius was to be his heir; that most people wrote their wills in this way
and that it was valid procedure and always had been valid. With these
and many similar arguments he won credence.... [198] He then passed
over to general right and equity; defended observance of the manifest
will and intention of the testator; pointed out what snares lay in words,
not only in wills but elsewhere, if obvious intentions were ignored;
what tyrannical power Scaevola was arrogating to himself if no one
hereafter should venture to make a will unless in accordance with his
idea. Trans. G.L. Hendrickson, *Cicero, Brutus,* Loeb Classical Library
[Cambridge, Mass., 1939], 165, 167, 169.) In 44 B.C.E., Cicero again concerned himself with this case in his treatise dedicated to the jurist Tre-
batius about correct argumentation, *Topica* (44), in which the testament
is cited again somewhat differently than in *De inventione* 2.122 and *Pro
Caecina* 53: "Si filius natus esset in decem mensibus isque mortuus pri-
usquam in suam tutelam venisset, <secundus heres> hereditatem
obtinuisset." ("In the event a son was born within ten months and died
before attaining his majority, <another heir> would have taken the
inheritance." Trans. Hubbell, *Cicero, De inventione,* 415.) Otherwise,
Quintilian mentions the trial in his *Institutiones oratoriae* 7.6.9f.; and
Boethius in his commentary on Cicero's *Topica*.

3. See primarily Franz Wieacker, "The Causa Curiana and Con-temporary Roman Jurisprudence," *The Irish Jurist* 2 (1967): 151–67; Ulrich Manthe, "Ein Sieg der Rhetorik über die Jurisprudenz—Eine vertane Chance der Rechtspolitik," in Manthe/Ungern-Sternberg, *Große Prozesse*, 74–84; and Andrea Lovato, "La voce del giureconsulto," in *Fides humanitas ius: Studii in onore di Luigi Labruna* (Naples, 2007), 5: 2975–86.

4. Cicero, *Pro Caecina* 69; also id., *De oratore* 1.180 end; and id., *Brutus* 197 end. Cicero often bears witness to his legal instruction with Scaevola the Augur: see, e.g., Friedrich Münzer, "Mucius 21," *RE* XVI 1 (1933), 434; and Matthias Gelzer, "Tullius 29," *RE* VIIA 1 (1939), 829f. After the death of Scaevola the Augur in early 87 B.C.E., Cicero became a disciple of Scaevola the Pontifex; Münzer, 440, lines 36–41.

5. This is emphasized correctly by Jan Willem Tellegen and Olga E. Tellegen-Couperus, "Law and Rhetoric in the Causa Curiana," *Orbis Iuris Romani* 6 (2000): 171–202.

6. The question was under dispute; however, the interpretation of *filius* in a gender-neutral sense soon prevailed; see Labeo and Proculus, in Javolenus, *Epistulae* 7 (*D.* 50.16.116); Pomponius, *Ad Quintum Mucium* 8 (*D.* 50.16.122); Julian, *Digesta* 71 (*D.* 50.16.201); Callistratus, *Quaestiones* 2 (*D.* 50.16.220.3); and Paul, *Ad Vitellium* 2 (*D.* 50.16.84).

7. *XII Tables* 4.4.

8. When a declaration of intent is interpreted, one must ascer-tain the true intention rather than adhere to the declaration's literal meaning.

9. Cicero, *De oratore* 2.24; and id., *Brutus* 198.

10. According to Manthe, "Ein Sieg der Rhetorik," 77 top, the testa-tor may indeed have considered this case but have forgotten to main-tain this notion in the will. Romans, however, usually devoted great care to their testaments. At the end, Manthe clearly emphasizes that this concerns the hypothetical will of the party, and heartily rebukes Crassus because he did not say so openly.

11. Cicero, *Brutus* 197 end.

12. *D.* 34.2.33 (from the law of bequest).

13. Evidence in Detlef Liebs, *Lateinische Rechtsregeln und Rechtssprich-wörter,* 7th ed. (Munich, 2007), 82f. = F 14.

14. *D.* 34.5.13.6, from his *De ambiguitatibus liber singularis* (Pamphlet on Ambiguities), a draft for students that was published by others; see Detlef Liebs, "Esoterische römische Rechtsliteratur vor Justinian," in *Akten des 36. Deutschen Rechtshistorikertages Halle an der Saale 2006,* ed. Rolf Lieberwirth and Heiner Lück (Baden-Baden, 2008), 40–79, here 49f. There Julian insisted, like Scaevola, that whoever wants something different has to express it unambiguously.

15. The concluding sentence, "Sed proclivior est" etc., contradicts the statements made previously. Furthermore, *proclivior* without a subject appears only in Justinian: e.g., 531 (*CJ* 4.31.14.1); compare Arcadius 396 (*C. Th.* 1.12.5), whereas the classical jurists use *proclivior* to refer to persons: e.g., Celsus (*D.* 12.4.16) and Ulpian (*D.* 24.1.32.4 and 32.11.15). Finally, the concluding sentence contains a conceptual error: words are interpreted, not intentions. Uncritical about this: Tellegen and Tellegen-Couperus, "Law and Rhetoric," 199–201.

16. *D.* 28.6.4 pr., from his *De heurematicis liber singularis* (Pamphlet on Found Solutions).

17. In this sense, however, see Manthe, "Ein Sieg der Rhetorik," 84.

18. The appointment as a subsequent heir, in case of doubt, also contains the appointment as a substitute heir.

6. CICERO THWARTS THE INTRIGUE
OF A POWERFUL MAN

1. Bernardo Santalucia, "Cic. pro Rosc. Am. 3, 8 e la scelta dei giudici nelle cause di parricidio," *IVRA—Rivista Internazionale di Diritto Romano e Antico* 50 (1999 [2003]): 143–51.

2. Cicero, *Pro Sexto Roscio Amerino* 42 and 45.

3. Cicero, *Pro Sexto Roscio* 96.

4. Cicero, *Pro Sex. Roscio* 6 and 35.

5. Cicero, *Pro Sex. Roscio* 17 and 87 end: *magnas rei familiaris controversias* (great disputes about family property).

6. Gustav Landgraf, *Kommentar zu Ciceros Rede Pro Sex. Roscio Amerino,* 2nd ed. (Leipzig, 1914), 26.

7. Cicero, *Pro Sexto Roscio Amerino.* Philological commentary, which also includes historical information: Landgraf, *Kommentar;* cf. Manfred Fuhrmann, *Marcus Tullius Cicero, Sämtliche Reden,* vol. 1 (Zurich, 1970, 1985²), 103–75 and 368–71; id., "Zur Prozeßtaktik Ciceros: Die Mordanklagen gegen Sextus Roscius von Ameria und Cluentius Habitus," in Manthe/Ungern-Sternberg, *Große Prozesse,* 48–61, esp. 54–57; and Olivia F. Robinson, *Penal Practice and Penal Policy in Ancient Rome* (London, 2007), 30–55.

8. T.E. Kinsey, "The Case against Sextus Roscius of Ameria," *L'Antiquité Classique* 54 (1985): 188–96, and in other articles; and Michael C. Alexander, *The Case for the Prosecution in the Ciceronian Era* (Ann Arbor, Mich., 2002), 145–72. Neither considers Fuhrmann's relevant works.

9. Cicero, *Pro Sex. Roscio* 19: *homo tenuis* (a man of slender build).

10. Fuhrmann, "Zur Prozeßtaktik Ciceros," 55–57.

11. Cicero, *Pro Sex. Roscio* 13 and 26–28.

12. Cicero, *Pro Sex. Roscio* 84.

13. Cicero, *Pro Sex. Roscio* 30, also 82 end.

14. Cicero, *Pro Sex. Roscio* 46.

15. Cf. the Scholiasta Gronovianus on Cicero's speech, in Theodor Stangl, ed., *Der sog. Gronovscholiast zu elf ciceronischen Reden* (Prague, 1884), 301: *quodam ex novis accusatoribus* (by someone from the new accusers).

16. Cicero, *Pro Sex. Roscio* 55.

17. Cicero, *Pro Sex. Roscio* 84.

18. Cicero, *Pro Sex. Roscio* 101.

19. Cicero, *Pro Sex. Roscio* 6, 17, 23, and 26 (twice).

20. Cicero, *Pro Sex. Roscio* 30 and 71f.

21. Landgraf, *Kommentar,* 24f.

22. Suetonius, *De vita Caesarum,* Augustus 33.1. According to Mommsen, *Strafrecht,* 644f., in the year 70 B.C.E. the parricide sack was replaced by the general death penalty, but this seems to be wrong; see Schilling, *Poena,* 108–13.

23. Cicero, *Brutus* 312; id., *De officiis* 2.51 end; Plutarch, *Vitae,* Cicero

3.2; Scholiasta Gronovianus, ed. Stangl; and Jerome, *Chronicon,* year 79 B.C.E., Rudolf Helm, ed., *Eusebius Werke,* 2nd ed., vol. 7 (Berlin, 1956), 152: *Roscio contra Chrysogono defenso Cicero Athenas secedit et inde post triennium Romam regreditur* (Having defended Roscius against Chrysogonus, Cicero set out for Athens and after three years returned to Rome). This obviously means that the defense was successful. Alexander, *Case for the Prosecution,* 172, claims, however, that only Plutarch states that Cicero won the case, yet this statement should be considered with caution, because Plutarch could have succumbed to the temptation of quickly extrapolating a tangible success from Cicero's brilliant rhetoric. Alexander construes, against all of the sources, that Sextus Roscius was probably actually guilty of the patricide.

24. Friedrich Vonder Mühll, "Roscius 7" (the younger Sex. Roscius), *RE* IA 1 (1914), 1117; id., "Roscius 12" (Roscius Capito), ibid., 1120f.; id., "Roscius 18" (Roscius Magnus), ibid., 1125f.; Friedrich Münzer, "Erucius 2," *RE* VI 1 (1907), 552 (Lucius Varenus was, however, not also accused by Erucius: Hans Georg Gundel, "Varenus 3," *RE* VIIIA 1 [1955], 374, lines 38–42); and id., "Mallius 12" (Mallius Glaucia), *RE* XIV 1 (1928), 911.

25. Plutarch, *Vitae,* Cicero 3.2; and Jerome, *Chronicon,* year 79 B.C.E., quoted above, n. 23.

26. Jerome, *Chronicon,* year 79 B.C.E., quoted above, n. 23.

7. DEFENSE AGAINST A LOVER'S MALICE

1. Valerius Maximus, *Facta et dicta memorabilia* 8.2: De privatis iudiciis insignibus, 2: Gaius Visellius Varro, gravi morbo correptus, trecenta milia nummum ab Otacilia Laterensis, cum qua commercium libidinis habuerat, expensa ferri sibi passus est, eo consilio ut si decessisset, ab heredibus eam summam peteret, quam legati genus esse voluit, libidinosam liberalitatem debiti nomine colorando. Evasit deinde ex illa tempestate adversus vota Otaciliae. Quae offensa, quod spem praedae suae morte non maturasset, ex amica obsequenti subito destrictam feneratricem agere coepit, nummos petendo, quos ut fronte inverecunda ita inani stipulatione captaverat. De qua re Gaius Aquil-

lius, vir magnae auctoritatis et scientia iuris civilis excellens, iudex adductus, adhibitis in consilium principibus civitatis, prudentia et religione sua mulierem reppulit. Quod si eadem formula Varro et damnari et adversariae absolvi potuisset, eius quoque non dubito quin turpem et inconcessum amorem libenter castigaturus fuerit; nunc privatae actionis calumniam ipse compescuit, adulterii crimen publicae quaestioni vindicandum reliquit. (Of remarkable private trials. Gaius Visellius Varro, being seized with a grave illness, let Otacilia, wife of Laterensis, with whom he had had carnal commerce, record a loan to himself of three hundred thousand sesterces. His plan was that if he died she would claim that sum from his heirs. He wanted it to be a sort of legacy, coloring a gift deriving from lust with the name of debt. Then, contrary to Otacilia's vows, he came out of the crisis. Annoyed that he had not speeded up the hope of her plunder by dying, from an obliging mistress she suddenly began to play the uncompromising creditor, claiming the money which she had tried to extract by a face of brass and an empty contract. Gaius Aquillius, a highly respected personage eminent in knowledge of civil law, was appointed arbiter. He called in leading members of the community as his assessors and, guided by his skill and conscience, rebuffed the woman. If it had been possible for Varro to be both condemned and in respect of his female opponent acquitted under the same formula, I do not doubt that Aquillius would gladly have chastised his shameful and illicit love. As it was, he quashed the chicanery of the private suit, leaving the charge of adultery to be pursued in a public court. Trans. adapted from Shackleton Bailey, *Valerius Maximus*, 2: 207 and 209 [see chap. 3, n. 3].)

2. On Varro, see Hans Georg Gundel, "Visellius 3," *RE* IX A 1 (1961), 355–58; esp. Cicero, *Brutus* 264. Varro's and Cicero's mothers were sisters.

3. On Otacilia, see Friedrich Münzer, "Otacilia 19," *RE* XVIII 2 (1942), 1866, according to which she was born circa 105 B.C.E. at the latest.

4. On the Iuventii Laterenses, father and son, see Friedrich Münzer, "Iuventius 16," *RE* X 2 (1919), 1365–67, esp. 1365, line 66–1366, line 7.

5. See Pomponius, *Enchiridii liber singularis* (*D.* 1.2.2.43).

6. On Gallus, see Elimar Klebs and Paul Jörs, "Aquilius 23," *RE* II

1 (1895), 327–30; and Wolfgang Kunkel, *Herkunft und soziale Stellung der römischen Juristen* (Weimar, 1952), 27f. = no. 43.

7. Cicero, *Epistulae ad Atticum* 4.14 (12).

8. Münzer, "Iuventius 16," 1366, lines 5f., sets the date circa 66 B.C.E.; circa 70: Ulrich von Lübtow, "Die Ursprungsgeschichte der exceptio doli und der actio de dolo malo," in *Eranion Giorgios Maridakis* (Athens, 1963), 1: 183–201, here 201; Max Kaser, *Über Verbotsgesetze und verbotswidrige Geschäfte im römischen Recht* (Vienna, 1977), 80; and Leon ter Beek, *Dolus—Een semantisch-juridische studie* (Nijmegen, 1999), 2: 609. None of the latter takes into account the fact that Gallus was most likely on Kerkena at that time.

9. Cf. the prices for land and building expenses, found in Wolfgang Szaivert and Reinhard Wolters, *Löhne, Preise, Werte—Quellen zur römischen Geldwirtschaft* (Darmstadt, 2005).

10. About this in detail, see Kaser/Hackl, *Zivilprozeßrecht*, 231–41 = §32 and 256–66 = §35.

11. About this procedure in detail, see Kaser/Hackl, *Zivilprozeßrecht*, 192–97 = §26 I.

12. Schilling, *Poena*, 80–85.

13. Peter Gröschler, *Die tabellae-Urkunden aus den pompejanischen und herkulanensischen Urkundenfunden* (Berlin, 1997), 258.

14. Von Lübtow, "Die Ursprungsgeschichte," 197f.

15. Kaser, *Über Verbotsgesetze*, 81f.; likewise ter Beek, *Dolus*, 610f.

16. Alan Watson, *The Law of Obligations in the Later Roman Republic* (Oxford, 1965), 32–35, extensively disproves von Lübtow, which Kaser, however, did not address.

17. *Si paret, Visellium Varronem Otaciliae sestertium trecenti milia dare oportere, iudex Aquilie Galle, Visellium Varronem Otaciliae sestertium trecenti milia condemnato; si non paret, absolvito.*

18. Kaser/Hackl, *Zivilprozeßrecht*, 350ff., esp. 359 and n. 47, and p. 11.

19. Kaser, *Über Verbotsgesetze*, 84f., downplays this possibility. He opined: "Dann wäre vor dem Judex Aquilius Gallus die Skandalgeschichte, die der Schenkung zugrunde lag, wohl nicht zur Sprache gekommen" (The scandalous tale that formed the basis for the gift then would probably not have come up for discussion before the

Judex, Aquilius Gallus). As it was a public trial, this was actually quite unlikely, and Gallus could also put two and two together.

20. Kaser, *Über Verbotsgesetze,* 85 bottom.

21. *Ea res agatur extra quam si ita negotium gestum est, ut eo stari non oportet ex fide bona,* according to Cicero's report (*Epistulae ad Atticum* 6.1.15) from January/February 50 B.C.E., written in Laodicea in his province of Cilicia.

22. . . . *everriculum malitiarum omnium, iudicium de dolo malo, quod Gaius Aquilius familiaris noster protulit;* Cicero, *De natura deorum* (written 45 B.C.E.) 3.74 end.

23. *Nondum enim Gallus Aquilius, collega et familiaris meus, protulerat de dolo malo formulas;* Cicero, *De officiis* 3.60. The episode can be dated based on the primary participant, the Roman equestrian Gaius Canius; on him, see Friedrich Münzer, "Canius a," *RE Suppl.* 1 (1903), 274.

24. Cf. von Lübtow, "Die Ursprungsgeschichte," 191–201; and Kaser, *Über Verbotsgesetze,* 86.

25. Ulpian, *Ad edictum praetoris* 76: *De doli mali et metus exceptione* (On the exception founded on fraud and fear) (*D.* 44.4.4.1).

26. Ulpian, *Ad edictum praetoris* 76 (*D.* 44.4.4.2).

27. Cf. Ulpian, *Ad edictum praetoris* 76 (*D.* 44.4.4.9), concerning the gift of a slave child by one who did not own said child.

28. For examples, see nn. 26–27 above.

8. CORRUPTER OF MORALS THROUGH POETRY, OR ACCESSORY TO A CONSPIRACY?

1. Eckhard Meise, *Untersuchungen zur Geschichte der Julisch-Claudischen Dynastie* (Munich, 1969), 223f., offers an overview, including five interpretations that he evaluates on pp. 224–35; since then, see, e.g., S. Georgia Nugent, "*Tristia* 2: Ovid and Augustus," in *Between Republic and Empire—Interpretations of Augustus and His Principate,* ed. Kurt Raaflaub and Mark Toher (Berkeley, 1990), 239–57; see also Anna Julia Martin, *Was ist Exil?—Ovids Tristia und Epistulae ex Ponto* (Hildesheim, 2004), 17f. On the dominance of the elegiac *I* in Ovid's poetry, see Burkard Chwalek, *Die Verwandlung des Exils in die elegische Welt—Studien zu den*

Tristia und Epistulae ex Ponto Ovids (Frankfurt am Main, 1996). It has even been claimed that the banishment is merely a poetic fiction: A. D. Fitton Brown, "The Unreality of Ovid's Tomitan Exile," *Liverpool Classical Monthly* 10 (1985): 18–22; and Heinz Hofmann, "Ovid im Exil? . . . sumque argumenti conditor ipse mei—Ovids Exildichtung zwischen Biographie und Fiktion," in *Latein und Griechisch in Baden-Württemberg—Deutscher Altphilologenverband Landesverband Baden-Württemberg, Mitteilungen* 29 (2001): Heft 2, 8–19. On this thesis, see Chwalek, *Die Verwandlung des Exils,* 28–30. But Ovid published a long petition for clemency addressed to Augustus with many afflictions caused by the emperor (*Tristia* 2).

2. Ovid states this in his first lament, *Tristia* 1.1.67f. and 105–12; also 2.239f., 345f., and 539; see also the anonymous, Late Antique *Epitome de Caesaribus* 1.24; and Apollinaris Sidonius, *Carmina* 23.158–61, who goes even further, hinting at an affair between Ovid and Augustus's daughter Julia.

3. See esp., besides Meise, *Untersuchungen,* Rudolf Christian W. Zimmermann, "Die Ursachen von Ovids Verbannung," *Rheinisches Museum für Philologie* 8 (1932): 263–74, esp. 269ff.; Marion Giebel, *Ovid* (Reinbek, 1991), 101–8; Michael von Albrecht, *Ovid—Eine Einführung* (Stuttgart, 2003), 23–25, 13–22 on Ovid's earlier biography, 9f. on methodological problems of filtering historical fact from elegies; Rolf Hochhuth, *Livia und Julia—Demontage einer Geschichtsschreibung* (Munich, 2005), 112–36, who insistently trumps weaknesses in older research; and Philipp Leitner, "Nasonis Relegatio: Zu den Hintergründen der Verbannung Ovids," *SZ* 122 (2005): 150–65.

4. *Tristia* 2.127–38; and 5.2.58.

5. *Tristia* 2.211f. and 345f.

6. Dating according to von Albrecht, *Ovid,* 20f.

7. On him, see Ernst Hohl, "Iunius 164," *RE* X 1 (1918), 1091; on this Julia, see Kurt Fitzler, "Iulius 551," ibid., 906–8; Meise, *Untersuchungen,* 40–48; and Elaine Fantham, *Julia Augusti: The Emperor's Daughter* (London, 2006), 108–16, which is somewhat confusing and makes insufficient note of scholarship in languages other than English.

8. On him, see Paul von Rohden, "Aemilius 115," *RE* I 1 (1893), 580; on

his eponymously named son, whom he had with Julia, see Richard D. Weigel, "Aemilius 115a," *RE Suppl.* 15 (1978), 4.

9. Meise, *Untersuchungen,* 234f. and n. 70, concludes this from *Tristia* 2.5f.

10. *Tristia* 1.6, written in spring 9 C.E., was addressed to her; *Tristia* 5.5 called for a celebration of her first birthday without him; and *Epistulae ex Ponto* 1.4 and 3.1, written 12–13 C.E., also address her.

11. *Tristia* 1.2.61–64; 2.127f. and 130; 4.4.45; and 5.2.55.

12. *Tristia* 2.207–10; see also 1.5.51f.; 3.6.27–33; 4.10.100; *Epistulae ex Ponto* 2.2.57–59; 2.9.75f.; and 3.3.73.

13. Tacitus, *Annales* 4.71.4. How seriously Augustus looked upon this offense can be concluded from an edict enacted in 8 C.E. in which questioning slaves about their masters was exceptionally allowed if such questioning was deemed absolutely necessary: Paul, *De adulteriis* 2 (*D.* 48.18.8 pr.).

14. This is ultimately learned from Suetonius, *De vita Caesarum,* Augustus 65.4. Julia could have been, according to her name, adopted by Augustus; however, she could also have been named Vipsania Julia, and our sources may have merely omitted her family name, as Fitzler, "Iulius 551," 906, lines 43–48, assumes. Legally, paternal authority over a daughter, or an adopted daughter, does not extend to her children, not even a child born out of wedlock. If the mother was married, her children were under the authority of the woman's husband; and after his death, they were free of this authority, illegitimate children in any case. This Julia's father, Agrippa, had died in 12 B.C.E., and her husband had just been executed. Thus Augustus simply assumed the function of paterfamilias without further ado.

15. Tacitus, *Annales* 3.24.

16. Suetonius, *De vita Caesarum,* Augustus 19.1; and on this, see Meise, *Untersuchungen,* 44–47; on the date, 233; and Leitner, "Nasonis Relegatio," 161f.

17. On Agrippa Postumus, see Viktor Gardthausen, "Iulius 128," *RE* X 1 (1918), 183–85; and Ralf Scharf, *Agrippa Postumus—Splitter einer historischen Figur* (Landau, 2001).

18. Early on, Augustus had made him a member of the college of

the Arval Brethren, which drew its members exclusively from the high aristocracy; however, young Paulus predeceased him in late 13 or early 14 C.E.; see Weigel, "Aemilius 115a."

19. *Tristia* 1.2.98–100; 1.9.51f.; 3.5.44–48; 4.4.43f.; and *Epistulae ex Ponto* 2.2.15f.

20. As a young man, Ovid had served in those offices that were considered the initial steps along the path to senatorial rank, *Tristia* 2.95f.; however, he had not striven for further political offices, and thus remained an equestrian, the rank his father and grandfather had held before him, *Tristia* 2.9; and *Epistulae ex Ponto* 4.9.18.

21. *Tristia* 2.131–34; and *Epistulae ex Ponto* 2.7.56.

22. This can be deduced from *Epistulae ex Ponto* 2.7.55f., in conjunction with *Tristia* 2.133f. and 207f.

23. Gathered from *Tristia* 1.1.21–26; 4.10.99f.; and *Epistulae ex Ponto* 2.3.85f.; Meise, *Untersuchungen*, 227 and n. 31. Therefore, one cannot state that Tacitus knew nothing about Ovid's exile, because in his *Dialogus de oratoribus*, published in 102 C.E., Curiatius Maternus, the rhetorician turned poet, praises the life of a poet around 75 C.E. in contrast to that of a rhetorician (*Dial.* 11–13), in particular as to how this affects personal security (*Dial.* 13.1); in *Dial.* 12.6 he had cited a poem of Ovid. Ovid's primary offense had nothing to do with his poetry.

24. I found only one further example: 62 C.E., Nero in the case of Octavia, according to Tacitus, *Annales* 14.63.1; cf. Augustus according to Flavius Josephus, *Antiquitates Judaicae* 16.163.

25. *Tristia* 2.340.

26. Cf. *Tristia* 2.244 and 247–56.

27. *Tristia* 2.347–52 (see also 211–18, and 239f.); and *Epistulae ex Ponto* 3.3.53f.

28. *Tristia* 2.539–46.

29. Thus Cassius Dio, *Historia Romana* 54.16.3–6.

30. *Tristia* 2.77f.

31. Raoul Verdière, "Un amour secret d'Ovide," *L'Antiquité Classique* 40 (1971): 623–48; in more detail: id., *Le secret du voltigeur d'amour ou le mystère de la relégation d'Ovide* (Brussels, 1992). This concerns the telestich in *Tristia* 5.8.1–4: *atei;* acrostic in 5.11.30–27 and 21–26; first and second

letters in 29, 26, 23, and 20; and second letters in 27–30: *naso inicit atteiu capito* (Ovid throws in Atteiu [vocative case] Capito).

32. L. Janssens, "Deux complexes d'acrostiches délateurs d'Ibis, alias C. Ateius Capito," *Revue de Philologie* 55 (1981): 57–71.

33. Zosimus, *Hostiria nova* 2.4.2: in 17 B.C.E., Capito's interpretation of the Sibylline oracle cleared the path for Augustus's Secular Games. His obsequious conduct under Tiberius is attested by Tacitus, *Annales* 3.70 and 75; and Suetonius, *De grammaticis* 22.2; a personal testimonial appears in Gellius, *Noctes Atticae* 13.12.1–4. Augustus appointed him consul in 5 C.E., if only as a second-tier suffect consul; first tier was Gaius Vibius Postumius, a significantly younger upstart and military officer.

34. Ovid, *In Ibin* 3, 8, 10, 13, 18, 11 (penultimate and final letters); 8 (first and second letters); 15, 14, 1, 2 (acrostics): *ateius ateius capito.*

35. *Tristia* 2.133f. (see also 127); and *Epistulae ex Ponto* 2.7.55f. (see also 2.2.19).

36. *Tristia* 2.207–10; 3.6.11–14, and 31–33; and *Epistulae ex Ponto* 2.2.55–60.

37. *Tristia* 1.5.41f.; 2.51f.; and 3.5.44–46.

38. *Tristia* 3.5.47f.

39. *Tristia* 1.2.98–100; 4.4.43f.; and 4.10.90.

40. *Tristia* 2.103–6; 3.5.49; and 3.6.28.

41. *Tristia* 1.2.99; 1.3.37; 2.109, and 207; 3.1.52; 3.5.52; 3.6.26; 3.11.34; 4.4.39; 4.8.40; 4.10.90; *Epistulae ex Ponto* 2.2.55 and 61; 2.3.66 and 91f.; 3.3.75; and 4.8.20.

42. *Tristia* 1.2.100; 1.5.42; 3.6.35; 4.4.39; and *Epistulae ex Ponto* 1.7.44; 2.2.17f.; and 2.6.5.

43. *Tristia* 1.9.63f.; and *Epistulae ex Ponto* 2.2.55.

44. Schilling, *Poena,* 86–88.

45. Cervidius Scaevola, *Regulae* 4 [*Ad legem Iuliam maiestatis*] (On the Julian Law Concerning Treason) (*D.* 4.4.4 beginning).

46. As to their alleged roles, Hochhuth, *Livia und Julia,* explains this as broadly and as rigorously as possible.

47. *Epistulae ex Ponto* 4.6–16; and on this, Zimmermann, "Die Ursachen," 265f. and 269; Hochhuth, *Livia und Julia,* 118f.; and Leitner, "Nasonis Relegatio," 163f.

48. Thus, cautiously, Zimmermann, "Die Ursachen," 269f.; and esp. Hochhuth, *Livia und Julia,* 116 and 138–40.

49. *Tristia* 2.127–30 and 135–38; 4.4.45f.; and 5.2.55–65.

50. I infer this from *Tristia* 2.127–30; 4.4.46; and 5.2.57.

51. *Tristia* 3.1.65–74; 3.14.5–18; and *Epistulae ex Ponto* 1.1.5–10.

52. *Tristia* 1.1.65–68 and 111f.; 3.14.5f.; and *Epistulae ex Ponto* 3.1.12.

53. *Tristia* 1.2.61; 2.127–30 and 135–39; 4.4.45f.; and 5.2.55–61.

54. Mommsen, *Strafrecht,* 691ff.; on the trial, 696–98; on the punishment, 698f.

55. Mommsen, *Strafrecht,* 98–101 and 91.

56. *Tristia* 2 and 5.2 are directed toward him. On this, see von Albrecht, *Ovid,* 25–28, 208–10, and 218.

57. Books 1–4, letter 5. On this, see von Albrecht, *Ovid,* 222–33.

58. *Tristia* 2.78, 238, 340, and 345–49.

59. *Tristia* 3.6.33f.

60. *Tristia* 2.43–50.

61. *Epistulae ex Ponto* 4.6.15f.

62. Tacitus, *Annales* 1.5f.; Pliny, *Naturalis historia* 7.150; and Cassius Dio, *Historia Romana* 56.30.1f.; and 57.3.5f.

63. Ovid, *Fasti* 1.3–26. Germanicus died shortly after Ovid of unknown circumstances.

64. *Epistulae ex Ponto* 4.13.17–39 (16 C.E. or later).

65. *Epistulae ex Ponto* 4.9.87–104 (16 C.E.).

66. Wolfgang Kunkel, "Über die Entstehung des Senatsgerichts" (first published in 1969), in *Kleine Schriften* (Weimar, 1974), 267–323, here 298 n. 51, denies this. His argument that Ovid acknowledged his guilt, and so was immediately treated like a convict, does not apply. The only publicly cited accusation, incitement of adultery through poetry, was not accepted by Ovid in any fashion.

67. This can be gathered from Suetonius, *De vita Caesarum,* Augustus 33.1f. Jochen Bleicken, *Senatsgericht und Kaisergericht* (Göttingen, 1962), 30 n. 4, discounts the two trials here cited as provincial proceedings, but the initial sentences in Suetonius proscribe this. However, Augustus allowed himself other liberties in these cases. Marcus Aure-

lius, too, is said to have heard delicate trials in camera, pronouncing only the verdict publicly; *Historia Augusta,* Marcus Antoninus 10.6.

68. On this, see Theodor Mommsen, *Römisches Staatsrecht,* 3rd ed., vol. 2.2 (Leipzig, 1887), 959f.; and id., *Strafrecht,* 260f.; he assumes unlimited jurisdiction residing in the *princeps* in criminal and civil cases. Hans Volkmann, *Zur Rechtsprechung im Prinzipat des Augustus* (Munich, 1935, 1969²), 63–93, summary 216–19 (see also the addendum to the 1969 edition, p. 220), did not go as far as Mommsen; nevertheless, he opined that the entire jurisdiction was transferred to Augustus at the beginning of the principate. John Maurice Kelly, *Princeps judex—Eine Untersuchung zur Entwicklung und zu den Grundlagen der kaiserlichen Gerichtsbarkeit* (Weimar, 1957), 24–70, believes that Augustus had general jurisdiction only in cases of treason. Bleicken, *Senatsgericht und Kaisergericht,* 66–124, does not accept any criminal jurisdiction on the part of Augustus; he interprets his action against Ovid as a coercive measure, p. 70. Cf. below, chap. 9, n. 28.

69. On this, Bleicken, *Senatsgericht und Kaisergericht,* 104–15. In general, Kaser/Hackl, *Zivilprozeßrecht,* 445–51 = §67.

70. Cf. von Albrecht, *Ovid,* 24f.; and already id., *History of Roman Literature,* 1: 789 (see chap. 3, n. 3).

9. A PRECAUTIONARY CRUCIFIXION

1. An overview of the political landscape is provided by Alexander Demandt, *Hände in Unschuld: Pontius Pilatus in der Geschichte* (Cologne, 1999), 20–31 and 36f.; on the organization of Judea, see Werner Eck, *Rom und Judäa* (Tübingen, 2007), 23–43.

2. On the year of Jesus's birth, see Demandt, *Hände in Unschuld,* 133f.

3. There is a large body of literature on the trial of Jesus, from which only a selection is presented here: Josef Blinzler, *Der Prozeß Jesu—Das jüdische und das römische Gerichtsverfahren gegen Jesus Christus auf Grund der ältesten Zeugnisse* (Regensburg, 1951, 1969⁴); Paul Winter, *On the Trial of Jesus* (Berlin, 1961, 1974²); Samuel G. F. Brandon, *The Trial of Jesus of Nazareth* (London, 1968); David R. Catchpole, *The Trial of Jesus—A Study in the Gospels and Jewish Historiography from 1770 to the Present Day* (Leiden, 1971); Haim Cohn, *The Trial and Death of Jesus*

(New York, 1971); August Strobel, *Die Stunde der Wahrheit—Untersu-chungen zum Strafverfahren gegen Jesus* (Tübingen, 1980); Rudolf Pesch, *Der Prozeß Jesu geht weiter* (Freiburg i. Br., 1988); John Dominic Cros-san, *Jesus—A Revolutionary Biography* (San Francisco, 1994), 123–58; id., *Der historische Jesus* (Munich, 1994), 469–519; Alan Watson, *The Trial of Jesus* (Athens, Ga., 1995); Peter Egger, *Crucifixus sub Pontio Pilato—Das crimen Jesu von Nazareth im Spannungsfeld römischer und jüdischer Verwal-tungs- und Rechtsstrukturen* (Münster, 1997); Demandt, *Hände in Unschuld*; Erika Heusler, *Kapitalprozesse im lukanischen Doppelwerk—Das Verfahren gegen Jesus und Paulus in exegetischer und rechtshistorischer Analyse* (Mün-ster, 2000); Guido O. Kirner, *Strafgewalt und Provinzialherrschaft—Eine Untersuchung zur Strafgewaltspraxis der römischen Statthalter in Judäa 6–66 n. Chr.* (Berlin, 2005), 246–90; Hans-Georg Knothe, "Der Prozess Jesu rechtshistorisch betrachtet," *Orbis Iuris Romani* 10 (2005): 67–101; Wolfgang Reinbold, *Der Prozess Jesu* (Göttingen, 2006); Otto Betz, *Der Prozess Jesu im Licht jüdischer Quellen* (Gießen, 2007); Adalberto Giovan-nini and Erhard Grzybek, *Der Prozess Jesu—Jüdische Justizautonomie und römische Strafgewalt: Eine philologisch-verfassungsgeschichtliche Studie* (Munich, 2008).

4. On them, see Demandt, *Hände in Unschuld*, 104f. and 215–24; on the canonical Gospels, 98–103; Knothe, "Der Prozess Jesu," 74–78; and Reinbold, *Der Prozess Jesu*, 19–31, 41–70, and 188–92; on the Gospel of Peter, 32–34 and 183–87.

5. Demandt, *Hände in Unschuld*, 180–83.

6. Summarizing Knothe, "Der Prozess Jesu," 75–78. On similar first elements of a biography, cf. Thomas Buergenthal, *Ein Glückskind* (Frankfurt am Main, 2007), 11f. For full discussion of the origin and date of the Gospels, see Gerd Theissen, *Die Entstehung des Neuen Testa-ments als literaturgeschichtliches Problem*, 2nd ed. (Heidelberg, 2011).

7. Heusler, *Kapitalprozesse*, summary, 259–66.

8. Tacitus, *Annales* 15.44.3.

9. Flavius Josephus, *Antiquitates Judaicae* 18.3.3 = 18.63f. For an assess-ment of this, see Reinbold, *Der Prozess Jesu*, 34–37.

10. Demandt, *Hände in Unschuld*, 75, lacking the places of publica-tion; Simon of Cyrene: M. Avigad, "A Depository of Inscribed Ossuar-

ies in the Kidron Valley," *Israel Exploration Journal* 12 (1962): 1–12, here 9f. (Ossuarium 9); Richard Wesfall, "Simon of Cyrene, a Roman Citizen?" *Historia* 59 (2010): 489–500.

11. Philo of Alexandria, *Legatio ad Gaium* 299–305; and Flavius Josephus, *Antiquitates Judaicae* 18.3.1f. = 18.55–64 and 18.4.1 = 18.85–87; on this, see Demandt, *Hände in Unschuld,* 83–92.

12. Detlef Liebs, "Das ius gladii der römischen Provinzgouverneure in der Kaiserzeit," *ZPE* 43 (1981): 217–23.

13. Demandt, *Hände in Unschuld,* 37–39. This does not mean, however, that the Jews did not sometimes impose a death sentence in the form of stoning, and execute the same; e.g., the stoning of Stephen in 35 C.E. (Acts 6f.; see Demandt, 195f.) and the stoning of James, the brother of Jesus, in 62 C.E. (Flavius Josephus, *Antiquitates Judaicae* 20.9.1 = 20, 200–203).

14. Thus, for example, on 17 July 180 C.E., the trial against the martyrs of Scilly in Carthage before the proconsul; see Herbert Musurillo, *The Acts of the Christian Martyrs* (Oxford, 1972), 86–89; Peter Guyot and Richard Klein, *Das frühe Christentum bis zum Ende der Verfolgungen* (Darmstadt, 1993), 1: 90–95 (commentary 351–54); and Detlef Liebs, "Umwidmung—Nutzung der Justiz zur Werbung für die Sache ihrer Opfer in den Märtyrerprozessen der frühen Christen," in *Märtyrer und Märtyrerakten,* ed. Walter Ameling (Stuttgart, 2002), 32–35.

15. On criminal trials in the provinces, see Nogrady, *Strafrecht,* 24–125, esp. 24–32 and 76–86; on punishment of new harmful conduct at the discretion of the authorities, 256–310.

16. Demandt, *Hände in Unschuld,* 43.

17. Thirty silver coins according to Matthew 26:15 (cf. 27:3 and 9), but this sum is suspiciously equal to that in Zechariah 11:12f.; Demandt, *Hände in Unschuld,* 147. On the arrest, see Demandt, 145–52; on Judas, 147 and 150–52.

18. Winter, *On the Trial of Jesus;* and Cohn, *Trial and Death of Jesus.*

19. Pesch, *Der Prozeß Jesu,* 32f. and 45f.

20. Horace Abram Rigg Jr., "Barabbas," *Journal of Biblical Literature* 64 (1945): 417–56; Hyam Z. Maccoby, "Jesus and Barabbas," *New Testament Studies* 16 (1969/70): 55–60; in more detail, id., *Revolution in Judaea—*

Jesus & the Jewish Resistance (London, 1973); and Pinchas Lapide, *Wer war schuld an Jesu Tod?* (Gütersloh, 1987), 84. Overly subtle on this: Pesch, *Der Prozeß Jesu,* 52–56; and id., *Das Markusevangelium,* vol. 2 (Freiburg i. Br., 1977), 459–68; according to Pesch, Pilate was not convinced of Jesus's guilt and hoped to solve the problem on the occasion of the Easter amnesty, which he hoped to direct in Jesus's favor; this failed, so that the governor "fell into a trap of his own, from which he could not escape without allowing the crucifixion of Jesus" (in eine selbstgemachte Falle geraten [sei]; aus der er nun nicht mehr herauskam, ohne Jesus kreuzigen zu lassen; *Der Prozeß Jesu,* 55; see already id., *Das Markusevangelium,* 2: 466). This is an overly complicated chain of thought; Pilate rarely dealt in a way that would lead to this type of constraint on his authority.

21. See also Remo Martini, "La condanna a morte di Gesù fra colpa degli Ebrei e responsabilità dei Romani," *SDHI* 69 (2003): 543–57.

22. On the day, see Demandt, *Hände in Unschuld,* 186–90.

23. Demandt, *Hände in Unschuld,* 75 top.

24. See the events as depicted by Demandt, *Hände in Unschuld,* 83–85. Cohn, *Trial and Death of Jesus,* 185f., wrongly rejects this.

25. Demandt, *Hände in Unschuld,* 64–68 and 80–91; and Reinbold, *Der Prozess Jesu,* 73–78, yet it is wrong to conclude, as Reinbold does on the basis of Pilate's relatively long term of office, that he was a prudent administrator, as long terms of office were quite common under Emperor Tiberius; see Tacitus, *Annales* 4.6.3; see also Demandt, 81. Cf. Seneca, *De ira* 2.5.5, who reports that a proconsul of "Asia" (western Asia Minor), after having three hundred people executed on a single day, strode through the rows of corpses exclaiming in Greek: "O majestic deed!"

26. For more detail on this, see Demandt, *Hände in Unschuld,* 160.

27. Cohn, *Trial and Death of Jesus,* 180f., also emphasizes this.

28. Thus esp. Klaus Rosen, "Der Prozeß Jesu und die römische Provinzialverwaltung," in *Festgabe für Hürtgen* (1988), 135 (non vidi; two years later, Rosen speaks of *cognitio de plano*—informal hearing, crucifixion for *contumacia*—obstinant behavior, and disciplinary proceedings; id., "Rom und die Juden im Prozeß Jesu," in *Macht*

und Recht—Große Prozesse in der Geschichte, ed. Alexander Demandt, 2nd ed. [Munich, 1996], 47–73, here 60 and 68–70); Joachim Ermann, "Ius gladii—Gedanken zu seiner rechtshistorischen Entwicklung," *SZ* 118 (2001): 365–77, here 372 n. 23; and Demandt, *Hände in Unschuld,* 170. They base their arguments on Theodor Mommsen's theory about the coercive powers of the Roman magistrate, which has been justly criticized by Adalberto Giovannini, "L'interdit contre les chrétiens: Raison d'État ou mesure de police?" *Cahiers du Centre Gustave Glotz* 7 (1996): 103–34; and Detlef Liebs, "Mommsens Umgang mit den Quellen des römischen Strafrechts," in *Theodor Mommsens langer Schatten—Das römische Staatsrecht als bleibende Herausforderung für die Forschung,* ed. Wilfried Nippel and Bernd Seidensticker (Hildesheim, 2005), 199–214, here 203–5.

29. See esp. Knothe, "Der Prozess Jesu," 96.

30. Schilling, *Poena,* 192f.

31. Demandt, *Hände in Unschuld,* 175 bottom.

32. Demandt, *Hände in Unschuld,* 83–88.

33. This is reported by Flavius Josephus, *Antiquitates Judaicae* 18.4.1f.; on this, see Demandt, *Hände in Unschuld,* 194f.

34. Suetonius, *De vita Caesarum,* Caligula 15.4.

35. Eusebius, *Historia ecclesiastica* 2.7; and Orosius, *Historia adversus paganos* 7.5.8; on this, see Demandt, *Hände in Unschuld,* 214f.

10. "THEY HATE MANKIND"

1. On the following, see, e.g., Léon Herrmann, "Quels chrétiens ont incendié Rome?" *Revue Belge de Philologie et d'Histoire* 27 (1949): 633–45; Harald Fuchs, "Tacitus über die Christen," *Vigiliae Christianae* 4 (1950): 65–93; Jean Beaujeu, "L'incendie de Rome en 64 et les Chrétiens," *Latomus* 19 (1960): 65–80 and 291–311; Valentino Capocci, "Christiana I: Per il testo di Tacito, Annales 14, 44, 4 (sulle pene inflitti ai cristiani nel 64 d.Cr.)," *SDHI* 28 (1962): 65–99; id., "Christiana II: Nota sulla persecuzione neroniana contro i cristiani in Roma l'anno 64 d.Cr. e sulla sua base giuridica," ibid. 36 (1970): 21–123; Giovannini, "L'interdit contre les chrétiens," 121–29 (see chap. 9, n. 28); Edward Champlin, *Nero* (Cam-

bridge, Mass., 2003), 121–26; Antonie Wlosok, "Die christliche Apologetik griechischer und lateinischer Sprache bis zur konstantinischen Wende," in *L'apologétique chrétienne gréco-latine à l'époque pré-Nicénienne,* ed. A. Wlosok (Vandœuvres, 2005), 1–37; and Nogrady, *Strafrecht,* 42–47.

2. Tacitus, *Annales* 15.44.2–4: Sed non ope humana, non largitionibus principis aut deum placamentis decedebat infamia, quin iussum incendium crederetur. Ergo abolendo rumori Nero subdidit reos, et quaesitissimis poenis affecit, quos per flagitia invisos vulgus Chrestianos appellabat. (3) Auctor nominis eius Christus Tiberio imperitante per procuratorem Pontium Pilatum supplicio affectus erat; repressaque in praesens exitiabilis superstitio rursum erumpebat, non modo per Iudeam, originem eius mali, sed per urbem etiam, quo cuncta undique atrocia aut pudenda confluunt celebranturque. (4) Igitur primum correpti, qui fatebantur, deinde indicio eorum multitudo ingens, haud proinde in crimine incendii quam odio humani generis coniuncti [*not* convicti] sunt. Et pereuntibus addita ludibria, ut ferarum tergis contecti laniatu canum interirent aut crucibus affixi aut flammandi atque, ubi defecisset dies, in usum nocturni luminis urerentur. (5) Hortos suos ei spectaculo Nero obtulerat et circense ludicrum edebat, habitu aurigae permixtus plebi vel curriculo insistens. Unde quamquam adversus sontes et novissima exempla meritos miseratio oriebatur, tamquam non utilitate publica, sed in saevitiam unius absumerentur. (But all human efforts, all the lavish gifts of the emperor, and the propitiations of the gods, did not banish the sinister belief that the conflagration was the result of an order. Consequently, to get rid of the report, Nero fastened the guilt and inflicted the most exquisite tortures on a class hated for their abominations, called Chrestians [*sic*] by the populace. [3] Christus, from whom the name had its origin, suffered the extreme penalty during the reign of Tiberius at the hands of one of our procurators, Pontius Pilate; and a most mischievous superstition, thus checked for the moment, again broke out not only in Judaea, the first source of the evil, but even in Rome, where all things hideous and shameful from every part of the world find their center and become popular. [4] Accordingly, an arrest was first made of all who confessed; then, upon their information, an immense multitude was united [*not* convicted],

not so much of the crime of firing the city, as of hatred against mankind. Mockery of every sort was added to their deaths. Covered with the skins of beasts, they were torn by dogs and perished, or were nailed to crosses, or were to be doomed to the flames and burnt, to serve as a nightly illumination, when daylight had expired. [5] Nero offered his gardens for the spectacle, and was exhibiting a show in the circus, while he mingled with the people in the dress of a charioteer and stood aloft on a car. Hence, even for criminals who deserved extreme and exemplary punishment, there arose a feeling of compassion; for it was not, as it seemed, for the public good, but to glut one man's cruelty, that they were being destroyed. Trans. adapted from Alfred John Church and William Jackson Brodribb, *The Complete Works of Tacitus,* [New York, 1942].) On Tacitus and the dating of this text, cf., e.g., Schanz, *Literatur,* 2: 603–43, esp. 627; Manfred Fuhrmann, "Tacitus I," *DKP* 5 (1975), 486–93, esp. 489, lines 40–44; von Albrecht, *History of Roman Literature,* 2: 1096–1145, esp. 1101 (see chap. 3, n. 3); and Egon Flaig, "Tacitus I," *DNP* 11 (2001), 1209–14, esp. 1210.

3. Suetonius, *De vita Caesarum,* Nero 16.2: *afflicti suppliciis Christiani, genus hominum superstitionis novae ac maleficae* (Punishment was inflicted on the Christians, a class of men given to a new and mischievous superstition; trans. John Carew Rolfe, *Suetonius,* Loeb Classical Library [Cambridge, Mass., 1914], 2: 111). On Suetonius, cf. von Albrecht, *History of Roman Literature,* 2: 1391–1411 (see chap. 3, n. 3); Klaus Sallmann, "C. Suetonius Tranquillus," *HLL* 4: 14–53 = §404, esp. 14–16 (bibliography), and 44–50 (texts); and, briefly, id., "Suetonius 2," *DNP* 11 (2001), 1084–88.

4. First Epistle of St. Clement, 5f. On this, see, e.g., John N. D. Kelly, *The Oxford Dictionary of Popes* (Oxford, 1986), 8; and Richard Klein in *Das frühe Christentum,* ed. Guyot and Klein, 1: 306–8 (see chap. 9, n. 14).

5. Tertullian, *Apologeticum* 4.4 (autumn or winter 197): . . . *definitis dicendo "Non licet esse vos!"* (. . . You lay it down, saying: "It is not allowed for you [the Christians] to exist!"); and 5.3: *Consulite commentarios vestros; illic reperietis primum Neronem in hanc sectam cum maxime Romae orientem Caesariano gladio ferocisse* (Consult your chronicles; you will find there that Nero was the first who assailed with the imperial sword this [the

Christian] sect, making progress then especially at Rome). See already id., *Ad nationes* 1.7.9 (spring 197, a preparatory work for the *Apologeticum*): *Et tamen permansit erasis omnibus hoc solum institutum Neronianum* (And although every other has been destroyed, yet this sole Neronian institution [that Christians should be condemned to death] has remained). On these writings of Tertullian, cf. von Albrecht, *History of Roman Literature*, 2: 1529f.; and Hermann Tränkle, in *HLL* 4: 433–49 = §474, W.1f.

6. Lactantius, *De mortibus persecutorum* 2.5f.; Eusebius, *Historia ecclesiastica* 2.25.5–7; and Sulpicius Severus, *Chronica* 2.29.1–3.

7. Karl Büchner, "Tacitus über die Christen," *Aegyptus* 33 (1953): 181–92, here 190.

8. Büchner, "Tacitus über die Christen," 183ff.

9. Thus already in 65 c.e., the praetorian tribune Subrius Flavus according to Tacitus, *Annales* 15.67.2.

10. The extant text reads: *ut ferarum tergis contecti laniatu canum interirent aut crucibus affixi* [sc. *interirent*] *aut flammandi atque . . . urerentur* (so that they perished covered in skins of deers by laceration of dogs or by being nailed to crosses or by being set on fire and burned [later in the night]). This is clearly tripartite.

11. Sulpicius Severus, *Chronica* 2.29.2.

12. Cf. Nogrady, *Strafrecht*, 75–86, esp. 79, on Seneca, *De beneficiis* 3.26.2; id., *Consolatio ad Marciam* 22.5; and Tacitus, *Annales* 4.34.

13. On this, see Detlef Liebs, *Hofjuristen der römischen Kaiser bis Justinian* (Munich, 2010), 159–64.

14. On the location of the imperial court, see Kaser/Hackl, *Zivilprozeßrecht*, 448 and nn. 19–24.

15. To hear the cases of the Pisonian conspirators in 65 c.e., Nero held court in the Servilian Gardens, where he was residing at the time (Tacitus, *Annales* 15.55.1 and 15.58.3); on this, see Bleicken, *Senatsgericht und Kaisergericht*, 81 n. 2. However, these trials were probably closed to the public. On the publicity of the trials against the Christians, see Champlin, *Nero*, 122.

16. Suetonius, *De vita Caesarum*, Nero 57.

17. Ulpian, *De officio proconsulis* 8: *De naufragiis et incendiariis* (On Shipwrecks and Arsonists); *Lex Dei* 12.5.1.

18. According to Gaius (writing in an eastern province ca. 160 C.E.), *Ad legem XII Tabularum* 4 (*D.* 47.9.9); Callistratus (writing ca. 200, likewise in an eastern province), *De cognitionibus* 6 (*D.* 48.19.28.12); and Pseudo-Paul (writing ca. 300 in a western province), *Sententiae* 5.3.6 and 5.17.3. On this, see Nogrady, *Strafrecht,* 207–9.

19. First Epistle of St. Clement 6.2. Martin Dibelius, "Rom und die Christen im ersten Jahrhundert" (first published in 1956), in *Das frühe Christentum im römischen Staat,* ed. Richard Klein (Darmstadt, 1971), 47–105, here 70–72, opined that Clement would have been the first to draw attention to the Danaides and Dirce in order to represent how magnificently the Christian women suffered under Nero; that they had been veritable Danaides and Dirces. However, in so doing, Dibelius omits the manner in which the Danaides were killed, and he suggests that they and Dirce would have been considered heroines, to whom it would have been appropriate for Pope Clement I to compare the Christian women.

20. On the mythological allusions, see Champlin, *Nero,* 122f.; on the suffering of the Christian women sketched out in First Clement 6, see p. 123f.

21. Büchner, "Tacitus über die Christen," 192.

22. See the authors listed in Dieter Flach, "Die römischen Christenverfolgungen—Gründe und Hintergründe," *Historia* 48 (1999): 446f. nn. 22–25. Correct thus far: Timothy D. Barnes, "Legislation against the Christians," *Journal of Roman Studies* 58 (1968): 32–50, here 34f.

23. Nogrady, *Strafrecht,* 44–47.

24. Cf. Lucianus, *De morte Peregrini* 12f.

25. John 21:18f.; Lactantius, *De mortibus persecutorum* 2.6; Eusebius, *Historia ecclesiastica* 2.25.5; and Sulpicius Severus, *Chronica* 2.29.3; see also First Clement 5.4, and on this, Dibelius, "Rom und die Christen," 66–70.

26. Lactantius, *De mortibus persecutorum* 2.6; Eusebius, *Historia ecclesiastica* 2.25.5; and Sulpicius Severus, *Chronica;* see also First Clement 5.5–7; and on this, Dibelius, "Rom und die Christen," 66–70. On his trial, see Heike Omerzu, *Der Prozeß des Paulus: Eine exegetische und rechtshistorische Untersuchung* (Berlin, 2002), 309–501.

27. On this in detail, see Omerzu, *Der Prozeß des Paulus*, 17–52.

28. Acts 21:27–23:11; and on this, Omerzu, *Der Prozeß des Paulus*, 309–95.

29. Acts 23:12–25:12; and on this, Omerzu, *Der Prozeß des Paulus*, 396–497.

30. Acts 24:25–25:12 and 27:1–28:16; cf. Omerzu, *Der Prozeß des Paulus*, 494f.

31. Acts 28:16, 23, and 30.

32. Omerzu, *Der Prozeß des Paulus*, 499–501.

II. A CRIMINAL ORGANIZATION?

1. On the following, see, e.g., Adrian N. Sherwin-White, *The Letters of Pliny: A Historical and Social Commentary* (Oxford, 1966), 691–712 and 772–87; Ute Schillinger-Häfele, "Plinius, ep. 10, 96 und 97: Eine Frage und ihre Beantwortung," *Chiron* 9 (1979): 383–92; Robert Muth, "Plinius d. J. und Kaiser Trajan über die Christen," in *Information aus der Vergangenheit*, ed. Peter Neukam (Munich, 1982), 96–128; Giovannini, "L'interdit contre les chrétiens" (see chap. 9, n. 28); Wlosok, "Die christliche Apologetik" (see chap. 10, n. 1); Nogrady, *Strafrecht*, 48–56; and Felice Costabile, "I processi contro i cristiani e la coerenza giuridica di Traiano," in *Fides humanitas ius: Studii in onore di Luigi Labruna* (Naples, 2007), 2: 1169–86.

2. On this Roman province, see, e.g., Carl Georg Brandis, "Bithynia," *RE* III 1 (1897), 524–39; and Christian Marek, *Pontus et Bithynia* (Mainz, 2003).

3. This is shown in particular in Trajan's harsh words in Pliny, *Epistulae* 10.34, 93 end, and 117.

4. Pliny, *Epistulae* 10.96.10 end. On Pliny's mission to Pontus et Bithynia, see, e.g., Sherwin-White, *Letters of Pliny*, 80–82, 84, and 526f.

5. Cf. 1 Peter 1:1, thus directed at numerous Christian communities, with those in Pontus appearing first; 1 Peter 1:14 and 18, 2:9f., and esp. 4:3 reveal that the letter was directed at Christian converts from paganism.

6. Pliny, *Epistulae* 10.96.9. Cf. Adam H. Becker, "Christian Society," in *Social Relations in the Roman World*, ed. Michael Peachin (Oxford, 2011), 567–86, esp. 573f.

7. Pliny, *Epistulae* 10.96.3f.

8. See Pliny, *Epistulae* 10.92 from Amisos, and 10.98 from Amastris. The letters are chronologically organized. Pliny was apparently traveling through the province dispensing justice.

9. Pliny, *Epistulae* 10.96.5f. and 2.

10. Pliny, *Epistulae* 10.96.10.

11. Pliny, *Epistulae* 10.96: Sollemne est mihi, domine, omnia de quibus dubito ad te referre. Quis enim potest melius vel cunctationem meam regere vel ignorantiam instruere? Cognitionibus de Christianis interfui numquam; ideo nescio quid et quatenus aut puniri soleat aut quaeri. (2) Nec mediocriter haesitavi, sitne aliquod discrimen aetatum, an quamlibet teneri nihil a robustioribus differant; detur paenitentiae venia, an ei, qui omnino Christianus fuit, desisse non prosit; nomen ipsum, si flagitiis careat, an flagitia cohaerentia nomini puniantur. Interim, in iis, qui ad me tamquam Christiani deferebantur, hunc sum secutus modum. (3) Interrogavi ipsos an essent Christiani. Confitentes iterum ac tertio interrogavi supplicium minatus; perseverantes duci iussi. Neque enim dubitabam, qualicumque esset quod faterentur, pertinaciam certe et inflexibilem obstinationem debere puniri. (4) Fuerunt alii similis amentiae, quos, quia cives Romani erant, adnotavi in urbem remittendos. Mox ipso tractatu, ut fieri solet, diffundente se crimine plures species inciderunt. (5) Propositus est libellus sine auctore multorum nomina continens. Qui negabant esse se Christianos aut fuisse, cum praeeunte me deos adpellarent et imagini tuae, quam propter hoc iusseram cum simulacris numinum adferri, ture ac vino supplicarent, praeterea male dicerent Christo, quorum nihil cogi posse dicuntur qui sunt re vera Christiani, dimittendos putavi. (6) Alii ab indice nominati esse se Christianos dixerunt et mox negaverunt; fuisse quidem sed desisse, quidam ante triennium, quidam ante plures annos, non nemo etiam ante viginti. Hi quoque omnes et imaginem tuam deorumque simulacra venerati sunt et Christo male dixerunt. (7) Adfirmabant autem hanc fuisse summam vel culpae suae vel erroris, quod essent soliti stato die ante lucem convenire, carmenque Christo quasi deo dicere secum invicem seque sacramento non in scelus aliquod obstringere, sed ne furta ne latrocinia ne adulteria committerent,

ne fidem fallerent, ne depositum adpellati abnegarent. Quibus peractis morem sibi discedendi fuisse rursusque coeundi ad capiendum cibum, promiscuum tamen et innoxium; quod ipsum facere desisse post edictum meum, quo secundum mandata tua hetaerias esse vetueram. (8) Quo magis necessarium credidi ex duabus ancillis, quae ministrae dicebantur, quid esset veri et tormenta quaerere. Nihil aliud inveni quam superstitionem pravam et immodicam. Ideo dilata cognitione ad consulendum te decucurri. (9) Visa est enim mihi res digna consultatione, maxime propter periclitantium numerum. Multi enim omnis aetatis, omnis ordinis, utriusque sexus etiam vocantur in periculum et vocabuntur. Neque civitates tantum, sed vicos etiam atque agros superstitionis istius contagio pervagata est; quae videtur sisti et corrigi posse. (10) Certe satis constat prope iam desolata templa coepisse celebrari, et sacra sollemnia diu intermissa repeti passimque venire carnem victimarum, cuius adhuc rarissimus emptor inveniebatur. Ex quo facile est opinari, quae turba hominum emendari possit, si sit paenitentiae locus. (It is my regular custom, my lord, to refer to you all questions which cause me doubt, for who can better guide my hesitant steps or instruct my ignorance? I have never attended hearings concerning Christians, so I am unaware of what is usually punished or investigated, and to what extent. [2] I am more than a little in doubt whether there is to be distinction between ages, and to what extent the young should be treated no differently from the more hardened; whether pardon should be granted to repentance; whether the person who had been a Christian in some sense should not benefit by having renounced it; whether it is the name Christian, itself untainted with crimes, or the crimes which cling to the name which should be punished. In the meantime, this is the procedure I have followed, in the cases of those accused before me as Christians. [3] I asked them whether they were Christians. If they admitted it, I asked them a second and a third time, threatening them with execution. Those who remained obdurate I ordered to be executed, for I was in no doubt, whatever it was which they were confessing, that their obstinacy and their inflexible stubbornness should at any rate be punished. [4] Others similarly lunatic were Roman citizens, so I registered them as due to be sent back to Rome. Later in the course of the hearings, as usually happens, the charge rippled outwards, and more examples appeared. [5] An anonymous document was filed containing the names of many. Those who denied that they were or had been Christians and called upon the gods after me, and with incense and wine made obeisance to your statue, which I had ordered to be brought in together with images of the gods for this very purpose, and who moreover cursed Christ (those who are truly Christian cannot, it is said, be forced to do any of these things), I ordered to be dismissed. [6] Others who were named by the informer stated that they were Christians and then denied it. They said that in fact they had been, but had abandoned their allegiance, some three years previously, some more years earlier, and some as many as twenty years before. All these as well worshiped your statue and images of the gods, and blasphemed Christ. [7] They maintained, however, that all that their guilt or error involved was that they were accustomed to assemble at dawn on a fixed day, to sing a hymn antiphonally to Christ as God, and to bind themselves by an oath, not for the commission of some crime, but to avoid acts of theft, brigandage, and adultery, not to break their word, and not to withhold money deposited with them when asked for it. When these rites were completed, it was their custom to depart, and then to assemble again to take food, which was however common and harmless. They had ceased, they said, to do this following my edict, by which in accordance with your instructions I had outlawed the existence of secret brotherhoods. [8] So I thought it all the more necessary to ascertain the truth from two maidservants, who were called deaconesses, by employing torture. I found nothing other than a debased and boundless superstition. [9] I therefore postponed the inquiry, and hastened to consult you, since this issue seemed to me to merit consultation, especially because of the number indicted, for there are many of all ages, every rank, and both sexes who are summoned and will be summoned to confront danger. The infection of this superstition has extended not merely through the cities, but also through the villages and country areas, but it seems likely that it can be halted and corrected. [10] It is at any rate certain that temples which were almost abandoned have begun to be crowded, and the solemn rites which for long had been suspended are being restored. The flesh of the victims, for which up to now only a very occasional buyer was found, is now on sale in many places. This leads me readily to believe that if opportunity for repentance is offered, a large crowd of people can be set right. Trans. adapted from Patrick G. Walsh, *Pliny the Younger, Complete Letters* [Oxford, 2006], 278f.)

Trajan's answer, Pliny, *Epistulae* 10.97, reads: Actum quem debuisti, mi Secunde, in excutiendis causis eorum, qui Christiani ad te delati fuerant, secutus es. Neque enim in universum aliquid, quod quasi certam formam habeat, constitui potest. (2) Conquirendi non sunt; si deferantur et arguantur, puniendi sunt, ita tamen, ut, qui negaverit se Christianum esse idque re ipsa manifestum fecerit, id est supplicando dis nostris, quamvis suspectus in praeteritum, veniam ex paenitentia impetret. Sine auctore vero propositi libelli in nullo crimine locum habere debent. Nam et pessimi exempli nec nostri saeculi est. (You have followed the appropriate procedure, my Secundus, in examining the cases of those brought before you as Christians, for no general rule can be laid down which would establish a definite routine. [2] Christians are not to be sought out. If accused before you and found guilty, they must be punished, but in such a way that a person who denies that he is a Chrstian and demonstrates this by his action, that is, by worshiping our gods, may obtain pardon for repentance, even if his previous record is suspect. Documents published anonymously must play no role in any accusation, for they give the worst example, and are foreign to our age. Trans. adapted from Walsh, *Pliny the Younger, Complete Letters,* 279.)

12. Official nomenclature: *Legatus pro praetore provinciae Ponti et Bithyniae consulari potestate in eam provinciam ex senatus consulto missus ab imperatore Caesare Nerva Traiano Augusto* (Envoy instead of a praetor for the province Pontus et Bithynia having the powers of a consul, dispatched in this province based on senatorial decision by the emperor Nerva Trajan); *Corpus inscriptionum Latinarum* V, no. 5262 = *Inscriptiones Latinae selectae,* no. 2927, lines 2–4.

13. On Pliny the Younger and his achievements, see Schanz, *Literatur,* 2: 656–73, esp. 656–58, and 666–69; Sherwin-White, *Letters of Pliny,* 69–84 and 525–55; and von Albrecht, *History of Roman Literature,* 2: 1146–57, esp. 1146f. and 1153 (see chap. 3, n. 3).

14. E.g., Pliny, *Epistulae* 10.29. Pliny attempts to deflect a death penalty incurred by a slave by stating circumstances that could be considered mitigating. While Trajan does not accept the stated circumstances as mitigatory (letter 30), he does react to the basic concern and lists conditions that, from his point of view, would allow Pliny to refrain from imposing the death penalty on a slave in this situation. Muth, "Plinius d. J. und Kaiser Trajan," 120, condemns this letter as overly cautious, which is hard to justify.

15. E.g., Pliny, *Epistulae* 10.31f., 56f., 77f., and 118f. In contrast, in 10.54f. he is in danger of neglecting provincial property rights in favor of imperial finances, and in 10.108f. and 112f. of passing over local laws in favor of asking for a general imperial ruling. Sherwin-White, *Letters of Pliny*, 546–55, defends Pliny decisively against the charge of unnecessarily bothering the emperor, which applies only rarely at best, perhaps with regard to letter 68.

16. Cf. Barnes, "Legislation against the Christians," 36f. (see chap. 10, n. 23), who imputes unauthorized actions to Pliny; he suggests that Pliny could have assumed that this was covered by *mos maiorum* (constituent custom), and his assignment to establish order in the province, thus, for example, to suppress private clubs.

17. Suetonius, *De vita Caesarum*, Nero 16.2; for literature on Suetonius, see above, chap. 10, n. 3.

18. Tertullian, *Ad nationes* 1.7.9; and id., *Apologia* 4.4 and 5.3. On Tertullian, cf. von Albrecht, *History of Roman Literature*, 2: 1528–54; Detlef Liebs, "Tertullianus," *HLL* 4: 123f. = §417.2; and Hermann Tränkle, ibid., 438–511 = §474, who, however, denies identity with the jurist, admittedly through an erroneous devaluation of Eusebius, *Historia ecclesiastica* 5.5.5, and further devaluations.

19. See, e.g., Antonie Wlosok, "Die Rechtsgrundlagen der Christenverfolgungen der ersten zwei Jahrhunderte," *Gymnasium* 66 (1959): 14–32; and Karl-Heinz Schwarte, "Intention und Rechtsgrundlage der Christenverfolgung im Römischen Reich," in *Spätantike und frühes Christentum: Ausstellung* . . . (Frankfurt am Main, 1983), 20–33. In contrast, and quite convincing: Olivia Robinson, "Repressionen gegen Christen

in der Zeit vor Decius—noch immer ein Rechtsproblem," *SZ* 112 (1995): 352–69, esp. 362f.

20. Mommsen, *Strafrecht,* 6 and 35, with reference to id., *Römisches Staatsrecht,* 3rd ed. (Leipzig, 1887), 1: 136–38, where (n. 2) he merely cites Cicero, *De legibus* 3.6; and Pomponius, *Enchiridii liber singularis* (*D.* 1.2.2.16). But these citations do not yield the comprehensive coercive power postulated by Mommsen; see Liebs, "Mommsens Umgang," 202–5 (see chap. 9, n. 28).

21. In Pliny, *Epistulae* 10.97.2: *si deferantur et arguantur, puniendi sunt* (If accused before you and found guilty, they must be punished). On the requirement of a proper accusation in provincial cognitive trials as well, which Mommsen, *Strafrecht,* 346–51, incorrectly negates, see Nogrady, *Strafrecht,* 76–78; and Pliny himself, *Epistulae* 10.96.2: *qui ad me tamquam Christiani deferebantur* (those accused before me as Christians).

22. Schillinger-Häfele, "Plinius, ep. 10, 96 und 97," 386; and Muth, "Plinius d. J. und Kaiser Trajan," 105, consider this to be impossible; governors were not authorized to do this. But neither has considered the vast discretion that was granted to criminal judges *extraordinarii* in the principate; see Ernst Levy, "Gesetz und Richter im kaiserlichen Strafrecht I: Die Strafzumessung" (first published in 1938), in *Gesammelte Schriften* (Cologne, 1963), 2: 433–508, esp. 448–51 and 478–80.

23. Schillinger-Häfele, "Plinius, ep. 10, 96 und 97," 387; and Muth, "Plinius d. J. und Kaiser Trajan," 124f.

24. Levy, "Gesetz und Richter," 433–508, esp. 448–51 and 478–80.

25. See Trajan in Pliny, *Epistulae* 10.97.2: *veniam ex paenitentia impetrare* (obtain pardon for repentance); and already Pliny himself, *Epistulae* 10.96.2: *haesitavi... an... detur paenitentiae venia* (I am... in doubt... whether pardon should be granted to repentance). Cf. Wolfgang Waldstein, *Untersuchungen zum römischen Begnadigungsrecht* (Innsbruck, 1964), 102f.

26. Pliny, *Epistulae* 10.96.3: *Neque enim dubitabam, qualecumque esset, quod faterentur, pertinaciam certe et inflexibilem obstinationem debere puniri* (For I was in no doubt, whatever it was which they were confessing, that their obstinacy and their inflexible stubbornness should at any rate be punished).

27. Thus Wlosok, "Die christliche Apologetik," 4f. (see chap. 10, n. 1).

12. BRUTAL SLAVE OWNERS

1. *Lex Dei* 3.3, from Ulpian, *De officio proconsulis* 8: De dominorum sae-vitia. Si dominus in servum saevierit vel ad impudicitiam turpemque violationem compellat, quae sint partes praesidis, ex rescripto divi Pii ad Aelium Marcianum proconsulem Baeticae manifestatur. (2) Cuius rescripti verba haec sunt: "Dominorum quidem potestatem in suos ser-vos illibatam esse oportet nec cuiquam hominum ius suum detrahi. Sed dominorum interest, ne auxilium contra saevitiam vel famem vel intolerabilem iniuriam denegetur his qui iuste deprecantur. (3) Ideoque cognosce de querellis eorum, qui ex familia Iulii Sabini ad statuam confugerunt, et, si vel durius habitos quam aequum est vel infami iniu-ria affectos cognoveris, veniri iube ita, ut in potestatem domini non revertantur. Qui si meae constitutioni fraudem fecerit, sciet me admis-sum severius executurum." (4) Divus etiam Hadrianus Umbriciam quandam matronam in quinquennium relegavit, quod ex levissimis causis ancillas atrocissime tractasset. (5) Item divus Pius ad libellum Alfii Iulii rescripsit in haec verba: "Servorum obsequium non solum imperio, sed et moderatione et sufficientibus praebitis et iustis operibus contineri oportet. (6) Itaque et ipse curare debes et iuste ac temperate servos tractare, ut ex facili requirere eos possis, ne, si apparuerit vel imparem te impendiis esse vel atrociorem dominatione saevitiam exer-cere, necesse habeat proconsul vir clarissimus, ne quid tumultuosius contra te accidat, praevenire et ex mea iam auctoritate te ad alienandos eos conpellere. Datum ... Glabrione et Omullo consulibus."

2. Gaius, *Institutiones* 1.53: De personis. ... hoc tempore neque civi-bus Romanis nec ullis aliis hominibus, qui sub imperio populi Romani sunt, licet supra modum et sine causa in servos suos saevire; nam ex constitutione sacratissimi imperatoris Antonini, qui sine causa servum suum occiderit, non minus teneri iubetur, quam qui alienum servum occiderit. Sed et maior quoque asperitas dominorum per eiusdem prin-cipis constitutionem coercetur; nam consultus a quibusdam praesidi-bus provinciarum de his servis, qui ad fana deorum vel ad statuas prin-cipum confugiunt, praecepit, ut, si intolerabilis videatur dominorum saevitia, cogantur servos suos vendere. Et utrumque recte fit, (regula:)

male enim nostro iure uti non debemus; qua ratione et prodigis inter-
dicitur bonorum suorum administratio.

3. Paolo Frezza, "La cultura di Ulpiano," *SDHI* 34 (1968): 363–75.

4. On this service of the emperors, see Detlef Liebs, "Reichskum-
merkasten—Die Arbeit der kaiserlichen Libellkanzlei," in *Herrschafts-
strukturen und Herrschaftspraxis: Konzepte, Prinzipien und Strategien der
Administration im römischen Kaiserreich*, ed. Anne Kolb (Berlin, 2006),
135–52.

5. On Ulpian, see esp. Tony Honoré, *Ulpian—Pioneer of Human
Rights*, 2nd ed. (Oxford, 2002); and, briefly, Detlef Liebs, "Domitius
Ulpianus," *HLL* 4: 175–87 = §424.

6. On this text, cf. Detlef Liebs, *Die Jurisprudenz im spätantiken
Italien* (Berlin, 1987), 162–74; Robert M. Frakes, *Compiling the Collatio
Legum Mosaicarum et Romanarum in Late Antiquity* (Oxford, 2011). Ambro-
sius in particular called upon the Old Testament whenever ques-
tions of Christian law arose; see Hartmut Leppin, "Zum politischen
Denken des Ambrosius—Das Kaisertum als pastorales Problem," in
*Die christlich-philosophischen Diskurse der Spätantike: Akten der Tagung . . .
2006 . . . Freiburg,* ed. Therese Fuhrer (Stuttgart, 2008), 33–49.

7. On Gaius and his writings, cf., briefly, Detlef Liebs, "Gaius,"
HLL 4: 188–95 = §426.

8. On this, cf., briefly, Liebs, *Römisches Recht*, 160–62.

9. Cicero, *De officiis* 1.41: Meminerimus autem etiam adversus infi-
mos iustitiam esse servandam. Est autem infima condicio et fortuna
servorum, quibus non male praecipiunt qui ita iubent uti ut mercen-
nariis, operam exigendam, iusta praebenda.

10. Seneca, *De clementia* 1.18 = 3.16.1: Servis imperare moderate laus
est. Et in mancipio cogitandum est, non quantum illud impune possit
pati, sed quantum tibi permittat aequi bonique natura, quae parcere
etiam captivis et pretio paratis iubet.

11. Seneca, *De beneficiis* 3.21.2: Est aliquid, quod dominus praestare
servo debeat, ut cibaria, ut vestiarium; and 3.22.3: . . . de iniuriis dominorum in servos qui audiat positus est, qui et saevitiam et libidinem et
in praebendis ad victum necessariis avaritiam conpescat.

12. Seneca, *Epistulae ad Lucilium* 47.

13. Columella, *De re rustica* 1.8.17f., trans. adapted from Harrison B. Ash, *Lucius Iunius Moderatus Columella, De re rustica*, Loeb Classical Library (Cambridge, Mass., 1941); the Latin reads: tantoque curiosior inquisitio patris familiae debet esse pro tali genere servorum, ne aut in vestiariis aut in ceteris praebitis [sc. a vilicis] iniuriose tractentur, . . . et rursus saevitia atque avaritia laesi magis timendi sunt. (18) Itaque diligens dominus . . . et ab solutis, quibus maior est fides, quaerit, an ex sua constitutione iusta percipiunt, atque ipse panis potionisque probitatem gustu suo explorat, vestem manicas pedumque tegumina recognoscit. Saepe etiam querendi potestatem faciat de iis, qui aut crudeliter eos aut fraudulenter infestent.

14. Suetonius, *De vita Caesarum*, Claudius 25.2. Antoninus Pius supposedly made this a general provision according to Gaius, cited above; cf. Olivia Robinson, "Slaves and the Criminal Law," *SZ* 98 (1981): 213–54, here 219f.

15. Modestinus, *Responsa* 3 (*D.* 48.4.11.2 and 1).

16. On Petronius Turpilianus, see Edmund Groag, "Petronius 75," *RE* XIX 1 (1937), 1229f.

17. Venuleius, *De officio proconsulis* 1 (*D.* 48.8.6).

18. Richard Gamauf, *Ad statuam licet confugere: Untersuchungen zum Asylrecht im römischen Prinzipat* (Frankfurt am Main, 1999), 130–35; see also id., "Ad statuas confugere in der frühen römischen Kaiserzeit," in *Das antike Asyl: Kultische Grundlagen, rechtliche Ausgestaltung und politische Funktion*, ed. Martin Dreher (Cologne, 2003), 177–202.

19. Ulpian, *Institutiones* 1 (*D.* 1.4.1.2): . . . quaedam [sc. constitutiones] sunt personales nec ad exemplum trahuntur: . . . si [sc. princeps] . . . quam poenam irrogavit . . . , personam non egreditur (. . . some [constitutions] are purely personal and not followed as setting an example: . . . if he [the prince] has imposed a special penalty, this does not extend beyond the individual).

20. Nogrady, *Strafrecht*, 256–60.

21. *Historia Augusta*, Hadrian 18.7.

22. *Historia Augusta*, Hadrian 18.8.

23. Obviously the same, the contents of which Gaius reproduces briefly in sent. 2.

24. These particulars were issued to several (*quidam*) provincial governors, as we learn from Gaius.

25. However, Gamauf, *Ad statuam licet confugere,* 98, is to be undestood thus.

26. That this was, however, often lacking can be noted from the robber chief, Bulla Felix (about 206 C.E.). A centurion was sent to capture him, but Felix overcame him and sent him back, ordering that he inform his rulers that they give their slaves enough te eat so that they would not become bandits, Cassius Dio, *Historia Romana* 76 (77).10.5; cf. Arthur Stein, "Felix 6," *RE* VI 2 (1909), 2167; Brent D. Shaw, "Bandits in the Roman Empire," *Past & Present* 105 (1984): 46–52; and Jens-Uwe Krause, "Bulla Felix," *DNP* 2 (1997), 841.

27. Ulpian, *De officio proconsulis* 8 (*D.* 48.18.1.27). He quotes the letter of Marcus Aurelius discussing the question of whether confession abrogates the need for further investigation. On Voconius Saxa, cf. Rudolf Hanslik, "Voconius 14," *RE Suppl.* 9 (1962), 1834f.

28. James H. Oliver and Robert E. A. Palmer, "Minutes of an Act of the Roman Senate," *Hesperia* 24 (1955): 333ff.

29. For details, see above, chapter II in this book.

30. E.g., Melito of Sardis according to Eusebius, *Historia ecclesiastica* 4.26.5.

31. Ulpian, *De officio praefecti urbi liber singularis* (*D.* 1.12.1.8). Gamauf, *Ad statuam licet confugere,* 89f., after having construed the statement of the source irresponsibly broadly, then narrows it, so that it reads contrary to the clear wording.

32. Bettina Eva Stumpp, *Prostitution in der Antike* (Berlin, 1998), 74f., 184f., 249, and 302.

33. On this, cf. Thomas A.J. McGinn, *The Economy of Prostitution in the Roman World* (Ann Arbor, Mich., 2004), 30–36. Ulpian, *Ad edictum praetoris* 15 (*D.* 5.3.27.1), mentions this deprecatingly.

34. Cf. McGinn, *Economy of Prostitution,* 76. On 21 April 428 in the Eastern Roman Empire Theodosius II enacted a law against fathers and slave owners who compel their daughters and female slaves to engage in prostitution, *C. Th.* 15.8.2, in which he threatened them with the loss of paternal power and of the authority to own slaves,

and beyond that with forced labor in imperial mines; on 6 Dec. 439 in *Novellae Theodosii* 18 punishment was limited to only public beatings and expulsion from Constantinople (with liberty for the prostituted female slaves). Emperor Leo then consolidated the laws circa 470 C.E. so that forced labor was applied only to low-class perpetrators and only as an alternative to expulsion; see *CJ* 11.47.7 and 1.14.4. Finally, Justinian enacted similar legislation on 1 Dec. 535 (*Novellae Justiniani* 14). Cf. Mommsen, *Strafrecht,* 699f. and n. 7; Robinson, "Slaves and the Criminal Law," 222f.; ead., *The Criminal Law of Ancient Rome* (London, 1995), 69f.; and Kyle Harper, *Slavery in the Late Roman World, 275–425 AD* (Cambridge, 2011), 309.

35. Gamauf, *Ad statuam licet confugere,* 97f.

36. On the numerous imperfections in his system, see Manfred Fuhrmann, *Das systematische Lehrbuch* (Göttingen, 1960), 104–21 and 184–88.

37. See, however, Gamauf, *Ad statuam licet confugere,* 95.

38. The penal section in this text was not directed at proconsuls merely in the narrow sense, that is, as governors of the ten senatorial, most Romanized provinces; Nogrady, *Strafrecht,* 19–21.

39. Nogrady, *Strafrecht,* 256–60.

40. Lactantius, *Divinae institutiones* 5.11.18f. and 5.12.1. Cf. Valerio Marotta, *Ulpiano e l'impero,* vol. 2 (Naples, 2004), 19–149.

41. *Lex Dei* 3.4, from the *Codex Gregorianus,* rubric "On Accusations." This *Codex* was a compilation of imperial instructions, in use in the Eastern Empire only until Justinian. It is significant that he did not adopt this rescript, even though he incorporated Ulpian's position, albeit in an abridged manner, and then only with regard to administrative law: *D.* 1.6.2.

42. Pseudo-Paul, *Sententiae* 5.23.6.

43. *Lex Dei* 3. It is true that the *Codex Gregorianus* and the Pseudo-Pauline *Sententiae* are extant only in fragmentary forms; however, had they had a corresponding rubric, the compiler of the *Lex Dei* would have used it and would not have had to search laboriously through other texts. *Lex Dei* 3.2 takes its rubric "On Homicide" from the Pseudo-Pauline *Sententiae;* and 3.4 "On Accusations" from the *Codex Gregorianus.*

44. Liebs, *Die Jurisprudenz*, 174; and in full Wolfgang Kaiser, *Die Epitome Iuliani* (Frankfurt am Main, 2004), 101f., 167–71, 396, and 631–37.

13. SELF-HELP IS PUNISHED

1. Leiva Petersen, *PIR* 5.2 (1983), 173, no. 209a.

2. Callistratus, *De cognitionibus* 5 (D. 48.7.7): [Ad legem Iuliam de vi privata] Creditores si adversus debitores suos agant, per iudicem id quod deberi sibi putant, resposcere debent; alioquin si in rem debitoris sui intraverint id nullo concedente, divus Marcus decrevit ius crediti eos non habere. Verba decreti haec sunt: "Optimum est, ut, si quas putas te habere petitiones, actionibus experiaris; interim ille in possessione debet morari, tu petitor es." Et cum Marcianus diceret: "Vim nullam feci!", Caesar dixit: "Tu vim putas esse solum, si homines vulnerentur? Vis est et tunc, quotiens quis id, quod deberi sibi putat, non per iudicem reposcit. Non puto autem nec verecundiae nec dignitati nec pietati tuae convenire quicquam non iure facere. Quisquis igitur probatus mihi fuerit rem ullam debitoris non ab ipso sibi traditam sine ullo iudice temere possidere eumque sibi ius in eam rem dixisse, ius crediti non habebit." ([On the Julian law on private violence] Creditors who proceed against their debtors should demand a second time through the judge, what they think to be due to them. Otherwise, if they enter upon the property of the debtor without permission having been given them to do so, the Divine Marcus decreed that they have no longer any right to their claims. The following are the terms of the Decree: "It is very proper, where you think that you have claims, that you should attempt to collect them by means of actions. In the meantime, the other party should remain in possession, for you are merely the plaintiff." And when Marcianus said that no force had been employed, the Emperor replied: "You think that force is only employed when men are wounded. Force is employed when anyone thinks that he can take what is due to him without demanding it through the judge. I do not think that it is consistent either with your character for reserve or your dignity, to commit an act which is unauthorized by law. Therefore, whenever it is proved to me that any property of the debtor was not deliv-

ered by him to his creditor, but that the latter boldly took possession of it without being authorized by a court, and he has declared that he was entitled to the property, he will forfeit his right to the claim." Trans. Samuel P. Scott, *The Civil Law . . . Translated* [Cincinnati, 1932], 11: 58.) On this text more recently, see José Maria Llanos, "Observaciones sobre D. 48, 7, 7," in *Liber amicorum Juan Miquel* (Barcelona, 2006), 605–15.

3. On Callistratus and his works, cf. Detlef Liebs, "Callistratus," *HLL* 4: 211–13 = §430.1.

4. By Emperor Justinian's *Digest* (533 c.e.), a systematic compilation of the still applicable texts from the writings of the classical Roman jurists. Book 48 concerns criminal law; the seventh rubric, the *Lex Julia de vi privata* (Julian law on private violence). The fragments in the individual rubrics of the *Digest* were found usually already in the— now mostly lost—original works under the same rubric. This fragment was utilized by Justinian's compilers once more: *D.* 4.2.13, here severely abridged; cf. Detlef Liebs, *Tijdschrift voor Rechtsgeschiedenis* 34 (1966): 265f.

5. Marcianus, *Institutiones* 14 (*D.* 48.7.1 pr.); see also Pseudo-Paul, *Sententiae* 5.26.4.

6. Cervidius Scaevola, *Regulae* 4 (*D.* 48.7.2); and Macer, *Publica iudicia* 2 (*D.* 48.7.3 pr. 1). Section 2 seems to contradict this; however, the introduction beginning with *sed* (but) and the lack of predicate verb in the main clause indicate that Justinian's compilers were at work here. As Mommsen noted in his edition of the *Digest,* at this point the compilers may merely have omitted a negative word at the end, perhaps *negamus* (we deny), to cause this confusion.

7. Kaser, *Privatrecht,* 222; and Kaser/Hackl, *Zivilprozeßrecht,* 28f.

8. This has been concluded from a *responsum* by Servius Sulpicius (active during the late Republic): *D.* 13.7.30, which his student, Alfenus Varus, imparted in his *Digesta* in the 30s b.c.e.; and the late-classical Paul republished these *Digesta* in greatly abridged form circa 200 c.e., including this *responsum.* A raftman owed a monetary sum to a creditor, who had, acting on his own authority, seized his debtor's raft; Servius and Alfenus merely emphasized that the creditor was liable if the raft was lost, even if due to an act of the gods. Additionally, the philosopher

Seneca considered configurations in which a benefactor could become a debtor. He formulated a case in which a creditor who had presumably guaranteed a loan in the past seized his debtor's animals, killed a slave, and pinched the silver, obviously in excess. Seneca, *De beneficiis* 6.4.4f., criticized only the lack of moderation in the creditor's behavior. Cf. Alfons Bürge, *Römisches Privatrecht: Rechtsdenken und gesellschaftliche Verankerung* (Darmstadt, 1999), 59–61.

9. Scaevola IV, *Quaestiones publice tractatae* (D. 42.8.24), beginning at *quid ergo,* where this is in fact recommended. On the dating of this text, see Liebs, "Esoterische römische Rechtsliteratur," 52–56 (see chap. 5, n. 13).

10. Marcianus, *Institutiones* 14 (D. 48.7.1.1; see also 2); and Modestinus, *Regulae* 8 (D. 48.7.6).

11. Thus, indeed, Kaser, *Privatrecht*, 222 n.15, which overinterprets the later development into the original decision against the clear wording.

12. Lucia Fanizza, "Senato e principe in età Tiberiana—I profili costituzionali," *Labeo* 27 (1981): 36–53; briefly, Kaser, *Privatrecht*, 208f.; Franz Wieacker, *Römische Rechtsgeschichte,* vol. 2 (Munich, 2006), 72; and, esp. on Julian, *Digesta* 90 (D. 1.3.11), see Rainer, *Römisches Staatsrecht,* 230f. (see chap. 2, n. 2).

13. Until the second century, if a man died without legitimate descendants, and the collateral relatives or other extraneous heirs had not yet acquired the inheritance, in which case it was considered ownerless for the time being, this estate could be plundered by anyone. Emperor Hadrian, however, granted a claim of surrender for the ultimate acquirer of the inheritance against those looters, and Marcus Aurelius even established a fine payable to the final heirs as an alternative. Both of these innovations took place through senate decisions initiated by the emperor; Gaius, *Institutiones* 2.57; and Marcianus, *Institutiones* 3 (D. 47.19.1).

14. *CJ* 8.13.3.

15. This text is much disputed, and even considered interpolated; cf. Kaser/Hackl, *Zivilprozeßrecht,* 624 and n.12.

16. Tony Honoré, *Emperors and Lawyers*, 2nd ed. (Oxford, 1994), 81–86, esp. 84ff.

17. Ulpian, *Ad edictum praetoris* 11 (*D.* 4.2.12.2, beginning at *quamvis*).

18. Modestinus, *De poenis* 2 (*D.* 48.7.8).

19. Diocletian, 8 Dec. 294 (then in Nicomedia on the Sea of Marmara, present-day Izmit), addressed to one Oplon (*CJ* 9.12.5). On the authorship of Hermogenianus, cf. Honoré, *Emperors and Lawyers*, 163–81, esp. 177ff. Diocletian's rescript from 30 Dec. 293, addressed to Euelpistus (*CJ* 9.33.3), concerned a violent robbery of property pledged to the creditor; however, the crime committed is not designated clearly; the main point was that the action could also be qualified as a minor offense to be settled only by punitive damages to be paid to the victim. The victim thus got four times his or her real damages, but only if he or she prosecuted the action within one year of the event; if later, he or she got just his or her real damages.

20. Pseudo-Paul, *Sententiae* 5.26.4 (on the punishments, 5.26.3) and 2.14.5. On the dating of the text, see Detlef Liebs, *Römische Jurisprudenz in Africa*, 2nd ed. (Berlin, 2005), 46–50.

21. See, on the one hand, *D.* 48.7.7 and 4.2.12.2, and, on the other hand, *D.* 48.7.8 and *CJ* 9.12.5. On the *Lex Romana Visigothorum* and its continuing in force in Frankish Gaul, see Detlef Liebs, *Römische Jurisprudenz in Gallien* (Berlin, 2002), 166–76, and 183–265.

14. PROTECTING A WARD PREVAILS OVER STANDARD PAYMENT PRACTICES

1. On this, see Antony Birley, *The African Emperor Septimius Severus*, 2nd ed. (London, 1988), 127f., 165f., and 199; and Jörg Spielvogel, *Septimius Severus* (Darmstadt, 2006), 99–104.

2. This happened often; cf. Ulpian, *Ad edictum praetoris* 35 (*D.* 27.9.5.11).

3. Claudius Telemachus is known from three inscriptions found in ancient Xanthus (southwestern Asia Minor, present-day Koca Çayi, Turkey): *Année épigraphique* 1981, nos. 842–44.

4. In the same sense, even if independent of a specific case, Hermogenianus, *Juris epitomae* 2 (*D.* 18.3.7).

5. On his life and works, cf. Liebs, "Iulius Paulus," *HLL* 4: 150–75 = §423.

6. Cf. *D.* 32.27.1, where Paul also speaks first, followed by the emperor, in a dialogue, until the emperor makes his decision; *D.* 49.15.50, where Papinian and Messius express their opinions first, and the emperor finally decides according to their reasoning; *D.* 29.2.97, in which Papinian speaks first, then Paul differently, and the emperor ultimately decides along the lines of Papinian's opinion; and finally, *D.* 14.5.8, in which the jurists speak first (Paul says simply *dicebamus,* "we said"), and then the emperor expresses his divergent opinion and gives the judgment according to his reasoning.

7. On the somewhat complex transmission of this work, see Fritz Schulz, *History of Roman Legal Science,* 2nd ed. (Oxford, 1953), 154 and 340 n. X.

8. *D.* 4.4.38 pr.: [De minoribus XXV annis] Aemilius Larianus ab Ovinio fundum Rutilianum lege commissoria emerat data parte pecuniae, ita ut, si intra duos menses ab emptione reliqui pretii partem dimidiam non solvisset, inemptus esset, item si intra alios duos menses reliquum pretium non numerasset, similiter esset inemptus. Intra priores duos menses Lariano defuncto Rutiliana pupillaris aetatis successerat, cuius tutores in solutione cessaverunt. Venditor denuntiationibus tutoribus saepe datis post annum eandem possessionem Claudio Telemacho vendiderat. Pupilla in integrum restitui desiderabat; victa tam apud praetorem quam apud praefectum urbi provocaverat. Putabam bene iudicatum, quod pater eius, non ipsa contraxerat; imperator autem motus est, quod dies committendi in tempus pupillae incidisset eaque effecisset, ne pareretur legi venditionis. Dicebam posse magis ea ratione restitui eam, quod venditor denuntiando post diem, quo placuerat esse commissum, et pretium petendo recessisse a lege sua videretur; non me moveri, quod dies postea transisset, non magis quam si creditor pignus distraxisset post mortem debitoris die solutionis finita. Quia tamen lex commissoria displicebat ei, pronuntiavit in integrum restituendam. Movit etiam illud imperatorem, quod priores tutores, qui non restitui desiderassent, suspecti pronuntiati erant. (Aemilius Larianus bought from Ovinius the Rutilian country estate

under a forfeiture clause and paid a part of the price, it being understood that, if within two months from that date he should not have paid half of the remainder of the price, the sale should be considered void; and also, if he did not pay the remainder within two months more, the sale should also be held to be void. Larianus, having died before the first two months had elapsed, was succeeded as heir by Rutiliana, a girl under twelve, whose guardians neglected to make payment within the specified time. The vendor, having served several notices upon the guardians, sold the same property to Claudius Telemachus after a year had elapsed. Later the ward applied for restitution, and having lost the case before the praetor, as well as the urban prefect, she appealed [to the emperor]. I gave the opinion that the judgment was correct, because her father and not she had made the contract; the emperor, however, was influenced by the fact that the day when the condition was to be fulfilled came during the time when the girl was a ward, and this was why the clause of the sale contract had not been observed. I stated that she was rather to be granted restitution for the reason that the vendor, by notifying her guardians after the time when it was agreed that the sale should be void, and by demanding the price, should be held to have abandoned his own [it was for his benefit] clause; I was not influenced by the fact that the time had elapsed afterwards [after a ward had become party to the contract], any more than I would have been, had a creditor sold a pledge when the day of payment had passed after the death of the debtor. Still, because the forfeiture clause was displeasing to the emperor, he decreed that restitution be granted. He was also influenced by the fact that the former guardians, who had not applied for restitution, had been convicted as liable as suspicious guardians.) On this text, cf. Detlef Liebs, "Der Sieg der schönen Rutiliana—Lex commissoria displicebat," in *Festschrift für Max Kaser zum 70. Geburtstag* (Munich, 1976), 373–89; and Francesco Musumeci, "Ancora sulla in integrum restitutio di Rutiliana," in *Cunabula iuris: Studi storico giuridici per Gerardo Broggini* (Milan, 2002), 245–61.

9. Musumeci, "Restitutio di Rutiliana," 252f., considers this to be certain; it is primarily for this reason that the restitution would be justified, for which he refers to Hermogenianus, *Juris epitomae* 2 (*D.* 4.4.35).

However, in our trial the immature plaintiff is not expected to pay financial compensation. The reason named in the text as the primary motivation behind the emperor's decision (that the forfeiture clause displeased the emperor) is discarded by Musumeci, who relates *ei* ("to him" or "to her") to Rutiliana (251f.), who, however, has not been mentioned for several lines. The emperor, in contrast, appears immediately before *ei* and thus is the more likely noun referent.

10. Adolf Schulte, "Fundus," *Dizionario epigrafico di antichità romane*, vol. 3 (Rome, 1906), 340.

11. Musumeci, "Restitutio di Rutiliana," 248f., overlooks this, assuming that the estate still belonged to Ovinius and that he still possessed it—that is, he had not yet transferred it to Telemachus.

12. Over the course of time the term was interpreted more and more broadly; Francesco Musumeci, "Quod cum minore … gestum esse dicetur—Formulazione edittale e la sua concreta attuazione in età imperiale," *RH* 84 (2006): 523–31, in which strangely enough this imperial decision is not mentioned, only the adverse position taken by Paul (524).

13. Cf. Musumeci, "Restitutio di Rutiliana," 260f., which, however, is less convincing.

14. Ulpian, *Ad edictum praetoris* 32 (*D*. 18.3.4.2), with reference to Papinian.

15. As referred to by Ulpian, *Ad edictum praetoris* 35 (*D*. 27.9.1 pr.–2); see also Emperor Severus according to Modestinus, *Excusationes* 1 (*D*. 26.6.2.2).

16. Ulpian, *Ad edictum praetoris* 35 (*D*. 27.9.1.4); on the dating of this part of his commentary, see Honoré, *Ulpian*, 158–76 (see chap. 12, n. 5).

17. On Musumeci referring *ei* to Rutiliana, see above, n. 9.

15. A DISPUTE AMONG CHRISTIANS

1. On the antecedent of the dispute, see Bernhard Kriegbaum, *Kirche der Traditoren oder Kirche der Märtyrer? Zur Vorgeschichte des Donatismus* (Innsbruck, 1986).

2. On Eusebius, see David S. Wallace-Hadrill, "Eusebius von Caesarea," *Theologische Realenzyklopädie* (1982), 10: 537–43; Friedhelm Win-

kelmann, *Euseb von Kaisareia* (Berlin, 1991); and Josef Rist, "Eusebios 7," *DNP* 4 (1998), 309f.; on Eusebius's *Historia ecclesiastica*, see, in addition, Dieter Timpe, "Was ist Kirchengeschichte? Zum Gattungscharakter der Historia ecclesiastica des Eusebius," in *Antike Geschichtsschreibung: Studien zur Historiographie* (Darmstadt, 2007), 292–328; on its historical reliability, 313–23.

3. On Optatus of Milev, see Schanz, *Literatur,* 4.1: 390–94; Erich Dinkler, "Optatus 16," *RE* XVII 1 (1939), 765–71; and Bernhard Kriegbaum, "Optatus von Mileve," *Theologische Realenzyklopädie* (1995), 25: 300–302.

4. Two students of Johannes Straub judge the authenticity of Optatus's documents differently. Ernst Ludwig Grasmück, *Coercitio: Staat und Kirche im Donatistenstreit* (Bonn, 1964), 251–56, considered all documents to be authentic, whereas Klaus Girardet disputes several of these documents; e.g., Klaus Girardet, *Kaisergericht und Bischofsgericht* (Bonn, 1975), 6–51; id., "Die Petition der Donatisten an Kaiser Konstantin" and "Konstantin d. Gr. und das Reichskonzil von Arles" (both first published in 1989), in *Kaisertum, Religionspolitik und das Recht von Staat und Kirche in der Spätantike* (Bonn, 2009), 1–26 and 43–72; and id., *Die Konstantinische Wende* (Darmstadt, 2006), 133–46.

5. On Augustine of Hippo, see Peter Brown, *Augustine of Hippo* (London, 1967, 2000²); Manfred Fuhrmann, *Rom in der Spätantike* (Zurich, 1994), 195–212; von Albrecht, *History of Roman Literature,* 2: 1664–1708 (see chap. 3, n. 3); Hartmut Leppin, *Die Kirchenväter und ihre Zeit* (Munich, 2000), 86–101; and James O'Donnell, *Augustine, Sinner and Saint: A New Biography* (New York, 2005).

6. New edition: Serge Lancel, ed., *Actes de la conférence de Carthage en 411,* vols. 1–3 (Paris, 1972 and 1975), with an extensive introduction in vol. 1.

7. Eusebius, *Vita Constantini* 1.44.2.

8. On this, see, e.g., Otto Mazal, *Justinian I. und seine Zeit: Geschichte und Kultur des Byzantinischen Reiches im 6. Jahrhundert* (Cologne, 2001), 195–242; and Mischa Meier, *Justinian: Herrschaft, Reich und Religion* (Munich, 2004), 86–92.

9. Ammianus, *Res gestae* 22.5.4: *nullas infestas hominibus bestias, ut sunt sibi ferales plerique Christianorum.*

16. THE EXECUTION OF HERETICS

1. On the following, see primarily Adhémar d'Alès, *Priscillien et l'Espagne chrétienne à la fin du IVe siècle* (Paris, 1936); Benedikt Vollmann, "Priscillianus 5," *RE Suppl.* XIV (1974), 485–559, esp. 495–514; Klaus Girardet, "Trier 385: Der Prozeß gegen die Priszillianer" (first published in 1974), in *Kaisertum, Religionspolitik,* 419–54 (see chap. 15, n. 4); Henry Chadwick, *Priscillian of Avila: The Occult and the Charismatic in the Early Church* (Oxford, 1976); Raymond van Dam, *Leadership and Community in Late Antique Gaul* (Berkeley, 1985), 88–117; Virginia Burrus, *The Making of a Heretic: Gender, Authority, and the Priscillianist Controversy* (Berkeley, 1995); Charles Piétri, "Häresie und staatliche Macht: Die Affäre um Priszillian von Avila," in *Die Geschichte des Christentums* (Freiburg i. Br., 1996), 2: 478–506; and Nicole Zeddies, *Religio et sacrilegium: Studien zur Inkriminierung von Magie, Häresie und Heidentum (4.–7. Jahrhundert)* (Frankfurt am Main, 2003), 83–108 and 140–46.

2. The law against the followers of Mani, enacted by Diocletian circa 300 C.E., is extant in *Lex Dei* 15.3.

3. *C. Th.* 9.16.5, from 4 Dec. 357; cf. also 9.16.7 from 9 Sept. 364; however, the latter is from the Eastern Empire.

4. *C. Th.* 16.2.23, from 17 May 376.

5. Sulpicius Severus, *Chronica,* 2.50.7: *viro acri et severo* (to a man of stern and severe character); and id., *Vita Sancti Martini* 20.4: *vir quo nihil umquam iustius fuit* (a man by whom nothing unjust was ever done).

6. On the exact date, see esp. d'Alès, *Priscillien et l'Espagne chrétienne,* 167–73; and Chadwick, *Priscillian of Avila,* 132–38.

7. We know nothing about her class or status. Arnold H. M. Jones, *The Prosopography of the Later Roman Empire,* vol. 1 (Cambridge, 1971), 983, does not list her, named Urbica (see below, n. 10); however, this does not rule out superior rank; cf. van Dam, *Leadership and Community,* 100f.

8. Sulpicius Severus, *Chronica* 2.46–51, esp. 2.49.6–2.51: . . . ubi Maximus oppidum Treverorum victor ingressus est, ingerit preces plenas in Priscillianum ac socios eius invidiae atque criminum. (7) Quibus permotus imperator, datis ad praefectum Galliarum atque ad vicarium Hispaniarum litteris, omnes omnino, quos labes illa involverat, deduci ad synodum Burdigalensem iubet. (8) Ita deducti Instantius et Priscil-

lianus; quorum Instantius prior iussus causam dicere, postquam se parum expurgabat, indignus esse episcopatu pronuntiatus est. (9) Priscillianus vero, ne ab episcopis audiretur, ad principem provocavit. Permissumque id nostrorum inconstantia, qui aut sententiam vel in refragantem ferre debuerant aut, si ipsi suspecti habebantur, aliis episcopis audientiam reservare, non causam imperatori de tam manifestis criminibus permittere. (50.1) Ita omnes, quos causa involverat, ad regem deducti. Secuti etiam accusatores Ydatius et Ithacius episcopi, quorum studium super expugnandis haereticis non reprehenderem, si non studio vincendi plus quam oportuit certassent. (2) Ac mea quidem sententia est, mihi tam reos quam accusatores displicere, certe Ithacium nihil pensi, nihil sancti habuisse definio; fuit enim audax. loquax, impudens, sumptuosus, ventri et gulae plurimum impertiens. (3) Hic stultitiae eo usque processerat, ut omnes etiam sanctos viros, quibus aut studium inerat lectionis aut propositum erat certare ieiuniis, tamquam Priscilliani socios aut discipulos in crimen arcesseret. (4) Ausus etiam miser est ea tempestate Martino episcopo, viro plane Apostolis conferendo, palam obiectare haeresis infamiam. (5) Namque tum Martinus apud Treveros constitutus non desinebat increpare Ithacium, ut ab accusatione desisteret, Maximum orare, ut sanguine infelicium abstineret; satis superque sufficere, ut episcopali sententia haeretici iudicati ecclesiis pellerentur; saevum esse et inauditum nefas, ut causam ecclesiae iudex saeculi iudicaret. (6) Denique quoad usque Martinus Treveris fuit, dilata cognitio est, et mox discessurus egregia auctoritate a Maximo elicuit sponsionem, nihil cruentum in reos constituendum. (7) Sed postea imperator per Magnum et Rufum episcopos depravatus et a mitioribus consiliis deflexus causam praefecto Evodio permisit, viro acri et severo. (8) Is Priscillianum gemino iudicio auditum convictumque maleficii nec diffitentem obscenis se studuisse doctrinis, nocturnos etiam turpium feminarum egisse conventus nudumque orare solitum, nocentem pronuntiavit redegitque in custodiam, donec ad principem referret. Gesta ad palatium delata censuitque imperator, Priscillianum sociosque eius capite damnari oportere. (51.1) Ceterum Ithacius videns, quam invidiosum sibi apud episcopos foret, si accusator etiam postremis rerum capitalium iudiciis astitisset—etenim iterari iudicium necesse erat—subtrahit se cognitioni, frustra callidus iam scelere perfecto. (2) Ac tum per Maximum accusator apponitur Patricius quidam, fisci patronus. Ita eo insistente Priscillianus capitis damnatus est, unaque cum eo Felicissimus et Armenius, qui nuper a catholicis, cum essent clerici, Priscillianum secuti desciverant. (3) Latronianus quoque et Euchrotia gladio perempti. Instantius, quem superius ab episcopis damnatum diximus, in Sylinancim insulam, quae ultra Britannias sita est, deportatus. (4) Itum deinde in reliquos sequentibus iudiciis, damnatique Asarivus et Aurelius diaconus gladio, Tiberianus ademptis bonis in Sylinancim insulam datus. Tertullus, Potamius et Iohannes, tamquam viliores personae et digni misericordia, quia ante quaestionem se ac socios prodidissent, temporario exilio intra Gallias relegati. (5) Hoc fere modo homines luce indignissimi pessimo exemplo necati aut exiliis multati; quod initio iure iudiciorum et egregio publico defensum postea Ithacius iurgiis sollicitatus, ad postremum convictus, in eos retorquebat, quorum in mandato et consilio effecerat; solus tamen omnium episcopatu detrusus. (6) Nam Ydatius, licet minus nocens, sponte se episcopatu abdicaverat; sapienter id et verecunde, nisi postea amissum locum repetere temptasset. (7) Ceterum Priscilliano occiso, non solum non repressa est haeresis, quae illo auctore proruperat, sed confirmata latius propagata est. Namque sectatores eius, qui eum prius ut sanctum honoraverant, postea ut martyrem colere coeperunt. (8) Peremptorum corpora ad Hispanias relata magnisque obsequiis celebrata eorum funera; quin et iurare per Priscillianum summa religio putabatur. At inter nostros perpetuum discordiarum bellum exarserat, quod iam per quindecim annos foedis dissensionibus agitatum nullo modo sopiri poterat. (9) Et nunc, cum maxime discordiis episcoporum omnia turbari ac miscere cernerentur cunctaque per eos odio aut gratia, metu, inconstantia, invidia, factione, libidine, avaritia, arrogantia, somno, disidia depravata, (10) postremo plures adversum paucos bene consulentes insanis consiliis et pertinacibus studiis certabant; inter haec plebs Dei et optimus unus quisque probro atque ludibrio habebatur. (When ... Maximus, as victor, entered the town of the Treveri, he [Ithacius] poured forth entreaties full of ill-will and accusations against Priscillian and his confederates. [7] The emperor, influenced by these statements, sent letters to the prefect of Gaul and to the lieutenant in Spain, ordering that all whom that disgraceful heresy had affected should be brought to a Synod at Bordeaux. [8] Accordingly, Instantius and Priscillian were escorted thither, and, of these, Instantius was enjoined to plead his cause; and after he was found unable to clear himself, he was pronounced unworthy of the office of a bishop. [9] But Priscillian, in order that he might avoid being heard by the bishops, appealed to the emperor. And that was permitted to be done through the want of resolution on the part of our friends, who ought either to have passed a sentence even against one who resisted it, or, if they were regarded as themselves suspicious persons, should have reserved the hearing for other bishops, and should not have transferred to the emperor a cause involving such manifest offenses. [50.1] Thus, then, all whom the process embraced were brought before the king. The bishops Hydacius and Ithacius followed as accusers; and I would by no means blame their zeal in overthrowing heretics, if they had not contended for victory with greater keenness than was fitting. [2] And my feeling indeed is, that the accusers were as distasteful to me as the accused. I certainly hold that Ithacius had no worth or holiness about him. For he was a bold, loquacious, impudent, and extravagant man, excessively devoted to the pleasures of sensuality. [3] He proceeded even to such a pitch of folly as to charge all those men, however holy, who either took delight in reading, or made it their object to vie with each other in the practice of fasting, with being friends or disciples of Priscillian. [4] The miserable wretch even ventured publicly to bring forward a disgraceful charge of heresy against Martin, who was at that time a bishop, and a man clearly worthy of being compared to the Apostles. [5] For Martin, being then settled at Trier, did not cease to importune Ithacius, that he should give up his accusations, or to implore Maximus that he should not shed the blood of the unhappy persons in question. He maintained that it was quite sufficient punishment that, having been declared heretics by a sentence of the bishops, they should have been expelled from the churches; and that it was, besides, a foul and unheard-of indignity, that a secular ruler should be judge in an ecclesiastical cause. [6] And, in fact, as long as Martin stayed in Trier, the trial was put off; while, when he was about to leave this town, he, by his remarkable influence, obtained a promise from Maximus, that no cruel measure would be resolved on with respect to the guilty persons. [7] But subsequently, the emperor being led astray by Magnus and Rufus, and turned from the milder course which Martin had counseled, entrusted the case to the prefect Evodius, a man of stern and severe character. [8] He tried Priscillian in two hearings, and convicted him of black magic and because Priscillian did not deny that he had succumbed to lewd doctrines; had been accustomed to hold, by night, gatherings of vile women, and to pray in a state of nudity. Accordingly, Evodius pronounced him guilty, and sent him back to prison, until he had time to consult the emperor. The matter, then, in all its details, was reported to the palace, and the emperor decreed that Priscillian and his friends should be put to death. [51.1] But Ithacius, seeing how much ill-will it would excite against him among the bishops, if he should stand forth as accuser also at the last trial on a capital charge (for it was requisite that the trial should be repeated), withdrew from the prosecution. His cunning, however, in thus acting was in vain, as the mischief was already accomplished. [2] Well a certain Patricius, an advocate connected with the treasury, was then appointed accuser by Maximus. Accordingly, under him as prosecutor, Priscillian was condemned to death, and along with him, Felicissimus and Armenius, who, when they were clerics, had lately adopted the cause of Priscillian, and revolted from the Catholics. [3] Latronianus, too, and Euchrotia were beheaded. Instantius, who, as we have said above, had been condemned by the bishops, was transported to the Scilly Isles which lie beyond Britain. [4] A process was then instituted against the others in trials which followed, and Asarivus, and Aurelius the deacon, were condemned to be beheaded, while Tiberianus was deprived of his goods, and banished to the Scilly Isles. Tertullus, Potamius, and Joannes, as being persons of less consideration, and worthy of some merciful treatment, inasmuch as before the trial they had made a confession, both as to themselves and their confederates, were sentenced to a temporary banishment within Gaul. [5] In this sort of way, men who were most unworthy of the light of day, were, in order that they might serve as a terrible example to others, either put to death or punished with exile. For that conduct which had been defended at first by the law of the tribunals, and by regard to the public good, Ithacius, harassed with invectives, and at last overcome, threw the blame upon those, by whose direction and counsels he had effected his object. Yet he was the only one of all of them who was thrust out of the episcopate. [6] For Hydacius, although less guilty, had voluntarily resigned his bishopric; that was wisely and respectfully done, had he not afterward spoiled the credit of such a step by endeavoring to cover the position which had been lost. [7] Well, after the death of Priscillian, not only was the heresy not suppressed, which, under him, as its author, had burst forth, but acquiring strength, it became more widely spread. For his followers who had previously honored him as a saint, subsequently began to revere him as a martyr. [8] The bodies of those who had been put to death were conveyed to Spain, and their funerals were celebrated with great pomp. Nay, it came to be thought the highest exercise of religion to swear by Priscillian. But between them and our friends, a perpetual war of quarreling has been kept up. And that conflict, after being sustained for fifteen years with horrible dissension, could not by any means be set at rest. [9] And now all things were seen to be disturbed and confused by the discord, especially of the bishops, while everything was corrupted by them through their hatred, partiality, fear, faithlessness, envy, factiousness, lust, avarice, pride, sleepiness, and inactivity. [10] In a word, a large number were striving with insane plans and obstinate inclinations against a few giving wise counsel: while, in the meantime, the people of God, and all the excellent of the earth were exposed to mockery and insult. Trans. adapted from Alexander Roberts, in *Nicene and Post-Nicene Fathers, Second Series,* vol. II: *Sulpitius Severus . . . ,* ed. Philip Schaff and Henry Wace [New York, 1894], 121f.)

9. On Sulpicius Severus, see, e.g., Gustav Krüger, in Schanz, *Literatur,* 4.2: 472–80 = §§1186–89.

10. Prosper Tiro, *Epitoma chronicon* (ed. Theodor Mommsen, in *MGH AA,* 9 (1892): 385–485), 462, no. 1187, on the year 385: Priscillianus in synodo Burdigalensi damnandum se intellegens ad imperatorem pronuntiavit, auditusque Treveris ab Euvodio praefecto praetorio Maximi gladio addictus est cum Euchrotia Delfidi rhetoris coniuge et

Latroniano aliisque erroris consortibus. Burdigalae quaedam Priscilliani discipula nomine Urbica ob impietatis pertinaciam per seditionem vulgi lapidibus extincta est. (When Priscillian realized that he would be convicted at the synod of Bordeaux [384 C.E.], he appealed to Emperor Maximus and was heard in Trier by Maximus's praetorian prefect, Evodius, and executed by the sword together with Euchrotia, the widow of Delfidius the advocate, Latronianus, and other likeminded persons of his heresy. In Bordeaux, a female disciple of Priscillian named Urbica was stoned to death by a crowd because of her persistence in this unbelief.) On Prosper, see Krüger, in Schanz, *Literatur,* 4.2: 491–501 = §§1194–1201.

11. Georg Schepß, *Priscilliani quae supersunt* (Prague, 1889), 1–147 (= *Corpus scriptorum ecclesiasticorum Latinorum* 18). Meanwhile, two further texts should be added, both easily accessible in Adalbert Hamman, ed., *Patrologiae cursus completus, Series Latina, Supplementum* 2 (Paris, 1960), 1487–1507.

12. Orosius, *Commonitorium de errore Priscillianistarum et Origenistarum* (ed. Schepß, *Priscilliani quae supersunt,* 149–57). On Priscillian's doctrine, see briefly Piétri, "Häresie und staatliche Macht," 479–84; stressing his leadership, van Dam, *Leadership and Community,* 88–117.

13. Vollmann, "Priscillianus 5," 513, lines 1–7; Girardet, "Trier 385," 600f.; and Piétri, "Häresie und staatliche Macht," 492f.

14. *C. Th.* 9.16.6, enacted 358 or rather 357 C.E. in Rimini.

15. Augustine, *De natura boni* 47. Vollmann, "Priscillianus 5," 513, also refers to Pacatus, *Panegyric to Theodosius* 29.2 (summer 389 after Maximus's conquest), in which it is said that Euchrotia had earned the punishment of being dragged through the streets on hooks (*ut unco ad poenam... raperetur*), and that the accusers had heard and seen the moans and torments of the others (... *gemitus et tormenta miserorum auribus ac luminibus hausissent*); however, both of these statements refer to the execution of the sentence, not to the hearing of evidence.

16. Sulpicius Severus, *Chronica* 2.51.4: ... viliores personae ... ante quaestionem se ac socios prodidissent (more common persons ... betrayed themselves and their companions before being questioned [under torture]).

17. Girardet, "Trier 385," 606f.; references, n. 146.

18. Pseudo-Paul, *Sententiae* 5.22.1 = *D.* 48.19.38.2 (the *Sententiae* date to ca. 300 C.E. and were particularly esteemed by Constantine; see *C. Th.* 1.4.2).

19. On the financial situation of the deported, see Bernardo Santalucia, "La situazione dei deportati in insulam," in *Iuris vincula: Studi in onore di Mario Talamanca* (Naples, 2001), 7: 173–90.

20. *C. Th.* 16.5.40 (22 Feb. 407) and 43 (15 Nov. 407), the latter completely: *Const. Sirm.* 12; Leo, *Epistulae* 15 pr.

21. Cf. Peter Stockmeier, "Das Schwert im Dienste der Kirche: Zur Hinrichtung Priszillians in Trier," in *Festschrift für Alois Thomas* (Trier, 1967), 415–28, esp. 425–28; Klaus Girardet, "Kaiser, Ketzer und das Recht von Staat und Kirche im spätantiken Trier," *Kurtrierisches Jahrbuch* 24 (1984): 35–50; and van Dam, *Leadership and Community,* 88–114.

CONCLUSION

1. Cf. Honoré, *Ulpian,* esp. 86–88 (see chap. 12, n. 5).

INDEX

Text   10.75 Janson MT Pro
Display   Janson MT Pro
Compositor BookMatters, Berkeley